A CHILDHOOD UNDER
HITLER AND STALIN

A CHILDHOOD UNDER HITLER AND STALIN

———⤐●⤐———

Memoirs of a "Certified" Jew

MICHAEL WIECK — Miriam Schneiders Brother

Foreword by Siegfried Lenz

Translated by Penny Milbouer

THE UNIVERSITY OF WISCONSIN PRESS

The University of Wisconsin Press
1930 Monroe Street
Madison, Wisconsin 53711

www.wisc.edu/wisconsinpress/

3 Henrietta Street
London WC2E 8LU, England

1   3   5   4   2

Printed in the United States of America

Library of Congress Cataloging-in-Publication Data

Wieck, Michael.
[Zeugnis vom Untergang Königsbergs. English]
A childhood under Hitler and Stalin : memoirs of a "certified" Jew /
Michael Wieck ; foreword by Siegfried Lenz ; translated by Penny Milbouer.
p. cm.
Includes bibliographical references.
ISBN- 0-299-18544-3
1. Wieck, Michael—Childhood and youth. 2. Jewish youth—Russia (Federation)—
Kaliningrad (Kaliningradskaia oblast')—Biography. 3. Holocaust, Jewish
(1939–1945)—Russia (Federation)—Kaliningrad (Kaliningradskaia oblast')—
Personal narratives. 4. World War, 1939–1945—Russia (Federation)—Kaliningrad
(Kaliningradskaia oblast') 5. Holocaust survivors—Russia (Federation)—Kaliningrad
(Kaliningradskaia oblast')—Biography. 6. Kaliningrad (Kaliningradskaia oblast',
Russia)—Biography. I. Title.
DS135.R95 W5413   2003
940.53'18'092—dc21   2002156544

Pictures credits: 1–16, 20, 31–35 are from the author's private collection; 17–19,
21–23, 26, 27, 29 are courtesy of Foto Krauskopf, Zeven (formerly Königsberg); 24,
25, 30 are courtesy of Keystone Pressedienst; 28 is courtesy of the City of
Konigsberg; 36, 37 are courtesy of Hugo Jehle.

Contents

Illustrations

Translator's Preface

Michael Wieck's book is not the work of a historian, but his memories are part of the historical record of the Holocaust. Why recall now, one and even two or three generations later, what happened then, or why mourn now those whose lives were lost or shattered? And why should English-language readers be interested in Wieck's account?

The translation of this book is an act of remembering. It is a small gesture against those who deny the Holocaust. It is a protest against otherwise perfectly upstanding citizens as well as hate-filled terrorists who bemoan or curse the influence of "the Jews." It is an attempt to call to mind the complexity and importance of the intersection of German and Jewish life before 1933. It is an acknowledgment that the question of Jewish identity is still, even in America, not purely a personal issue.

The challenge for this translator is to render the original faithfully while making it sound like contemporary American English. This task often requires making several sentences out of one without losing the rhythm of the original. It requires finding *le mot juste* or the perfect phrase in the second, third, and nth revision. It requires that the translator—an American woman born after World War II—become the voice of a German man born in 1928. The English must reflect the surprising number of shifts of voices and styles: the contemporary military reports the author quotes, whose matter-of-factness about armaments and troop movements recalls Julius Caesar; the puffery found in the quotations from articles by the contemporary Nazi professor who "scientifically" proves the necessity of protecting the purity of German blood; the lapidary legal formulations found in the Nazi ordinances and decrees, forbidding, for example, the sale of ice cream to Jews; and the sheer Orwellian linguistic perversion and pomposity in the phrases spoken by ardent Nazis.

There are all sorts of choices I made in this translation. For example, should I use German titles? I choose to use "Herr," "Frau," and "Fräulein" instead of "Mr.", "Mrs.", and "Miss." Use metric or American measures? I generally choose metric for weights and American measure for everything else. Literally translate the profanity of soldier's curses? This is a lovely little story in itself. I considered first a literal translation, but that would convey nothing to the American reader; then I considered current phrases of profanity; but that would conjure up the wrong historical period. Finally, I realized I needed to consult a contemporary source. I interviewed an American veteran from World War II. The elderly vet insisted that American soldiers never ever cursed and then, reluctantly, admitted to me, a "lady," that American boys might, under duress of course, use certain expletives; and these are the expletives I chose to use. At the request of Michael Wieck, I translate the word "Christus" as "Jesus."

There are also all those words and phrases from a vocabulary not normally familiar to me: military terms, ordnance and weaponry, woodworking terms, electrical vocabulary, Russian phrases, and so on. It's a treasure hunt to find the correct and suitable English equivalent. There are dictionaries, friends, relatives, and a spouse to help.

The glossary started as a didactic measure. How could an American be expected to understand the emotional resonance of "Dr. Oetker's Pudding Powder" or "the Battle of Gumbinnen"? But it soon became obvious to me that providing the glossary is a key to catching the echoes of the German-Jewish symbiosis before 1933. The history is so rich and at the same time so unfamiliar to anyone who isn't a scholar in the field. The tragedy that was the Third Reich now looms even larger and more poignantly once one grasps how intertwined Germans and Jews were in literature and politics and culture and what has been irretrievably lost.

I thank Dan Berman and John Fetzer, who first brought the book to my attention and who were the first to encourage me to undertake the project. My deepest thanks for "lending me a cup of elegance" goes to Susan R. Eilenberg, professor of English at the State University of New York, Buffalo. Susan heroically and patiently gave me and my prose the benefit of hers. To my husband, Shep Glass, I owe thanks beyond words for support, encouragement, and, above all, the willingness to be my first reader. The very patient and persistent reference librarian of Bryn Mawr College, Andrew Patterson, has my admiration and gratitude for finding the unfindable. I am grateful to friends and strangers, who scrutinized the Oxford English Dictionary for me, who provided me with helpful replies to my questions, or referred me to the next archive, where a patient librarian scoured sources unavailable to me otherwise. I am forever indebted to the author Michael Wieck, whose enthusiasm and graciousness and patience about the whole translation process were exemplary. I am also grateful for the encouragement of the author's brother-in-law, Hans Schneider.

Penny Milbouer
Houston, Texas

A CHILDHOOD UNDER
HITLER AND STALIN

Foreword

"This community"—that is, the Jewish community of Königsberg—
"originated with two Jews—physicians—in 1540" and "with the evacuation of two Jews in April 1948 an urban religious community of 408
years standing perished, in all likelihood never to rise again."
   The man who reminds us of this, the author of this book, was one of
the last survivors to leave the city. He survived by a miracle. A marked
man in a time when delusion and madness reigned, he was threatened
by so-called laws under which crimes were legal. He survived the war
and the agony of the postwar period, relentlessly hounded and imperiled. Whoever has managed to live through this must obey the ancient
imperative: Go and tell what you saw and heard and bear witness. We
have this obligation to those who are voiceless now. It is our task to
see that certain things will never be forgotten.
   Michael Wieck, who had to wear the Star of David as a child, learned
first-hand how a delusional theory of race allotted radically different
fates to members of his own family. Having been declared outside
the law, he had among his relatives not only victims of Auschwitz and
Theresienstadt, but also *Wehrmacht* officers and even a dinner companion of Hitler. What an era when such an outrageous and tragic
constellation of individual fates was possible!
   The youth Michael Wieck responds to the world he finds at hand
with a prematurely developed sensibility born of mortal danger. He
loves his native city of Königsberg; holidays on the Spit or on the
Samland seacoast are his greatest delight; the friendships at school are
important to him; but suddenly he becomes aware—and it's a blow to
his heart—that in the eyes of his classmates he's an outsider, he can
never be one of them. The poison of official propaganda produces the
desired effect. He puts up with the bullying and degradations, he bears

3

the full range of officially sanctioned animus. He endures, at first aghast, and then is aided by a power that offers solace: music. Fortified by his belief in God, the youth discovers the wondrous and life-sustaining world of art. Art becomes the miracle that saves his soul at the nadir of his existence.

He doesn't retreat from the world; what the real world has in store for him is too terrible. He observes everything that power gone mad does to humans: from existential misery to deportations and industrially organized murder. When the race laws intensify after the war begins, this youth discerns how precarious his own situation is: his life can be counted in mere days. The composure he exhibits under these restrictions and the burdens he takes upon himself isn't the only source of our astonishment. It underscores that waiting for the last days doesn't necessarily mean resignation or paralysis.

The youth with the Star of David is spared nothing—neither forced labor nor hunger, neither anxiety for his family nor the clutches of the absurd, as when blind bureaucracy orders him to the induction office. As the people he knows are gradually taken away from his Jewish community—marked for death by a policy of murder—he develops his strategy for survival despite the fact that he is scared and uncertain. The longer the war lasts and the more apparent it becomes that the German armies are being routed by their victories, the more hope there is that he will survive the days of darkness. But this hope is not so easily fulfilled nor does it happen quite as expected. Allied bombings of the city, the weeks of siege by the Soviet Army, and not least of all, encounters with the victors make clear that he is at risk just as much as before. After the war is over, the knowledge awaits him that all the suffering he has borne will be completely ignored.

Cunning, guile, and even violence flourish where life is reduced to finding enough to eat, staying warm, and just surviving in the cold ruins until the next day. The youth who has escaped the worst and for whom music is still comfort and refuge discovers abilities that surprise even him. A survival strategist becomes a survival practitioner who craftily and fearlessly takes from the victor what is necessary for bare survival. It's only human that he makes a vow at his lowest point: if he ever succeeds in surviving this misery—so he swears—he will be "happy, thankful, and content" as long as he shall live. He does survive, and, as we are told, he is one of the last allowed to leave his native city.

The author describes the euphoria of this emigration, his high expectations, settling down and starting a family, and the course of his professional and personal life. These final chapters seem abbreviated, or at least seem to work as an afterword. The central experiences of his life are intimately associated with the city of Königsberg. Here he became who he is. Here he underwent trial by fire. Here he learned to survive.

Michael Wieck is a thoughtful portraitist of his own fate. He juxtaposes contrasting incidents, he ponders the coincidence of events. For example, he shows us that at the time of his religious ceremony of consecration (bar mitzvah), as he was being dedicated to God, Göring gave Heydrich the order to prepare the "financial and material matters for a total solution of the Jewish question." Or he enables us to perceive the tragedy inherent in a visit a relative makes in his decorated officer's uniform while the author, wearing his Star of David, eavesdrops. Offering himself as representative, he describes the effects of anti-Semitism. He seeks to understand its roots: he challenges those who have refined the craft of repressing what they've done and quite frequently, he comes to a devastating conclusion. He tells his story in the past tense but switches to the present for those scenes with special significance—as if he feels a key experience has become a permanent one or to signal that what happened is still happening to him.

The judgments he passes—on those in power and their attendants, on the victims and the victors—reveal a striking intelligence about justice. The author who is making these judgments never loses sight of the fact that what happens in history is always subject to causality. He asks himself, for example, while he is shivering in a cellar in the ruins of his city, whether shells and bombs that have rained death on Königsberg aren't a response to what the German invaders did in Leningrad and in hundreds of other towns and cities in the Soviet Union. He asks and asks, sometimes outraged or stoically, and sometimes diffidently or courageously. All questions lead him to the insight that only reason and tolerance offer hope for our continued existence. Michael Wieck sets forth a shattering tale and in that spirit his book is an appeal to us.

Siegfried Lenz

Prologue

I never knew either of my grandfathers. I happened upon an auto-biography of Arnold Hulisch, my maternal grandfather, and found it took up only one typewritten page. Grandfather speaks with notice-able pride of his forebears who were descended from a long line of rabbis. He mentions his engineering degree and his first job as a construction engineer for the railroad, but even in the list of his most important accomplishments I heard dark chords resonating: "and I may add," he writes, "when I matriculated in 1864 I was the first Jew in a long time to become an academically trained construction engineer. I even had to sign the Simonian Declaration that held such dire conse-quences for Jews. This document, however, vanished from my records after Hanover was annexed. Thus, I, appointed as the first Jewish gov-ernment master builder in Prussia in many years, considered it my duty to avoid all opportunities for profit—perhaps more than necessary or prudent—in view of conventional anti-Semitic suspicions. There is no doubt, however, that tenacity to my faith and, particularly the anti-Semitism of the eighties and nineties seriously damaged me in every possible way." And then resignation and the end coming rapidly:

Of our six children, only three daughters named in my will are still alive. In 1890, my marriage was dissolved by the court on (the base-less) petition by my wife (on the grounds of—alleged—insurmount-able antipathy). I subsequently arranged for a Jewish divorce.

In the spring of 1897, I quietly and honorably took retirement due to my sorely diminished capacity for work so that I could thence-forth devote my life to my health and children.

The "avoidance of opportunities for profit" meant refusal of suitable compensation, and the "insurmountable antipathy" was a legally recognized phrase of divorce proceedings.

Poor Grandfather. By the age of fifty-two he had exhausted his energy, his spirit was broken, and his marriage had failed.

I did get to know Grandma Jenny—his wife. I was six when she died. I vividly remember how domineering she could be in spite of her reserved personality.

Mother, blonde and blue-eyed, was slight of build, but her movements and her walk always gave the impression of being expansive. Although she was endowed with a good mind, feelings were more important to her. Her speech, her music, and everything she did expressed the emotion she felt. She was idealistic, modest, and impractical. She was entirely the musician, not much of a housewife, sometimes ascetically frugal, but also very stubborn. Events shall bind us closely together.

How different, on the other hand, my Grandparents Wieck. Self-assured, well-off, respected by all. Grandfather Wieck was also an engineer and, coincidentally, active in building the railroad in Romania at the same time as Grandfather Hulisch. Maybe they even knew each other. Later he became director, department head, and chief district official in Berlin-Grunewald, where for a long time there was a street named Bernhard-Wieck-Strasse in his honor. Today it's a park. Compared to him, Grandmother Wieck faded into the background. She was Swedish, née Palme, the great-aunt of Olof Palme, the head of the Swedish Social Democrats who was assassinated in 1986.

In his best years, Father looked like the men Manet so often painted. He had a good build, was always impeccably groomed, had dark hair, wore a beard, and dressed smartly. You might believe he wanted to parade the fact that he was a cultivated man of intellect and high standards. He often spoke of his childhood home, where Brahms and Clara Wieck-Schumann, a distant cousin, came to visit and Joseph Joachim practiced with his string quartet. My Grandparents Wieck lived in a spacious house, Hertha-Strasse 4, and not far away stood the villa belonging to the Mendelssohn family, where artists likewise lodged and played music.

These two houses, so my father said, were the meeting places—indeed, they were almost the center—of all musical activity in Berlin. My father, who was born in 1880, was impressed by the artists Max Liebermann and Adolph von Menzel. When he recalled earlier times, everything was always splendid and lovely or important and significant. His generation still had great difficulty talking about the dark side of life, about weaknesses or even possible failures. The serene pride Father displayed took on a positive meaning for me: namely, you didn't need to first wonder if you had ability or talent. Whoever belonged to such a family was called to something higher, no matter what. Nothing could go wrong here, and that wasn't such a bad inheritance after all; it was a most beneficial fallacy that bestowed strength, and not just for a nascent musician.

Happily, the war memoirs (1870/1871) of my grandfather Bernhard Wieck fell into my hands only much later. What a surprise. Now my sainted forebear is transformed into a conservative, nationalistic German philistine, although by the standards of his day he was no such thing. He composed his war memoirs in rhyme. Stanzas 8 and 9 of his many-stanza'd epic read like this:

> Fritz gave the pack of riff-raff
> A good one on his backpack;
> Willem put the *grande nation*,
> Frossard, Bazaine, Mac-Mahone
> Canrobert, Napoleone
> One and all in *prison*.

> Then there was the *Republique*
> With, once more, a robber *clique*
> Turkos, Spahi, Gum, Zephyr.
> All of them were bashed and flayed
> We're still drubbing them today
> Great and long then our *plaisir*.

Even if, as he says, this was meant as a humorous occasional poem, what ominous notes are sounded here! Jingoism, war heroics, the sense of being, in every way something better, and contempt for everyone else. Weren't these the seeds from which subsequent excesses were to grow? In fact, only two generations later, my half-brother Peter—my father's son from his first marriage—became a successful army officer who set out to dominate the world, an ardent believer in National Socialism, while I only barely escaped the efforts of the Nazis "to eradicate" me. "Eradicate" was a term that the later Nobel laureate Konrad

Lorenz used when he called for the "preservation of the race," the "eradication" of alien species through breeding, and "an even more intense
eradication of those who are ethically inferior than is the case at present" (1940). This was one year after the euthanasia program began
carrying out murders and one and a half years before the Wannsee
Conference, where the physical destruction of all Jews became official
policy.

To be related to celebrated personalities on the one hand and to
belong to those officially condemned on the other was confusingly
paradoxical to me, an enthusiastic and cheerful boy. The daughter of
my father's brother, Cousin Dorothea Wieck—who was a popular
movie star of the thirties—was Hitler's dinner companion on several
occasions, while not much later my Aunt Fanny perished in Auschwitz
or Riga, Aunt Rebekka died in Theresienstadt, and Mother's cousin
Lotte Beth took her life rather than be deported. And if you think
this might be an anomaly within one branch of the family, I can
also enlighten you with another variant of the mad schism in those
days with the example of my Aunt Betty. My Grandparents Hulisch
had three daughters, Betty, Miriam, and my mother, Hedwig. Betty
married a man from Munich and in 1934 demanded that her mother
(Grandmother Jenny was eighty-four years old) sign a document she
presented that said that she, Betty, was not her birth child, but a foster
child, and further, that she was not of Jewish descent. After hesitating
at first, Grandmother signed it but did not long survive what was for
her a terrible shock. Aunt Betty needed this declaration so that her
sons could join Hitler's SA or SS. (To Betty's credit, I must add that
her husband and two sons forced her to do this.)

Needless to say, all contact was broken off, and I don't know what
happened either to her or to her two sons after that. It is even conceivable that my cousins were the ones who hauled off their own close
relatives to their deaths. Truly a subject suitable for a classical tragedy.

Shortly before I was born in July 1928, Mother met with Rabbi
Lewin of Königsberg. She asked him what religion her children would
be. "Every child born of a Jewish mother is Jewish," was his answer.
So my sister, who was born in 1925, and I were registered with the
Jewish community and raised as Jews. For this reason, the Nazis later
designated us as "certified" Jews. We were subject to all laws concocted
for Jews and later had to go around marked with the yellow Star of
David. Those born to mixed marriages, *Mischlinge*, who had been

raised as Christians were spared all this and perhaps for this reason were cynically called "privileged."

According to the book *Königsberg in Preussen* (*Königsberg in Prussia*) by Fritz Gause, I'm not actually supposed to be alive today. He wrote: "Their fate (the fate of the Jews) is as unknown as the destination and details of their transports. None of them survived the horror. To the extent that Königsberg Jews are still alive, they are those who succeeded in emigrating before the war." In fact, there are only four people from Königsberg who wore the Star of David and survived persecution, war, and the Russian occupation.

By another account, I'm supposed to have been saved as one of the civilians in the besieged city of Königsberg by the noble actions of the Festungskommandant (Fortress Commander), General Lasch. In his book, *So fiel Königsberg* (*How Königsberg Fell*), one can read, "The most compelling factor for my decision that had to be made now [to surrender] was, however, the recognition that I would only be senselessly sacrificing thousands of my soldiers and civilians if I continued to fight. I could not answer for this to God or my conscience. So I made the decision to halt the fighting and bring the horror to an end."

Unfortunately, he wasn't that considerate. The very reason we civilians had to suffer the heavy attack of 250,000 Russian soldiers and the accompanying murderous bombardment was that he did not surrender soon enough. Surrender came only when the battle for Königsberg was lost after months under siege and three days of street fighting with heavy casualties, and only after the Russians had reached General Lasch's well-secured bunker.

The destruction of the Jewish community and thereafter of the entire city will remain, in the end, a series of events that is beyond the power of words to describe. Many things that happened are like evil spirits, which, once they are conjured up, cannot be so quickly dispersed. This is true for the memory of what a thirteen-year-old boy feels when compelled, under the penalty of death, to wear a Star of David—a mark of Cain that singles him out from the community of his fellow men and turns him into fair game.

I just barely escaped the "Final Solution" only to fall into Stalin's hands after the Red Army's conquest of Königsberg. During my three-year Russian imprisonment, I shared the misery and the deprivations that reduced, almost annihilated, the remaining Königsberg population by 80 percent. The Jews of East Prussia were systematically killed, first under Hitler, and then, if any survived, under Stalin. In the cellars of the Soviet concentration camp Rothenstein all the pain and anguish reached a climax. Twenty-five years later, when I was the concertmaster of the Stuttgart Chamber Orchestra and we had just given successful concerts in Moscow and Leningrad, Stalin's comrade and long-time Culture Minister Yekaterina Furtseva greeted me as a guest of honor.

Before that, my days had been filled with demanding academic studies; it was the time of the Blockade of Berlin. I had married and, sustained by ardent hope, was devoting myself to encouraging a cultural rebirth in a bombed-out Germany. Fricsay, Klemperer, Ansermet, and Celibidache, along with many others, conducted the Radio Symphony Orchestra of Berlin, which I joined as its youngest member. Our first concert tours took us to foreign countries that not so long before had been attacked and destroyed by Hitler. These tours were a way of diffidently seeking forgiveness and reconciliation. Before the concerts we were jeered; afterwards we were enthusiastically applauded. These were heartening examples of the power of music to bring about reconciliation.

However, the bitter memories, my own inner conflict, and the construction of the Wall that closed off West Berlin motivated me to accept an offer from the University of Auckland in 1961. While on a concert tour, I was invited to teach the first violin class in New Zealand.

But then, after searching for a homeland at the other end of the world for seven years, after I discovered how very much alike people are all over the world, I was drawn back to Germany again. Only there, in the land of poets, philosophers—and unfortunately perpetrators, too—do I find the nourishment I need to live, what my musician's soul requires.

My relationship, fated to be equivocal, to "the Jews," "the Christians," "the Germans," and "the Russians" will, I hope, keep me from reporting one-sidedly. I can rely on the accuracy of my memories for all the significant events and for what I felt. These memories are still very much alive and all too real. I won't be entirely free of emotion. Especially toward two people who were active in Königsberg: Professor Konrad Lorenz and General Otto Lasch. I condemn them and through them the many others they represent. Afterwards, each managed only too well to establish his image as that of a moralist, or even a martyr, although both played a part in my misery and in the misery of many others. Indeed, they did so in a fateful way that was typical of that time—in the one case intellectually, and in the other militarily.

The terrible events of yesterday cannot emphasize forcefully enough that perpetrators of violence first perform their work in thought, in speech, and in print before moving on to finish the work of torture and killing with fists and weapons.

With immense and profound sadness, I think of all my schoolmates who perished so young, of relatives, and of the many millions of victims of humanity's mad delusions and its inexhaustible abuse of power. Perhaps I can contribute to their memory. Even they still have much to say to us!

Aunt Fanny

When I try to recall my earliest memories, Aunt Fanny is more vivid and brighter in my mind than my mother. I find this astonishing.

I clearly see my aunt, a perpetually slightly nervous woman, pushing me around in a baby carriage, and I hear her soft voice. She often comes to visit; it could be every day. She's always pleasant. Someone is annoyed with her awkwardness; there's someone scolding. When dressing me, she sometimes has to ask for help. The ties on the pants, the shoes, and other items of clothing are difficult for her. When we are alone on the street, in a nearby park, or in the sandbox I am filled with joy, with a feeling of happiness.

Mother was often in a nervous rush, busy with something important. She was always dashing off to rehearsals and concerts, and was really only at home when practicing her violin. Only then was I allowed to play in the same room. I would lay my head in her lap and suck my thumb: contentment.

There's a black grand piano from which tones emerge. Magic. I have the feeling that Grandma Jenny wants something from me; a slight feeling of unease. There's a carpet on whose pattern I can play with my blocks and wooden figures. Now Mother reappears. She gives me a vigorous but tender hug. Mother-love stashed away for the future? There are no memories of my father. After all, he lived across the street.

It's strange that in all these images my sister Miriam, three years older than I, doesn't appear. Even Grandma remains somewhat obscure. I more easily recall dogs, cats, birds, and horse-drawn carts.

Mother's apartment on the corner of the Goltzallee and the Old
Pillauer Road had a long hallway, and my room was in the back at the
end. At night I felt abandoned. I don't know why, but I was afraid and
fear caused me my first terrible hours.

Something's moving everywhere. There are mysterious lights on the
walls—harbingers of cars approaching from afar long before they can
be heard. There are sounds and animal noises. I always feel threatened,
and my sense of helplessness intensifies every imaginable danger to
something unbearable. Desperate and terrified, I'm calling—screaming.
Mother comes only seldom, as her room is at the other end of the
hallway; quite often she's not home at all.

She was the violist and Father played second violin in the Königsberg Quartet. He organized everything, planned the rehearsals and the
concerts. They performed the Beethoven cycle and traveled as far as
Berlin. They even founded a society for the new atonal music. After
forty or more rehearsals, they premiered Hindemith and Schoenberg
quartets. My parents also had a lot of pupils and were always practicing. The rooms weren't soundproof so they maintained separate
apartments.

When I was three years old—so I was later told—I crossed the street
and rang the bell or knocked on the door of my father's apartment.
When someone opened the door, I asked, "Is Wieck at home?" Mother
addressed my father as "Wieck" out of a longstanding habit of working together. Nonetheless, no matter how much I try, my first years
of memories are fatherless ones and "Wieck" remained something of
a stranger to me his whole life long.

Some time later it's Easter. The neighbors I'm sometimes taken to visit
let me find a small candy egg in a stuffed bunny sitting under the chest
of drawers. But for the most part I rock back and forth in a swing
fastened to the door frame. I find this absolutely delightful.

Every now and then the neighbor's wife goes to check if the bunny has
laid something. I never see her hiding the new eggs I'll find the next time
I look. There's always something remarkable, astonishing happening,
and, in a different sort of way, that hasn't changed to this day.

We celebrate Chanukah. A new candle is lit every day. Eight candles,
eight days of Chanukah. (Chanukah commemorates the struggle for

freedom of the Maccabees and the reconsecration of the Temple. It was 165 B.C. when, to the amazement and joy of all, the sacred lamp burned for eight days without oil, for they had none.) We're expecting Aunt Rebekka. Always dressed in somber colors, she's a serious and composed woman. Everything Grandma and Rebekka do is done in a deliberate and dignified fashion. How very much alike these two sisters are. Then there is a sense of unease about what I can recall of my father, who squeezes into my memory in the form of a vague, moody figure decorating the Christmas tree. Little things cause him to grumble and complain: disappointment, the smell of cigars.

I remember lots of snow and snow forts, snowmen, and huge horse-drawn sleighs ringing with bells. Sometimes—quite a bit later—children's sleds would be hooked onto the back of the sleigh. My sister Miriam makes an appearance here. She's nimble and clever. Three years older than I, she knows how to chase after these chains of sleighs and hook up the sled I'm sitting on. Glorious delight as I lurch to and fro on these journeys. Later, I thaw out my cold and aching fingers under running water. Pins and needles tickle my cold, cold feet. Hot chocolate and sugar cakes provide solace.

Only seldom did I enjoy attention and affection from my father, who suffered under the stress of his professional commitments. Perhaps my father's cares—cares that increased daily—blocked the connection I yearned for, or maybe a child has to grow up first before taking part in a meaningful conversation with a father; I don't know. Only after 1933 does the memory of my father become clear—that is, after I'm five years old. His influence is perceptibly stronger at that point.

Somewhat later only my mother was at home. She was no longer allowed to play in public concerts and performances. As a result, her quartet disbanded. Lack of money forced my parents to set up one household in the less expensive apartment. For all of us this was the point when our lives began to deteriorate ever more rapidly, both externally and internally.

That my first impressions and explorations are so conspicuously tied up with Aunt Fanny is proof to me that we shared a special bond. As she had never married, she felt, I suppose, I was like her own child. At any rate, she spent a lot of time with me. My father once remarked that Fanny wasn't very smart. That's probably why no one showed her much respect. If anybody asked me today when I first felt human affection, it was on those excursions with tender, loving, thoughtful Aunt Fanny. The particularly bitter pang I feel whenever I think of her derives from one single moment during this time of terrible persecution that stunned us both.

I was probably thirteen when I did something to her that was quite, quite reprehensible. She asked for and needed my help—which I didn't give. That was the time when we were in a long column of frightened people accompanied by armed guards being marched from a collection point—the old riding school—to the freight train station at Königsberg's North Station. The transport of Jews had begun some months before, mostly in relatively inconspicuous contingents. In those early days, the people of Königsberg could choose not to notice what they didn't wish to see—and they preferred not to. This day was different. Hundreds of people had been ordered to a designated central collection point. Every person had been sent detailed instructions. You could take no more than thirty kilograms of baggage. Everyone had more. It was an unbelievable sight, what people thought they could carry. No doubt about it: there were many bad consciences in Königsberg that day. Some people were obviously in shock. This campaign of expulsion was too large to remain concealed from anyone any longer. All morning Jews trudged through the city, loaded down with their bundles. Many had to stop every few steps, others took advantage of small carts. Their faces were expressionless, tense, resigned. They looked like prey, creatures without hope. They were a pitiful sight, resembling only in outward appearance the streams of refugees that were later to pour from bombed-out cities. The condemned passed through the streets, and with few exceptions, their former fellow citizens, patients, customers, friends, or neighbors watched passively or turned away. Some Königsbergers certainly must have had bitter feelings or were aware of the terrible wrong taking place and their own helplessness. And those without scruple easily took advantage of the opportunity to profit from what had been abandoned: estates, houses, apartments, furniture, books, and positions now vacant.

Not only were many of my school friends in this transport, but also my revered German teacher Rosa Wolff and the no less revered and beloved Ruth Marwilski with her whole family. There too was my school chum Manfred Echt who sat next to me in class. Also there were Herbert Schimmelpfennig, Siegfried Veit, Heinz Markowsky, Rita Jordan, Julius Rosenstein, Rahel Schlabowski, Irmgard Augstuschalsky:

familiar faces were everywhere. I was completely confused—I wanted to help and to remain among them and even go with them, disappointed that I had not received the order to go to the collection point.

All morning long people were arriving at the collection point. The weather was good, but rather cold. A broad, open door led into the large riding school. Here SS men were standing around or were buzzing around tables with lots of papers and files. They were very polite; a few were even friendly, or rather professionally polite. Inside chaos reigned. People sat on their suitcases or lay on their coats or blankets. It was so crowded that it was almost impossible to pass through. The compulsory Star of David dotted the somberly clothed mass of people milling about, the yellow spots forming a decorative pattern. I too wore this star, in strict accordance with the law. But even with my yellow star I wasn't one of these people here on this day. I wasn't on any list yet that would mean a sentence of death—a fact that no one could yet grasp. I had sneaked in to say good-bye. Perhaps because I was still a child, the guards let me pass back and forth through the barrier. I was frequently asked to do small favors. There were hurriedly written letters to take care of. Some people suddenly wanted pocket change for bills—I have no idea why. I would eagerly scurry off each time to find stores that would break the bills. The proprietors and sales clerks saw the yellow star and helped me get the desired change. The coins I brought back were carefully tucked away.

There they sat or lay, torn from their familiar surroundings and fearing for their fate. The courage to think about this completely failed them. Yet it wasn't lack of courage, of course; it was the sense of the utter uselessness to speculate about the inevitable. We knew of acquaintances who had committed suicide—Dr. Gottschalk, my mother's physician, a woman—but wasn't that premature surrender?

Aunt Fanny was somewhere in the huge hall. I'd lost sight of her. The terrible pain of saying farewell choked me, and the choking sensation wouldn't go away.

And then the moment came when there were only a few minutes before everyone had to leave. I found myself near Fräulein Wolff and immediately picked up her luggage. It was way over the thirty kilogram limit. I wanted to stay with them for as long as possible and not be left behind. I wanted to help. Only now, I had to leave the building. I had no notion then of the danger I was in. The guards were no longer neutral or even polite. Suddenly there was a lot of shouting and yelling of orders. A whole company of uniformed men appeared out of nowhere. Registration was over. Those about to be transported were isolated. I should've long since gone outside, but instead, as the tide of people began to move, I was still there, carrying Fräulein Wolff's luggage. No one knew, of course, that in a few hours the larger pieces of baggage would be loaded onto a separate car, which would be uncoupled and left in the train yard. (We saw this with our own eyes when another transport left the main train station.) What they looted from the baggage was distributed to bombed-out German citizens of the Third Reich, *Volksgenossen,* after anything of value had been picked over.

But where was Aunt Fanny? She must have been in the front part of the column of people, because we hadn't gone very far—accompanied by guards to the right and left of us, armed with bayonets—when suddenly I saw her sitting on the curb, her face red from her exertions and looking at me with imploring eyes. She couldn't manage another step. I didn't know what to do. I hesitated too long. Already I was a few steps beyond her, loaded down with all the heavy luggage my old teacher couldn't carry. The column of people pushed me forward and made it difficult to stand still. Very quickly I turned around once more and once more our eyes met, her look pleading with me, then—for the last time—her look reproaching me, and I never saw her again.

What could I have done? What should I have done? Stepped out from the column of people? Taken care of her? Hugged her? Tried to comfort her? Stayed with her until she got help no matter what our guards commanded or threatened? Unable to do anything, I marched along. The moment had become traumatic, wounding two hearts past healing. And my guilt made me feel agonizingly worse.

Once we reached the train station, which was heavily guarded, I remembered my parents. They had no idea where I was or what I was doing. Then I put the large suitcase next to the sinister baggage cart, which was in the process of being loaded by railway personnel. Extremely anxious, Fräulein Wolff ordered me to somehow leave the station at once. It was obvious to us that the guards assumed everyone here belonged to the transport. The explanation I tried to give to one of the guards was therefore totally useless. I was turned back by a second and then a third guard. I had almost resigned myself to my fate when a soldier standing at a bend in the row of guards nodded to me to disappear as quickly as I could. I heard him having words with another guard ten paces away who had seen what happened, but I was running as fast as my legs could carry me, soon reaching a little bridge that was out of their line of sight and out of immediate danger.

A suffocating sense of grief almost robbed me of breath. It was a sadness beyond tears, beyond description. My undeclared beloved—Ruth—was gone, too. Utterly annihilated, I went home. I haven't been able to talk to anyone about this before now.

Someone must have brought Aunt Fanny to the station. At that time, they weren't shooting anyone where the people of Königsberg could see; that came later, for no one escaped "eradication."

I tried to imagine all these people dying. Were they abandoned and alone? How much did they suffer? Why does dying have to be painful? I quarreled a long time with God, who bears responsibility for our fate. For, of all His wrongs in this world, that one dies a hard death and another an easy one is the one thing I resent Him for the most—much more than a life that may be hard for one and easy for another.

It was never learned where this transport went. Perhaps to Chelmno, the concentration camp not so far from East Prussia in which they carried out their first gas chamber trials—or perhaps to Riga, or maybe even to Auschwitz.

These people belonged to me, and I to them. Their removal meant part of me was amputated.

But I've run way ahead of myself, probably to free myself from this part of my tale right at the beginning in one fell swoop—to deliberately face these very painful memories.

Nidden

Father, Mother, my sister Miriam, and I are boarding the train in the North Station. This train is pulled by a wheezing, smoking, whistling locomotive spitting forth soot. From the open platform, the villages look like what we build at home with our toys. Farmhouses and barns form a courtyard for ducks and chickens to run around in. Right nearby is the usual fenced-in vegetable garden and directly in back the various fields begin. Dogs and horses are the main companions to people everywhere, and everything fits harmoniously into the rolling countryside. This district is called the Samland, and East Prussians are justifiably quite fond of it.

We go as far as Cranz, where we reach the harbor. There I'm awed by the sight of a steamboat, which seems gigantic to me and will take us to Nidden on the Courland Spit. As I go up the gangplank to the bobbing boat, I'm all excited and happy.

Wilhelm von Humboldt rhapsodized about the Courland Spit and Nidden, which later became something of an eastern Worpswede: Lovis Corinth, Schmidt-Rottluff, Waske, and Pechstein among the many painters; and Humperdinck, Otto Besch, Erwin Kroll, and my parents from the musical and composing guild. They met at the guest house Blode. The pictures hanging at Blode's would be the pride of many a museum today. Thomas Mann had his vacation house in Nidden. Agnes Miegel, who loved nature, but was easily overcome by *völkisch* feelings for the homeland, should not be left unmentioned. Käthe Kollwitz relaxed in Rauschen, another idyllic place on the Samland coast.

For several years we spent our vacations on the Spit. In my mind, they blend together into one glorious memory, and my primary feelings from those years are intense, varied, and indelible: the calm, shallow lagoon on one side of the narrow strip of land, the billowy Baltic on the other. There were elk on this strange spit of sand dunes and forests, rare birds, too, and quaint old fishing villages on the lagoon. One of these was Nidden. A collection of picturesque little houses, some of them thatched, set down in the middle of lovingly cultivated gardens. On the banks of the lagoon, you could always hear the plashing and the gentle smacking of waves that slapped constantly against the thick wooden sides of the fishing boats known as *Keitel-* and *Kurenkähne*. These are clumsy, broad boats without keels, equipped with lea boards for shallow water. On top of these masts they had Courland pennants as weather vanes: an artistic hand-carved image filled with symbols and depictions of everyday objects, and at the same time serving as a sort of family coat of arms. Everywhere there were tiny docks, nets stretched out, oar-racks, fishermen smoking their pipes, and dogs and cats. Everything reeked of fish drying in front of the houses or cleaned on the beach and smoked. To smoke the fish, we children gathered *Kruschken*, which were dry pinecones handily lying about by the bushel. In payment, we were given a small, freshly smoked fish; nothing could be more delectable.

Every day we made a pilgrimage to the other side of the Spit to go swimming in the Baltic. We swam in the nude. Only in the afternoon did we children have the glorious liberty of running after the fisher boys, who for the most part were busy finishing their chores. We helped them or watched; more often than not, we were simply pests. They felt superior to us city folk and they were. After all, they could ride without a saddle, maneuver their boats skillfully with a long pole; they could make butter, mend nets, feed pigs and chickens, run barefoot across fields of stubble, and repair roofs. They also cleaned out the latrines, and that wasn't so easy. The boys were a hardened lot who dealt us some rough shocks. The latrine incident illustrated this the best. Picture the latrines: they stood behind the houses, some distance away in the potato fields. They were simple wooden shacks with two doors that had steps leading up to them. Hearts carved in each door, which served as both window and ventilation, hadn't been omitted, and inside was the bench with the round hole. A good distance below were the removable buckets that had to be emptied at regular intervals. You could reach the buckets from the back by opening large flaps that not only revealed the buckets to view but also the circular openings of the seats. You only had to look up from below at an angle. With diabolical pleasure, Hans Fischer had waited for the moment when both toilets were occupied to sneak me quietly into position. Then he carefully lifted the flap—one glance was enough to leave an indelible impression.

We had adventures of a different sort when we took boat trips to look for fish or horses. Horses were allowed to run free whenever they weren't needed. They weren't in danger on the narrow strip of land at all, but when they were needed again, you did have to search for them for hours, sometimes even for days. For transporting freight or people, the horse-drawn wagon was the only vehicle available if you didn't count the leisurely boat. (Motor vehicles were completely prohibited on the Spit.) Once we had found our horses, catching them was the next impossible task, especially if the horses had been given a treat.

My father's brother, Karl, was a talented and highly esteemed painter. But my father also liked to paint. I frequently accompanied him with paper and pastels, and he carefully taught me to open my eyes in order to really see. I began to recognize the colors in shadow, form, line, and contrast, and it was he who awakened in me a feeling and love for painting. He also made me aware of the many species of birds, their calls, and their melodies. It was the storks that intrigued us children most of all. They nested on the roofs, where they clacked raucously and were easy to observe. We gave them names and hunted frogs for them.

Excursions always ended up at the Thomas Mann house, a lovely vacation cottage on an overgrown rise at the edge of Nidden. The Schepses sometimes went along on these walks. The Schepses were our friends and had a daughter my age—Renate. Renate was my first love. I demonstrated this by teasing her constantly, sometimes making her cry. This fascinated me; why, I don't know.

The uniquely beautiful landscape of the Spit delighted us anew each day. The fine golden sand formed huge towers of walking dunes, which dropped off almost vertically toward the lagoon on the side facing away from the sea. They could reach up to 240 feet in height, and on the crest, on windy days, the blowing sand stung like needles. You couldn't stand it unless you wore the right kind of protective clothing. Sometimes we slid down the steep wall, setting off sand avalanches. That was frowned on, as the loosely-packed mountains of sand shifted quickly enough by themselves. Relentlessly, they buried everything in their path. Behind the bare dunes heaped up so picturesquely were hills

overgrown with grass. Adjacent to the hills were piney woods and mead-
ows filled with flowers. And always above us was the ever-changing
sky, bright blue with splendid cloud formations. Beetles, dragonflies,
lizards—we came to know and love them all. Only the elk hiding in
the woods were something of a mystery. You had to rise at the crack
of dawn if you wanted to see them drinking at the edge of the lagoon.
We crept along quietly in the soft beach sand, past the wooden docks
in the reeds, past the boats, the dories at anchor whose smell of tar and
fish (everything on the Spit smelled of fish) wafted ashore. The waves
continued to break gently. But the shy elk quickly caught our scent and
bolted off.

Every morning and evening a white steamboat appeared on water
that was almost always as smooth as glass, chugging back and forth
between Cranz and Memel. Its ugly plume of smoke always left a
streak of pollution across the sky, even after the dirty little fellow had
chugged past the horizon. The natives, mostly fishermen, combined
eastern cordiality with Frisian phlegm. They could be relied on; their
word was their bond. It really seemed beyond our imagination that
peace on the Spit could ever be disturbed. And in fact, it did take a
while longer before the first nasty songs suddenly reverberated here,
too, and before the tinker who went from village to village was reviled
as a "Yid." The trips to Nidden now came to an end, although "Nida"
remained as before under the "Lithuanian Administration."

Our vacations on the Courland Spit are my loveliest childhood
memories. Most assuredly they enabled me never to lose hope and
always to love life. In my darkest hours these memories were a source
comfort and courage.

School Days 1

Other memories call up an array of shifting scenes, often of seeming inconsequence. Nonetheless, they play a definitive and important part in my development, for early impressions are critical to the inner life of a child. The first feelings of fear, first relationships, the first concert at home, the first visit to the zoo, to kindergarten, to the art museum, and so forth.

> Grandmother Jenny is helping Mother and not only sees to proper household management by fussily straightening the beds—which I then proceed to mess up again—she also recites from memory poems and ballads, some of which she even sings in a quavery voice.

Grandmother was a well-educated woman with an astonishing memory and also a good pianist with perfect pitch. She encouraged me to improvise on the sweet-sounding Blüthner grand piano and stirred my imagination with stories. Alas, for all too short a time. One day, there was a crash in the corridor; Grandmother had fallen. She had to go to the hospital with a broken hip and then into a nursing home, where she lived for a few years. We children would visit her on occasion. She was always lying in bed and would delight us with little gifts and would recite something. But from one visit to the next she became frailer, softer, paler, until one day her time was up. This was devastating and made a very deep impression on us. It was my first encounter with death.

Visits to Aunt Rebekka are abiding memories too. "Cookie," as she was affectionately called, had white tousled hair, wore a brooch decorated with the bust of a woman. She lived surrounded by books, pictures, old-fashioned furniture, photographs, and hand-painted porcelain. We, that is my sister Miriam and I, were permitted to play carefully with her typewriter. We learned rummy and were given hot chocolate with an "American" (a sugary pastry). At Aunt Rebekka's were also Aunt Fanny and other relatives from the Jewish side of the family. I found out later that our get-togethers—always without Father—were Sabbath festivities. As religious but not Orthodox Jews, they had the custom of meeting with the family on Friday evenings and of eating a braided poppy seed cake with butter by the light of two candles.

By tacit agreement, all of these Sabbath family get-togethers took place under the long-standing custom "to be as harmonious and friendly with each other as you can be at least on this evening." As a result, an atmosphere of security and comfort is etched in my mind. Everyone showed a lively interest in one another and was peaceful and patient. Social harmony and Sabbath festivities belonged together, and that was the basis for my proclivity to the Jewish faith. Of course, general political developments constituted the definitive factor in my relationship to Judaism. This relationship will be a recurring theme in these reflections, in which my concept of God, always changing throughout my life, will play an important role.

We spent memorable hours sledding on the toboggan-run in Luisenwahl and skiing on the Veilchenberg. I learned to swim in the Hammer Ponds; excursions took us to Juditten and to the Samland. The Hufen was truly a beautiful neighborhood to live in! Then school began, which in my case is divided into two parts. For one year I went to the public elementary school, and afterwards to the Jewish private school. Two schools, two worlds—just as different as different could be. It is revealing of my parents' attitude that they believed even in 1935 that I would feel at home in a "German" school.

Klaus, the boy next door, went to the same school as I did, and we walked to school together. It didn't bother good-natured Klaus that later I wasn't a member of the *Jungvolk*, didn't wear the *Jungvolk* uniform, and didn't attend other National Socialist events—and not a month went by without National Socialist *Volkfests*, parades, and assemblies. But other children noticed me standing more and more often off to the side or being shut out, and they began to react to that. Besides, Jew-baiting could be seen everywhere or heard on radio. Unfortunately, there were also many adults, of course—teachers, sometimes even clergy—who weren't shy about making defamatory remarks. Often they were "only" the usual turns of phrases and little jokes about the "haggling Jew" or "Jew Itzig." But now such remarks collaborated in the official demonizing of the Jew and made the most perverted propaganda credible. Since it was now forbidden to protest or even to express an opinion that was pro-Semitic, the rabble-rousing propaganda could drip into the soul like concentrated acid.

To my misfortune, I was assigned to an enthusiastic National Socialist young woman as my class teacher. Her name was Frau Koske. She sticks in my memory because of several unpleasant incidents: Frau Koske greeted the class with a snappy "Heil Hitler," to which we were supposed to reply standing up. As she took down names, she immediately noted that there was a boy in her class of "Mosaic" religious affiliation and didn't miss an opportunity to speak with contempt, or even with disgust, about Jewish people. Like most anti-Semites, she most certainly didn't know a single Jew herself. In the daily lessons, the script usually followed was this: Frau Koske: "Heil Hitler, children, today I need to fill out a questionnaire with your help. I have to put down your fathers' military rank and their war medals to see if they fought on the front or if they served behind the lines." Except for three boys and me, every seven-year-old knew what his father had been in the First World War. The three who didn't know were permitted to bring the information the next day. I, however, was told to leave the room to go home immediately to find out. My astonished mother instructed me to say that my father hadn't been a soldier on the front but had been posted to a military hospital. Back at school, I repeated what I had been told. At first I didn't understand what Frau Koske meant when, turning to the other children, she said, "You see, that's just what I thought. Such a man is no frontline soldier!" This humiliation was proof of my inferiority. This, and the fact that I was supposed to realize I had been humiliated, affected me so strongly that to this day I still feel the sting. It hurts me too for my parents' sake.

Another time, she stood at the top of a long flight of stairs in school. It was just before class was to begin and we all had to come up these steps. When we arrived at the top, we greeted her in a friendly way, some of us saying "good morning," and others "Heil Hitler." When I said "good morning," she hissed at me furiously: "March down those steps and then we'll just see if you don't know how you're supposed to greet your teacher in the New Germany." I knew what she meant and in front of my curious schoolmates and other pupils, I came up the stairs a second time. Once again deeply hurt, but obedient, I said

when I got to the top, "Heil Hitler, Frau Koske." But that did not satisfy her at all. Enjoying her power and the drama, she ordered me to
come up the steps yet again and would I kindly raise my right arm to
greet her, "like a decent boy." I even did this—what choice did I have?
My schoolmates, incited by this, began to torment me more and more
and became increasingly violent.

One day it was announced: "The Führer is coming!" Hitler was visiting Königsberg that day and all the school children were lined up
along both sides of the main routes. Just in front of the section about
four yards wide that had been assigned to our class, Frau Koske had
us march up in rows of six. The streets were already lined with brown-
uniformed SA troops who stood at their posts like a chain in front of
the excited crowds. We came marching up the sidewalk and at the
appointed place, the order came, "Everyone, halt!" and "Left face!" Now
we stood, still in our rows of six, on the curb. By chance I was in the
first row, which offered an unrestricted and direct view of the great
event advancing toward us. We were told it would occur in half an
hour. Meanwhile the whole length of the approach was filling up
with people, uniforms, and flags. Since every household had to hang
at least one flag from the window, Königsberg had become a billowing
ocean of swastikas. Every fifty steps banners with slogans hung over
the street: "*Ein Volk, ein Reich, ein Führer*" and "Long live our beloved
Führer" and others. Probably my parents had to send me to school that
day, and quite certainly they had no idea that all school children were
being pressed into a theatrical backdrop of cheering supernumeraries.
In any event, I was once again in a precarious situation. Of course, the
giant spectacle captured my imagination too, and the general excitement and anticipation swept me along with the others. Certainly there
was the secret wish to belong and to be allowed to yell my heart out
along with everyone else. Every now and then, shiny cars carrying ex-
ceedingly self-important black and brown uniformed miniature Hitlers
raced past. Each time, I thought that the great historical moment—
that's what Frau Koske called it—had arrived. But the half hour of
waiting turned into one and a half hours, then two. In the meantime,
the streets had become packed with people. Now it really couldn't be
much longer. I can still clearly remember the sense of intoxication that
gripped everyone. All at once everyone was enjoying a new feeling of
pride, and anyone who hadn't felt so before, did so now. We were once
again a dynamic, wondrous *Volk*, strong and great, and had a genius

sent by God as Führer. A genius in the position to solve every problem—be it one of identity, meaning of life, education, culture or race, law or values, the economy or unemployment—he knew the right answer to everything. He, the greatest Führer of all times, as the faithful called him, promised to make Germany the center of the cosmos.

Suddenly there was a roaring in the distance that poured from a thousand throats screaming "Heil." At last. The great moment had arrived. Then Frau Koske's harsh, piercing voice stabbed me like a knife (she had just then come to the front to be as close as possible to her beloved Führer): "What, the Jew boy is in the first row? That's out of the question! Get back there in the last row now and you, Horst, come up here!" I still see the horrified, incredulous look of the Storm Trooper standing in front of me. Fortuitously at that moment everyone's attention turned again to the din approaching closer and closer and the almost hysterical screaming. There still wasn't anything to be seen. Once again deeply hurt, I was delivered up to a storm of inexplicable feelings and wanted only to evaporate into thin air. I could still see between the heads of others. The sounds of those baying "Heil" had reached our section of the street—first a few cars and then the dictator sanding in the car in a rigid pose that aped stern manliness, his right hand raised in greeting. All of a sudden everything became unreal and remote to me. But looking back on it, it was fortunate that I, too, didn't break out screaming in exultation at that moment like everyone else around me. I would never have forgiven myself later. In retrospect, every "Heil Hitler" that I was forced to say seemed a cowardly failure on my part or blasphemy, forgivable only because I was a child of seven or eight at the time. Surely responsibility is apportioned to the extortioner for what one does when under dire threat. A theme that would very much continue to occupy me.

Needless to say, such massive humiliations were not without consequences. The many little remarks, gibes, and insults hurled in the heat of an argument that somehow always included the word "Jew" had left wounds. I became sick more often and—as Mother told me later—my sleep became more and more disturbed. Although my parents probably only knew a small portion of what was happening to me, they did see my emotional turmoil and—thank God—took me out of the German elementary school to enroll me in the Jewish private school. This put an end to an agonizing school year. I couldn't know, or at best only guess, that everything would soon get much worse. My first reaction to being transferred to the Jewish school was one of relief. This reminds me of a saying of my mother's. She gruffly rejected my complaints and would say, "Just remember that it is more honorable to belong to the persecuted than to the persecutors."

My first school days were not necessarily typical for all German schools. My sister's experience in a girls' school was proof of that. She suffered very little from anti-Semitism and transferred to the Jewish school only when forced to do so by law.

School Days 2—
The Jewish School

Königsberg was a city that fired a child's imagination. It was almost a fairy-tale city for children, with an imposing castle in the center. In front of the castle stood a statue, larger than life, of the crowned Kaiser Wilhelm I, holding up a saber. In the square courtyard of the castle there was a wine cellar with the hair-raising name "Court of Blood." Not very far away there was a lovely pond belonging to the castle, with ducks and swans, where you could rent boats. There were picturesque bridges everywhere spanning the Pregel River and drawbridges leading to an island in the center city that often made us late for school. The dignified old cathedral, in which, utterly overwhelmed, I first heard the *St. Matthew's Passion,* dominated the "Kneiphof," as the island was called. The philosopher Immanuel Kant, whose words were engraved onto a plaque on the castle wall, was buried beneath the cathedral walls. The words were full of admiration for the starry heavens above, which I empathized with, and a moral law within, for which I later looked in vain and in which I no longer believe.

Many old warehouses had cranes in front always unloading something. The narrow, crooked lanes and heavy gates in the fortified walls of the old city testified to a long history. They turned the city into a stage set for sagas and fairy tales—far better than the pictures in my storybooks could. The opera house, too, seemed mysterious. My father played violin there. (In 1935 he had to give up conducting the seminar he had founded for music teachers, and his Königsberg String Quartet was no longer permitted to give concerts.) I found the university impressive too, as well as the bookstore, several stories high, of Gräfe & Unzer—which we called *Grunzer* (grunter).

Every evening my mother read to my sister Miriam and me. The things I read, saw, or experienced blended together into a world full of variety, colors, and sometimes agonizing questions. Now and then my imagination carried me away into the world of the story being read, transforming me into someone important. Here I was always somehow helpful and successful, or at least admired and loved.

When Mother registered me in the Jewish school, I couldn't believe these new teachers or this new school had anything in common with the school where I'd been. Right off, Herr Kaelter, the principal, gave me a piece of cake. He had married the day before and was in a merry mood that spilled over onto us. He introduced his young wife first thing and asked her to put on her wedding dress just like the day before, and after first refusing, she did so. Everything was so intimate and friendly. Principal Kaelter didn't behave like a drill sergeant, which is what I'd been used to. With my arrival at the Jewish school, a whole new, important period began for me. How satisfying I found the religion class, the study of Hebrew, the Jewish holidays, and the "Sabbath lessons" held every Friday. The classes were small, boys and girls together. That was highly unusual in those days. There were no favored or out-of-favor children, only congenial or difficult ones. Heini Herrmann, for example, was a difficult pupil. He defied the rules and ran away from the teachers, who for some reason or other, wanted to catch him. To the delight of everyone present, a cat-and-mouse chase over tables and benches ensued, which always ended with the teacher giving up. Manfred Echt, Manfred Hopp, Erwin Pätzold, and Werner Grumach became my friends; Liesbeth Dannenberg, Hella Sass, Hella Markowsky, and Ruth Marwilski appeared in turn in my dreams. The magnetic currents in the constellation of personal relationships confused me and ruled my life, bringing me both happiness and sorrow. The more threatening the Nazis became, the more we needed our friendships and mutual support. Most assuredly, there were already fierce stirrings of love.

The Jewish school was housed in the back rooms of the great synagogue, which wasn't all that far from the old cathedral—not on the island itself but just beyond on the other bank of the Pregel. I recall our teachers with gratitude: Herr Erlebacher, Herr Nussbaum, Fräulein Wolff, Fräulein Hiller, and later Herr Weinberg and Fräulein Treuherz. All of them really made an effort to give us as much as possible and to create something as a substitute for the unfriendly world outside.

It isn't easy for me nowadays to put into words the feelings that for me were bound up with the Hebrew texts, bible lessons, prayers, and

bright and cheerful holidays. Reading the Torah on the Sabbath, blowing the shofar on Yom Kippur, the Chanukah candles, matzo at Pass-
over, the Purim costumes—all gave me a deep sense of satisfaction and
allowed us children to feel, at least for a few years, that we mattered.
We couldn't ignore political reality. That was certainly taken care of by
the continual farewells from the children who were emigrating. Herr
Kaelter conducted the farewells most impressively during the Sabbath
class by tying a symbolic "heart string" on the departing child and
reading aloud the letters of those who had already emigrated. Each
farewell was a depressing occasion, frequently accompanied by tears.
These ceremonies were repeated week after week.

Day by day the malevolence intensified and the likelihood that we
might learn of some yet unconsidered place of safety to which we
might escape evaporated. The obstacles to emigration thrown up by
countries unwilling to give a new homeland to the disenfranchised
German Jew—this applied to nearly every country—were beyond
belief. The whole world knew about the Jewish laws that became more
draconian by the month. Laws that deprived these people of their ability to live and to exist.

Even so, I must say looking back that my young soul was so nur-
tured in the years from 1936 to 1938 by what I experienced and dreamt.
It is only now that I'm aware of how my whole life—especially my
inner life—was formed by these years. We children profited from the
activities of the adults, which shifted more and more to spiritual and
cultural concerns. In those years I still played with other children on
occasion in the street, and went to a movie every now and then—the
more radical bans weren't issued until later. But it certainly wasn't any
fun for me or other Jews to encounter National Socialist propaganda
everywhere. For example, nasty and slanderous attacks were regularly
inserted in the newsreels or previews. It was particularly bad in East
Prussia under the regime of the infamous Gauleiter Erich Koch. But
we children could ignore these things, at least to some extent. I practiced my violin and enjoyed listening to classic books read to me. We
also rehearsed whole plays that were normally appropriate for considerably older children. Intellectual pursuits and music transported us
from an appalling reality to a more beautiful world, albeit an abstract
one, but a world that did exist.

With violin pieces by Bach and Mozart, with the works of Shakespeare and Schiller (in those days we learned whole ballads by heart);

with Jewish history, prayers, and biblical texts; with gym classes or dance lessons; with attending synagogue together; and with natural history in the school courtyard or on the occasional school excursions—not one of us children had a reason to completely lose our belief in goodness. At least not just then.

It made for excitement, of course, when whole bands of *Jungvolk* ambushed us after school—sometimes whole gangs of them—and we were beaten up, although a few of us sometimes managed courageously and successfully to defend ourselves. Nonetheless, Herr Erlebacher, who was a trained boxer, frequently had to be called to box free the pupils who were pinned down or surrounded. Since I didn't look "Jewish," I suffered less from these attacks than my schoolmates. Later, when we all wore the yellow Star of David, I too was the target of cowardly and brutal attacks. I well remember a particularly nasty incident when someone landed a heavy blow to my unsuspecting head and immediately ran off.

In truth, the story of this tense period, with its incremental escalation of dictatorial abuses and preparations for war on the one hand, and my awakening to the first stirrings of love, spirituality, and artistic affinities on the other could fill an entire book by itself.

My father was interested in sinology and liked to hold philosophical discussions with me. Probably this is how I came to think intensely about God and even death at a relatively young age. I would say that my relationship to God at that time was a childlike and personal one, appropriate for my age, as the thought of death was overwhelmingly frightening to me.

This fear climaxed—it's hard to believe—in a performance of the *Freischütz* at the Königsberg Opera. I don't recall the exact year or how old I was. But it was just before summer vacation, when the opera was poorly attended. Father wanted to introduce my sister and me to the *Freischütz*. Mother was afraid to go to the theater or opera at that point, so Father put us children by ourselves in the first row. If we peered over the balustrade, we could see him playing in the orchestra pit. We also had the conductor State Kapellmeister Reuss directly in front of us. Then the lights went down, and my first opera performance began to unfold. It utterly engulfed me. I was so immersed in the music and what was happening on stage that when it came to the Wolf's Glen scene, waves of terror I had never experienced before and never would again swept over me. The agony was so acute that I can recall even today my full sense of fright. I felt like someone drowning or hurled from a tower; I will absolutely never again resist possible death so vigorously as I did then. I have no explanation for why this musical experience was so powerfully bound up with the fear of death. When my fear had become so great that I thought it impossible to escape death or something far worse, something curious happened. Something that today I believe and trust happens at a certain point to all who are dying or horribly suffering: out of despair and exhaustion I surrendered myself, I totally gave up, putting myself in the hands of a seemingly inescapable fate, and—oh, wonder!—I was released from my terror, out of the blue. It was as if the unbearable pain had all of a sudden ceased and I was cured and at the same time, armed for all the real death threats that were yet to come. It is possible that this was the most important moment of my life—I had overcome the fear of death, and as a result, perhaps the fear of anything. Today, I no longer have any doubt that someone who is dying experiences a similar sort of release, only much more encompassing and cathartic.

At that time I was much too young to follow the plot of an opera accurately, and the slightly kitschy "Don't shoot, Max, I am the dove" didn't have anything to do with the last stage of my great transformation. These were internal workings I surrendered to, triggered by the music and the stage setting. I became feverish that evening and I am told that I was pale as a ghost. I didn't become sick. I was already well; it was over or behind me. I don't know how to describe what happened. In retrospect I see myself as sort of a Siegfried, who was immersed in something that evening that made me invulnerable for all time. Everything that happened after this—be it a hail of bombs, imprisonment, hunger, or illness—couldn't touch me in my deepest core of self. Fear and worry were rather superficial from that point on. This experience not only gave me strength but also formed the basis of a fundamentally optimistic outlook—my joy and gratitude in being alive.

Kristallnacht and After

How could the ill-will—as I would define anti-Semitism—that one encountered on occasion grow to be so great an individual hatred, a psychosis of hatred?

As early as 1933, after Hitler had eliminated democracy with his *Ermächtigungsgesetz* (Enabling Act) and a flood of new decrees, the persecution of Jewish people began. The first measures taken were boycotts of Jewish businesses and legislation to exclude Jews from the civil service (April 7, 1933), from the Reich Chamber of Culture (September 22, 1933), and from the media with the *Schriftleitergesetz* (Editors' Law, October 4, 1933). After that there followed a period of systematic propaganda before the Nuremberg Laws decreed the total exclusion of the Jews in 1935. The *Reichsbürgergesetz* (Reich Citizenship Law) and the *Gesetz zum Schutz des deutschen Bluts und der deutschen Ehre* (German Law for Protection of German Blood and German Honor) essentially banned any intimate contact with Jews; later the laws added the penalty of death. These, along with the distinction between "Reich citizens" and the citizens with diminished rights who were called "subjects of the state," were the first official acts of discrimination against a minority and the first steps that culminated in the extermination camps. In the years before 1939, before the war began, more than 250 anti-Jewish measures were enacted.

As so often is the case, a powerful person need only reveal what he wants for vast numbers of opportunists immediately to materialize who overzealously try to curry favor. Government officials, judges, professors, schoolteachers, artists, journalists, even a few theologians suddenly were spouting anti-Semitic slogans. There was nothing bad for which the Jews weren't responsible. By participating in such abuse many could access perquisites and procure professional favors or promotion.

Failure to participate subjected others to indescribable agony and, ultimately, ruthless mass murder.

It's absolutely true that no one in Germany could ignore the
National Socialist propaganda. Radio, press, posters, and circulars in-
doctrinated everyone. Anyone going to a movie saw a sign at the
entrance, "Jews Not Welcome." Moviegoers then heard over and over
again in the newsreel before the feature, "Jews are our catastrophe—
responsible for everything—are preparing for the next war." Then
the same thing could be read in the newspaper or heard again at the
party gathering or company meeting. Even park benches, businesses,
and restaurants had signs saying "No Jews Allowed." Caricaturists,
photomontage artists, song composers, and versifiers contributed to
the inflammatory anti-Semitic rhetoric. Schoolbooks and texts were
edited as quickly as possible and woe to anyone who even cautiously
tried to speak up for the Jews. Books, pictures, compositions—everything that indicated the great Jewish contribution to German culture
was either burned or banned. The "Aryan paragraph" could be used
by any professional organization to exclude Jews. Laws and court decisions stripped Jews of protection under the law. Most Germans could
still maintain the belief that it wouldn't end in mass murder. But is
it decent that such total disenfranchisement and complete abasement
of fellow German citizens of a different religious belief—even if they
were baptized Jews—is accepted without protest?

Thus, it should come as no surprise that it wasn't only children and
young people who all too readily believed that the Jews were proto-
typically evil. Indeed, the bogeyman, the witch, and the devil were
harmless in comparison. It wasn't much better for Communists or
gypsies. When criminal, political, and Jewish prisoners were later designated differently in the camps, the intent was to inflict the worst
treatment, food, work, and shelter on the Jews. As this was happening,
these measures were unfortunately legitimized by the pseudoscientific
excuses of ambitious scientists; "race experts" played a particularly
shameful role.

In his position as Professor of General Psychology in Königsberg,
Konrad Lorenz, who would later be awarded the Nobel Prize, wrote
in 1940, "consequently preservation of race would still have to be
concerned with an even more rigorous eradication of those who are
ethically inferior than is the case at present. . . . Just as with cancer . . .
nothing can be recommended to the suffering human being other than

the earliest possible diagnosis and eradication of the disease ... we must—and may—rely on the healthy sentiments of the best among us and entrust them with the selection that determines whether our race thrives or decays." (I'll come back to this in more detail later.) The "best"—at that time they were undeniably criminals and murderers—needed just such scientists to justify what they were doing to the mentally and physically handicapped, to the Jews, to the gypsies, and of course to anyone who opposed the regime, whom they simply designated as "enemies of the people." The countless victims who were compelled to die for their dissenting beliefs should be remembered here. No one can accurately say who all witnessed these atrocities and escaped the malignant mass psychosis. At the beginning, of course, there were many who were shocked, intimidated, threatened, and persecuted. But sadly the number of those who were duped grew larger and larger—unbelievably large.

Mandating identification cards for Jews, making compulsory the use of the names "Sarah" and "Israel," placing a prominent "J" in passports meant that an important line had been crossed; these changes unambiguously identified those who were to be "eradicated." The yellow Star of David, which was introduced in 1941, could only be the next step in a series of similar measures designed to completely isolate Jews in camps and ghettoes. These were places from which almost no one ever escaped, and where "eradication" began in grand style. But first of all, there were the synagogues to burn, Jewish businesses and Jewish schools to destroy. This was the logical consequence of the vicious propaganda and the stream of new decrees. It's easy to see how such events weighed down upon a child my age between eight and eleven.

It's only partly a contradiction to say that while all this was happening, the late 1930s was an intense and, for many reasons, a lovely period. A child enjoys the privilege of a certain degree of autonomy in many ways. I mustn't forget the storekeeper, for example, who handed me candies when no one else was in the store, or the neighbor here and there who made an effort to be friendly and generous. Much relieved, I always made a mental note of these warm gestures.

That they all were very much afraid, or could have been, was no secret to me. Later, after the introduction of the Star of David and martial law, they would have had to fear for their jobs or even for their lives. The time when protest could've been effective was past and the opportunity to object was gone. The official representatives of the church, more than others, must stand accused of having missed their chance: when they energetically protested the removal of crucifixes from the classrooms and killing the mentally ill, it most definitely had an effect. Wasn't the cry from the people, "Crucify him," and hadn't the sufferings of Jesus tolled the warning against the evil humans could do? What then had devout Christians under Hitler's regime learned from Golgotha if they watched in silence and tolerated the way the word "Jew" became the occasion for persecution and extermination of innocent fellow citizens? Maria, Joseph, Jesus, and the Apostles were, after all—and who didn't know this—Jews.

You saw more and more often *Juda verrecke!* (Death to Jewry!) scrawled on the walls of buildings. We had no choice but to see every day on synagogues and schools these slogans that wished us dead. Hitler, who was already systematically preparing the next war, said (in the Reichstag speech of January 30, 1939), "If international finance Jewry inside and outside Europe should succeed in plunging once more the nations into another world war, the consequence will not be the Bolshevization of the earth and thereby the victory of Jewry, but the annihilation of the Jewish race in Europe!"

Consequently, the winter of 1938/1939 was unusually tense. Everyone feared the worst. The brief, illusory respite around the time of the Berlin Olympics lay two years in the past.

Of course we children only had the vaguest notions of what was happening politically, but I sensed my parents' worry and the looming danger. Ultimately, conversations always focused on some disquieting event, on new decrees against the Jews that fully affected Mother, my sister, and me as unbaptized Jews or individuals of mixed race brought up as Jews. One day Mother told me that the Herrmann family had emigrated and I could have several Märklin model kits, but only on the condition that someone went that very day to pick them up. I set out at once to retrieve four heavy kits with metal parts, screws, nuts, and wheels. But these kits were so heavy I almost had a heart attack dragging them down the long Schrötterstrasse with enormous effort, from the streetcar stop at Luisenkirche, and back home to Steinmetzstrasse. My joy, however, was all the greater afterwards when I began to build cranes and machines. The boy who lived next door, Klaus, always came over to play with me. His family, the Norras, ignored the propaganda. They had always known and liked us. Naturally, Klaus had to conceal his visits and keep them secret. That wasn't difficult because only the

Norras and our family lived on the fourth floor. And so, Hitler Youth Klaus—often in his brown uniform—and Jew boy Michael played with the Märklin kits or some other toy. Fortunately, my sister Miriam, three years older than I, and Klaus's sister Lilo, four years older, also got along well. Sometimes we set up a "magic lantern" and retold familiar stories about Longnose the Dwarf, Sleeping Beauty, and others, falling under their spell each time. When Mother told me to practice my violin, Klaus played by himself in the next room while I played "La Follia," variations by Corelli. I loved the violin and most of the time I enjoyed practicing. I also enjoyed being read to every evening; Mother knew how to make even the most distinguished classics exciting and interesting for us children. I was far too young for Goethe's *Iphigenie* and certainly for *Torquato Tasso*. Schiller's *Robbers* and *Wallenstein* were absolutely perfect for us. Anyway, I liked going to school and my books gave me pleasure, too. In the Jewish sports club Bar Kochba I was one of the best athletes in track and field. On the other hand, I was rather weak in spelling and arithmetic. But I was interested in all the other subjects: Hebrew, religion, music, German, biology. My painting, poetry, and composing always found an appreciative audience.

The Jewish ceremony of consecration, called bar mitzvah, usually had a long period of preparation for the thirteen-year-old to learn to chant or sing the texts from the Torah. This ceremony takes place in front of the entire congregation during the Sabbath services. I was already going to my bar mitzvah lessons and was learning my *mapach, pashto, munach, segol*. These are the musical tropes used to sing the Hebrew text of each Torah portion, of which there are over fifty, one for each Sabbath of the year. The Torah—the five Books of Moses inscribed by hand on a scroll of parchment—is marked with these pre-scribed chants in such a way that precludes any arbitrary or individual emphasis that could distort the intended meaning. However, the Torah doesn't have these musical marks for reading, so they must be memorized from special books. This is not so easy to do. (The Torah is sacred to the Jews. No one knows exactly how old it really is. It is assumed that it derives from the tenth to the fifth century B.C.) The two scrolls, covered with velvet, silver, and gold, are always handled as the holiest of holies in the synagogue and are kept in a splendidly carved ark. Reading from the Torah is always the high point of the Sabbath service. On the Sabbath of his bar mitzvah, the thirteen-year-old Jewish boy is permitted to chant a Torah portion for the first time all by himself. He wraps himself in a white tallith, which is often worked with black and silver threads. I would be ready in two years. I took my bar mitzvah lessons seriously and felt obligated to do my part well. I could already say the *Shema Yisroel* and a dozen Hebrew blessings.

It has been taken for granted that since the Jewish woman has no function to play in the bar mitzvah service, which consecrates only the Jewish man, she is delegated to a subordinate role. This discrimination does not mean less respect. Rather the opposite. Since the woman primarily takes care of the family, the position of the Jewish woman who is unmarried is particularly unfulfilling. Of course the married woman must agree to the role assigned to her. All these habits of behavior come from the interpretation of the Torah; that is, they are derived from the five Books of Moses. The pious Jew tries to live his or her entire life according to the commandments of the Torah, an almost impossible undertaking. The dietary laws alone and those concerning cleanliness are absurd in the context of today. As absurd as if regulations for desert caravans were to be applied to our modern traffic. But if you want to be a good Jew, you try to follow as many commandments as possible, with each Sabbath presenting certain difficulties. You aren't supposed to work (now, what exactly is work?); you aren't supposed to drive, carry money, or buy anything; and much more. Inconsequential things and the difficulty of interpretation made me rather ill, but I felt myself to be Jewish and accepted in this community.

One morning, my parents were very upset and worried. They wouldn't allow me to go to school that day, and told me that the synagogue—and that meant our school too—had been burned and destroyed. The children from the orphanage right next door had been chased out into the street in their pajamas. Herr Wollheim, the assistant cantor and head of the orphanage, had been badly beaten and they had tried to toss him in the Pregel on the other side of the street. Also countless Jewish men had been arrested and thrown into Gestapo prisons. Early the next morning, Frau Winter, an acquaintance, had gathered up the orphan children and taken them home. We knew that she still had a large house.

I was completely stunned and longed to get in touch with my schoolmates. But on this day, people feared for their lives, their freedom, and their health, and I wasn't allowed to leave the apartment. The radio and press reported a murder in Paris. Herschel Grynszpan had assassinated a German diplomat. Grynszpan wanted to avenge the deportation action that had forced seventeen thousand "stateless" Jews to be expelled to Poland on October 28, 1938. Göring and Goebbels immediately seized the opportunity now at hand to finally "eradicate" synagogues and Jewish businesses from German cities wherever possible. At the same time, the pogrom, carried out by the SS and SA dressed in civilian clothes, was declared to be the spontaneous outburst of the people's anger, and was supposed to show the world the "true" attitude of Germans toward their fellow Jewish citizens. The Jews had to pay material damages incurred in the *Kristallnacht*—even though only Jewish property was affected—in the form of monetary penalties of more than a billion marks.

Let us remember that one and a half years later Konrad Lorenz wrote, "We must—and may—rely on the healthy sentiments of the best among us and entrust them with the selection that determines whether our race thrives or decays." Could Lorenz possibly have known at the time that Hitler had granted in a letter to the chief of the Führer's personal Chancellery, Philipp Bouhler, and to his personal physician, Dr. Karl Brandt, full discretionary power to kill the mentally ill? There were similar actions already in full swing. Bishop Theophil Wurm, Pastor Friedrich von Bodelschwingh—and many others—protested most vigorously on their behalf. In a public sermon on August 3, 1941, Archbishop Count von Galen threatened legal proceedings on account of murder. In contrast, Lorenz's sentence, "consequently preservation of race would *still* have to be concerned with an even more rigorous eradication of those who are ethically inferior than is the case at present," must be understood as the demand to apply even more effective means of annihilation, in other words an Auschwitz. (I will quote his words at more length further on.)

When I was allowed to go out again, I went directly to the synagogue. Shaken, I stood out in front and saw for the first time a burnt and destroyed building. Only a few years later Königsberg looked exactly like this and, if you wanted to, you could see this as God's judgment. I couldn't. What happened "punished" us and many others in the same way and often more harshly than those who were really guilty.

When I saw my teacher Fräulein Wolff, she told me that they had desecrated the Torah scrolls by ripping them apart and throwing them into the street. The orphanage could be rebuilt and then we would take up our school lessons there. We must never give up. But the school remained closed for some time. We worked hard and gradually most of those who had been arrested were released. This police action was probably intended as a dress rehearsal—a taste of what was yet to come. Even if the Gestapo used the euphemism "protective custody," we were all aware of the mortal danger. During his imprisonment, the lovely voice of my Hebrew teacher at that time, Cantor Dr. Rudolf Pik, did not go unnoticed. His daughter Ursel told me this later. The Gestapo officers told him to sing the Horst Wessel song, and Pik then sang the "Techesaknah," a Jewish song. Annoyed, they forced him to translate the words: "Strengthen then your arms, brothers, who cultivate land wherever you are. Don't let your spirit fall. Happy and courageous, come shoulder to shoulder, to the help of your people." With that they set on Pik, beating his face to a pulp.

Everyone was very depressed. Everybody was trying to emigrate but for the most part with no success. When we went back to school, we saw the hulking ruin of our historic old synagogue each day, now a silent, accusatory memorial, a memorial to suffering. I believe it was only when the Jewish houses of worship were destroyed that many at home and abroad took notice of what was happening. Even those who had believed up until now that the worst couldn't happen in a civilized state like Germany took note. Burning synagogues as cries of alarm! The governments of other countries still didn't ease restrictions on Jewish immigration. Private associations, individuals, and religious groups in neighboring countries helped. Quakers offered tuition-free admission to house thirteen-year-old Jewish children in English boarding schools. The costs were underwritten in part by anonymous donors.

Our friends the Schepses had been given such a boarding school slot for their daughter Renate. But Renate was too young, and besides, one of their relatives managed to get her a visa to America. They offered my sister, Miriam, the place now available at the boarding school. My parents immediately agreed, and one day my little big sister went off to the train station with her baggage and violin, to leave us for who knew how long. We saw each other again only after ten years. Her lonely fate, among strange people in a strange land, without knowing the language might well have saved her life and most definitely spared her the gruesome rapes and deportation by the Russians, but her early exile was not at all easy for her, and her accounts of that time later affected me greatly.

After Miriam left, I flung myself into my religion more than ever, and that created even more intense bonds with my school friends, both boys and girls. My heart fastened particularly onto Liesbeth Dannenberg, a blonde, freckled girl with delicate breasts, who was somewhat older and certainly much more mature than I was. I fell in love again and became unsure of myself, confused, and filled with longing. It required quite an effort to look as if nothing were wrong, but somehow I figured out how to always have my seat directly behind hers when classes changed and we switched classrooms. In this way, I sometimes had her gorgeous long braids in front of my seat, which made me ecstatic.

If only it hadn't been so difficult for me to catch her eye! She simply wouldn't take notice of me at all, until an idea occurred to me that was to have serious consequences: it was in Fräulein Wolff's German class. I had by chance—or intentionally—a few thumbtacks and just as Liesbeth's braids were lying on my desk, I jammed them down securely with several thumbtacks. Mission barely accomplished, and Fräulein Wolff was already asking her a question. According to the custom of the day, you were supposed to stand up immediately to answer. But when she tried to stand up, her head violently jerked back before the thumbtacks popped loose. Like the smart girl she was, she took in the situation at once. Before I could blink, I got such a vigorous slap that my cheek was still red when I got home. Fräulein Wolff also took in the situation astonishingly quickly and, since she felt that the punishment fit the crime, she overlooked the incident as if nothing had happened. She only threw herself a little bit more into the lesson. I immediately grasped that I had done something serious. Something that I would always remember. Some time after this class, I fell in love Ruth Marwilski.

The War Begins

Father's outbursts of temper are terrifying. One time it's the heat that's gone off, then it's the tableware that's not clean enough, or the afternoon nap that's been disturbed, or someone has feasted on his late afternoon piece of cake—that would be me—or the food has been badly seasoned. There's always some new unexpected shock. He doesn't accept an invitation from his relatives in Sweden. It would have been our salvation. Almost sixty years old, he lacks the courage to move to a strange country where he would have to begin anew. His conscience torments him. He studies Chinese furiously and talks with me about Lao Tze and Confucius.

All of us retreat into other worlds. Mother practices her violin as often as possible, and plays sonatas with a pianist. She urges me to make use of my time—whatever she means by that—and checks my school-work to make sure it's done correctly. In the few moments I have to myself I try to figure out on my own what I can about sex. I seek counsel from our multivolume *Meyer* encyclopedia. With the help of cross-references—"*see* Woman," "*see* Vagina," "*see* Intercourse," "*see* Birth," and so on. I hope to figure out what no one will explain to me. I don't put much faith in the obscene comments of other children. There are certainly plenty of questions, but this method works, too. If it would all somehow fit together! *Meyer's Lexikon,* Jesus's injunction to "love thy enemy," "String up the Polacks," Mozart sonatas, "The SA Is Marching," Goethe's "Noble be man, helpful and good,"—but not toward Jews, gypsies, homosexuals, Jehovah's Witnesses, the French, Slavs, or enemies of the people.

Germany became swollen as it swallowed country after country. The *Wehrmacht* marched into Vienna.

46

Austria becomes a part of the Third Reich. Then it is the Sudetenland's turn; six months later the remainder of the Czech state is occupied. And, in the same month almost as an afterthought, so is the Memel region.

The Western Powers were trying to preserve peace at all costs.

Herr Dossow, the grocer across the street, and Herr Rogalli, who lived on the second floor—our block warden, are now wearing SA uniforms.

Dossow threatens my father that there will be consequences if Jews continue to come visit us. We pay no attention.

Later Father was about to lose his appointment as a violinist with the city orchestra, and he asked his famous niece, Dorothea Wieck, for help. She succeeded in getting an order from Göring directed to the city administration of Königsberg. Immediately, Father's dismissal was provisionally withdrawn.

In school we put on a performance of *Wilhelm Tell*. I'm allowed to play the part of Tell and construct a crossbow for myself. There are many lines to learn, but we're used to that. We've always had to memorize poems, ballads, songs, prayers, and vocabulary. On Friday after Sabbath class, the last class of the week, Herr Weinberg teaches dancing to anyone who wants to learn. He plays the piano splendidly for the lesson. I'm really too young, but that doesn't bother Herr Weinberg, and besides, he knows how much I like his playing. He's very talented and can play symphonies and everything he knows by ear.

Once he put a sheet over the keys and played just as well. We were so amazed and awed that he even brought along his bedclothes one day. He proudly gathered us children around the piano, again with a sheet covering the keys. This time he completely wrapped himself up in the bed covers with a flourish and a great deal of hocus pocus. It was all white and spooky, especially when he worked himself up into a rage under the sheet. He was a terrifying ghost, but the fact that he couldn't see us at all inspired us to high jinks. First, Manfred Echt held a battered beaked cap over Herr Weinberg's head. Then someone fetched the teacher's big felt hat from the coat rack. We could scarcely contain our laughter. No one was listening to his playing anymore,

which at this point was getting ever more out of hand. Then it happened: Erwin, who was holding the hat just over his head, sometimes
this way and sometimes that, suddenly dropped it. At the height of our
merriment, the ghost crashed to a halt. Not only was Herr Weinberg
terribly frightened, he was hurt and deeply offended. It took weeks, if
not months, before he touched a piano again.

The Stocks lived on Steinmetzstrasse directly across the street from
us. Dr. Stock was also not quite "racially pure" from the point of view
of the master race. He also suffered for it. But his wife and daughter
looked like the typical ideal German woman of the time: the mother
was blonde with her hair pulled back in a bun and parted in the
middle, the daughter had braids coiled into a bun over each ear. As was
fitting, both played the piano. The daughter Ute—two years older than
I—also played the recorder. Charmed, I eavesdropped on her playing.
Sometimes I practiced in front of an open window in the hope of
inspiring her admiration. So I was quite satisfied when Father told me
that the Stocks had been very impressed by my progress. That wasn't
enough for me. I wanted to paint something important and, if possible, better than Michelangelo. Inspired by copies of the ceiling frescoes
of the Sistine Chapel, I painted philosophical pictures of the under-
world and heavenly paradise. My room stank of cheap oil paints.

Father generally celebrated Sunday mornings with a long walk, often
taking me along with him. Mother scarcely left the house anymore.
On these walks we discussed, among other things, deep philosophical
ideas, often from ancient times. Maybe this helped him ignore the dis-
tressing fact there were more and more people on the streets in uniforms: HJ (Hitler Youth), BDM (League of German Girls), SA and
SS, army, air force, and navy. Uniforms in all possible colors and with
every imaginable insignia. Like any boy, I found it fascinating to identify the outfit and the officer's rank. Whenever someone uniformed
went by, I said to myself: second lieutenant, Hitler Youth sergeant, army
corporal, German *Jungvolk* troop leader, and so on. Without a doubt,
most of those in uniform enjoyed having their rank documented for
all to see, and there were unquestionably moments when I regretted
never being able to wear a handsome uniform. The military element
on the street became more and more pronounced. I was fascinated by
the ever more frequent parades with tanks and cannons. In all honesty,
I sometimes had the feeling I could've been on the other side. It was
my fate, however, to be persecuted, although it certainly wasn't what I

deserved. Had I not been a Jew, even I would have had to join some sort of group with a uniform and unfortunately, I can't exclude the possibility that the general zeal would have infected me. How mature is a child, after all, I was eleven years old.

The toys and paraphernalia in my room reflected conflicting influences: a small Torah scroll and busts of Hitler in my stamp collection, a Chanukah menorah and a toy cannon, my violin and a carton of Christmas tree decorations, tin soldiers and teddy bear, a catapult and a four-volume set of poetry, an Indian costume and a little later a tallith, the Jewish prayer shawl.

In those tumultuous times, the Stocks took me along to the cathedral. There the *St. Matthew's Passion* was being performed.

I'm cautioned to be careful and to avoid anyone I know or who might know me. In the crowded cathedral the magnificent music washes over me and grips my soul. And so, sitting next to Ute, Bach's *Passion* was the second musical experience to overwhelm me. Only the words I found heinous. (I see a direct psychological link from "Judas, who betrayed Him" to "Judas, die" to Auschwitz.) Whenever the Evangelist sings the name of Judas, I cringe, and I think he's referring to me.

Primitive human emotion can be quite raw indeed. Besides the Romans, mostly Jews (Semites) lived in Jerusalem. But Jews are linked with Judas, not with Jesus as Christ. Judas's name even sounds like the word "Jew." The answer to the question "Why do you hate the Jews?" is often "They crucified Christ and Judas betrayed him." Christ is equated to Christians and Judas with Jews. Even today, after everything is over—or is it?—the words of the Evangelists give rise to the same sense of dread whenever I play or hear the *Passion.*

Military parades to demonstrate power and to menace neighboring countries and at the same time religious services preaching the gospel of Jesus and portraying his sufferings (such as *St. Matthew's Passion* in the cathedral) are emblematic of the juxtaposition and, frequently, the fusion of church and war. Instead of courageously advocating peace and love and consistently rejecting any manifestation of hatred, the Church came to terms with those filled with hate. As a consequence, they could act as if they had the blessing of the Church. Sadly, the question must be asked: Just how many wars has the Church been actively and successfully able to prevent? Aside from those, of course, waged in its name!

Tensions worsened daily. Hitler provoked other countries, risking war. The arms industry had long since been building up for war, autobahns were being built for moving troops, young men were being trained, propaganda was being systematically churned out. Even the surprise of a signed Non-Aggression Pact with the Soviet Union could only mean disaster for others, and so it was indeed.

After many years, Jew-baiting was suddenly augmented with vehement Pole-baiting. Loathing for the Poles and the invective "filthy Polack" suddenly appeared and quickly became progressively worse. With Hitler's announcement on September 1, 1939, "As of today, fire will be returned" (as if weak Poland had attacked strong Germany), the Second World War was set in motion. And the penultimate chapter of the disaster could now begin. The quick victory over Poland and over the other neighboring countries attacked next—Denmark, Norway, Holland, Belgium, even the surrender of France—propelled Hitler and his followers to the pinnacle of their power. Everyone around us was roaring approval. Victories and capitulations were always being celebrated. Every household was required to hang at least one flag with the swastika out the window. Everyone was gushing over Hitler as the greatest statesmen, the greatest commander, the greatest German of all times. All of Germany was deluded. All of Germany was drunk. All of Germany was intoxicated with the certainty of absolute superiority, of nobility, of being more important than anyone else. Before such aberration ended in catastrophe, there was much too much time for a great deal of misfortune.

Bar Mitzvah

The months leading up to my bar mitzvah and those afterwards were filled with events, each one of which, if taken by itself, made us tense with anxiety. Each blow imposed adjustments and restrictions. Food rations for Jews were continually being cut and, as an extra restriction, the ration cards were also stamped with a "J." We could buy food only in special shops at given times. We weren't allowed to take part in air raid drills. A curfew prohibited Jews from being on the street after eight o'clock in the evening. At fourteen, all Jews were drafted to work, mostly in dangerous jobs, such as in chemical factories, mines, or collecting garbage. My mother was already working ten hours a day in the chemical factory of Gamm & Son.

The invasion of Russia on June 22, 1941, resulted in air raid alarms for the first time and a few minor explosions from some Russian aircraft. For the time being there were only victories, and at first, the war served to feed Nazi egos. Except for Switzerland, all of central Europe was occupied, even part of the Balkans. In May, Yugoslavia and Greece were invaded. Norway and Denmark laid down their arms. And Hitler would certainly have marched into Sweden had it refused to allow transports and deliveries of iron ore across its territory. Against Hitler's acts of aggression, the world seemed defenseless.

Despite regulations directed at Jews and the war news, my violin and young love, Confucius and Karl May, it was my bar mitzvah that defined the month of July for me; it became the overriding concern that pushed everything else into the background.

In a residential neighborhood in the old part of Königsberg, where the buildings were jammed together, there was Seilerstrasse (formerly Synagogue Street), and there, in a narrow side street, stood the synagogue Adas Israel. Adas Israel was founded by an independent group of Orthodox Jews who had broken off between 1899 and 1921 from the Königsberg Jewish congregation that seemed too liberal even for them. This came after years of differing opinions about religion and finances. Although *Kristallnacht* had destroyed the building and religious objects, the desecrators hadn't been able to set it ablaze. They would have endangered the entire neighborhood. The damage therefore could be repaired, and services held again. But those in charge—unlike those at the synagogue that had been torched—were Orthodox Jews. They insisted on strict observance of commandment and tradition.

My rather liberal teacher had emigrated in the meantime, and the devout Herr Benjamin took over my instruction. He was a kindhearted man, who believed that by observing every commandment he could achieve a sort of invulnerability. He lived in such a manner that he could assume in good conscience God was pleased. And since everything happens by God's will, he was calmly able to entrust himself to God. He firmly believed God's will revealed itself in the fate of mankind. So there were scarcely any problems except the one of how one should behave in order to be the recipient, if possible more so than others, of God's good will.

This God-fearing man made a great impression on me, and he certainly handed his religiosity and way of thinking down to me. He even knew the brother of my grandfather, Israel Hulisch, whom he held in high esteem as a pious rabbi. He probably thought that the nephew of such a great-uncle must also possess the wherewithal to become a pious Jew. He often invited me home after Sabbath services. Before we sat down to a festively presented midday meal (there was precious little food), everyone washed one's hands and gave the blessing and benediction, the *b'rucha*. The same ritual occurred before the first bite and before the first sip: "Blessed art Thou, O Lord, our God, King of the Universe, who has brought forth bread from the earth" or "who has brought forth the fruit of the vine." Understandably, the good Lord being called on so much, all conversations were mostly religious in nature. The sermon, a psalm, Jewish history, the commandments of Moses and their interpretation were the favored topics.

I became an Orthodox Jew. I laid tefillin (leather straps for saying the morning prayers) every morning, studied Hebrew assiduously, and prepared for my bar mitzvah. I alienated my parents during this time, and I still remember my father's horrified look when he caught me at my morning prayers. I was very embarrassed when he winced. Mother didn't know quite what to say. I had actually wanted to follow, and should have followed, all the dietary restrictions but there I came up against insurmountable difficulties. After all, it wasn't I who did the cooking and food of any sort was scarce. I had no other choice but to follow the rule that had always held in our house: you ate what was on the table.

On the Sabbath the pious Jew is not permitted to ride, but it was so far to the synagogue that I would've had quite a long walk. During Pesach, one is supposed to eat only unleavened bread (matzo) and on Yom Kippur, one must fast. To scrupulously keep all these commandments would have taken my parents' support. Lukewarm tolerance alone wouldn't have helped. This meant I was constantly shifting between observing commandments and breaking them—an ambiguous situation. Since I took my relationship with God absolutely seriously, this hypocrisy depressed me. For the time being I had no other choice but to live with the contradictions and broken commandments; I was compelled to lead a sort of double life. In school, at synagogue, or with Jewish friends I was an Orthodox Jew. At home I neither kept kosher nor could I follow other commandments with any consistency. Herr Benjamin saw in me the good Jew and my parents saw the good son.

When the day of my bar mitzvah finally dawned I was so thoroughly steeped in forms of Jewish veneration of God that God could not be separated from Jewish ritual. The day I was to step before the "countenance of God," as Herr Benjamin put it, was the day that God's countenance had Old Testament attributes. As a God-fearing Jew, I bowed before Him. I remember the day.

The morning was lovely and the sun hot. It was the end of July and Mother had carefully put out my suit with long pants. I said my morning prayers as devoutly as I could, neither ate nor drank, and put my tallith in a small blue velvet bag. Father had an orchestra rehearsal and, so it seemed to me, he didn't want to have too much to do with my bar mitzvah. Everything was strange to him and perhaps not even very agreeable. I don't know but I prefer to assume that as a gentile he didn't want to disturb my Jewish dedication to God. I told Mother I was walking to synagogue and not, as I usually did, riding half way.

I leave the house way too early, and Mother's parting words are at the same time—I am sure of this—her blessing. In the synagogue we are sitting apart according to Jewish custom, and I will see her only after everything is over.

All sorts of thoughts go racing through my head on the long walk to the synagogue—so many that the distance seems twice as long. When I turn off into the Seilerstrasse, I meet some school friends. Ruth, blushing and embarrassed, hands me a flower. She is a quiet and very sensitive girl, and I love her with ever changing emotions.

It's truly my day. How lucky I am to be the only one bar-mitzvahed. We enter the synagogue's sanctuary through a narrow corridor, and someone shows me to my special seat. Everyone is attentive and is treating me like a worthy adult. I'm getting more and more nervous. I'm sort of worried about whether I've really learned everything right. My text is a rather long passage from the Torah. I'm not really aware of the beginning of the service. I'm becoming paralyzed with stage fright. My big moment is taking forever. Now it's here.

The Torah is solemnly taken out of the ark and laid on the altar-like table. I know I must wait for some paragraphs to be read before I begin, but I'm beginning to feel a little bit more confident. I've been studying for years. Wearing a velvet yarmulke and tallith, I step forward when I'm called. The cantor steps aside, and I touch the two wooden handles of the Torah scroll, I genuflect and utter the Hebrew blessing: "Blessed art Thou, O Lord our God, King of the Universe, who has given us the Law of truth." Rabbi, cantor, and assistant readers glance over to me, nodding encouragement, as I step up to the left side of the Torah. It's still not my turn to read. I'm now standing next to the cantor, who chants the last paragraph—just before the one I've learned—in a loud and resonant voice. Then, suddenly, there's a silence that I'm supposed to fill. All ears and eyes are now focused on what will be coming out of my mouth. The recitation of the *b'rucha* was only a preliminary step to the big moment that is now at hand. The Torah is written in Hebrew without vowels; I have to know the vowels and the marks indicating the melodies by heart. When I sing the first words, they sound slightly hoarse and faint to me. I hear this at once and force myself to sing loud and clear. It works. I chant my portion flawlessly. Then I step to the right side of the Torah, and the cantor continues with the next paragraph of the Torah portion. It only takes a few minutes, then I make another genuflection and recite another *b'rucha*. The rabbi blesses me and says a prayer for my parents. We've arranged this beforehand. Afterwards I go back to my seat and await the end of the Torah reading. Then comes the very pointed sermon, which is directed to me. The rabbi talks much of the expression of faith and constancy. He speaks of a wanderer who wraps himself in his coat when it is stormy and snows, but who takes it off when warmed by the sun. The rabbi's metaphor refers to Judaism, to the Jewish religion that always provides shelter in times of need. In the course of my life I will often think of this and take issue with it. In this moment I believe he is right. I am extremely moved, excited, and happy. Afterwards everyone is congratulating me. It's now late, and Mother tries to persuade me to take the streetcar back home. I really don't want to do this today, and again the long walk home gives me the chance to reflect about things.

I definitely hear the words of the sermon that doubt I will remain true to my Jewishness. What else could such a warning mean?

At that time I understood the expression of faith to be the observance of lots of commandments I couldn't do much with. In addition to the dietary laws, many commandments didn't have logical reasons. To perform illogical acts only because Moses had called for certain ways of behaving several thousand years ago seemed to me to be extremely difficult. It could be that I really would soon wear the coat of Jewishness somewhat more loosely.

I had no doubt that in difficult times God's good will would be essential—and everyone felt that even more difficult times would be coming. Today I find the idea quite troubling that in the face of threatened mass destruction, people were thinking and worrying about the proper observance of biblical commandments. Assuring a future by not using the streetcar on the Sabbath; passively surrendering to fate as the worship of God.

How many millions of people of all faiths who died horribly endeavored beforehand to win God's good will through self-sacrifice? To those who studied what happened in the concentration camps, speculation that God burdens those he especially loves with a difficult faith would be cynical mockery of the dead. The devastation that a mother, a father, or a child feels when they are separated from each other as death nears—as often was the case before being gassed or shot—is so indescribably immense and profound that this form of suffering can no longer be included in the category of a divine test. Such a terrible punishment would make the tester into the most brutal being that human imagination could think of. God would be no "Father in Heaven," who deserved the attributes of merciful, just, or loving ... these thoughts, however, stirred only later, and with them the "countenance of God" began to alter.

The bar mitzvah ended quite unfestively, although with all sorts of presents. Without question, the day was of great significance. Even though with increasing maturity, more experience, and more insight into life I imagined God differently, my bar mitzvah remained an important part of the struggle with my belief in God. There were other confrontations when I was in the danger of dying; even during my intense search for Him. Even in the flashes of clairvoyant knowledge of myself, the future, or of other people, a certain something beyond the imagination was revealed—God. Little by little, God became a force for me, a primal energy that dwells in all things. Spinoza's *Ethics*, the *Bhagavad Gita*, Buddhism, Jesus' gospel of love, and even natural reason became various lenses that modified my view of God and diverted me from rituals with which I hoped to attract God's attention.

As I was celebrating my bar mitzvah, Göring was charging Heydrich with preparing "financial and material matters for a total solution of the Jewish question" in all the territories under German control in Europe. Just a few weeks later the first gassing experiments took place in the concentration camp of Chelmno near Posen and in Auschwitz. Thirty-four thousand people were killed in the massacre of Jews near Kiev at Babi Yar.

The Star of David

Mother saw to it that I kept up my interest in literature and poetry, ensuring that it was a source of hope and a refuge. Revealing its power, as it always does in times of need, music became the source of consolation. The wisdom to be found in proverbs sustained our belief in goodness. Any expression of human warmth made us happy and nourished our souls. Although I couldn't yet know the last months of school and time with my friends had begun, what we did and felt was extraordinarily intense. This could only be explained by a sense of foreboding of the impending disaster. Erwin Pätzold was working on an essay, already over a hundred pages long, on a Jewish subject. Manfred Hopp's phenomenal memory for historical dates was awesome and I tried my hand at deep philosophical prose. At home, painting after painting ensued and I practiced the Mendelssohn Concerto and the Rhode Études. Fräulein Wolff invited us to her house after school to read Shakespeare, each of us taking a role. I also found excuses to go into town on my bike; all my thoughts were of Ruth, whom I hoped to meet on the way. If we did happen to meet, each of us tried to appear as nonchalant as possible. If the devil was at work, then we snubbed and wounded each other. But more often we betrayed that we liked and understood each other. On occasion, we caused each other not only pain and doubt— as if there weren't enough of that—but also great happiness too, which we both longed for.

Our neighbor Klaus came over regularly. When I visited him to play with his wonderful toy train, the playroom was locked from outside so that no visitor or relative happening by could discover the Norras had contact with Jews. We children could handle the defamatory statements, anti-Semitic posters, and decrees. Up until this time, circumstances unknown to me were shaping and misshaping my life. They were perhaps worthy of note, but as far as I was concerned nothing extraordinary. A child who squints or is handicapped in some way will suffer just as much disparagement and disappointment.

The details of politics and the war itself meant little to me. They were something that I was powerless to do anything about, like the weather. I did follow the advance into Russia with strange fascination, marking each newly conquered city with pins on a map on the wall in my room. Now why did I do that?

In those days my half-brother Peter visited his (my) father. Peter was a Nazi and a highly decorated officer, who had been in a tank on the frontlines in the Polish, French, and Russian campaigns. Understandably, there was a great deal of tension between Father and Peter, and we didn't know how he would react to Mother and me. He was haughty and very cool toward us, rejecting every gesture of pleasantness. While he was speaking with Father in the living room, his officer's cap was hanging next to the mirror in the corridor. Mother was in the kitchen. Carefully and stealthily, I took his cap off its hook, put it on, and stared in the mirror for a long time. What was I thinking of? Today I can't say, but one thing is certain: without the inclination to the same vanity with which so many young men wore uniforms and medals of bravery, I wouldn't have put on the cap. We weren't, after all, as different as the Iron Cross and Star of David were supposed to indicate.

It took Father a few days before he repeated to us the shocking details his son had told him. I was particularly shaken by the mention that they—who were they? surely not Peter—had poured gasoline over a Russian wearing his war medals and had set him ablaze. Peter was wounded at Moscow; most likely he survived the war because he was reassigned as an instructor. After Germany collapsed, he remembered his Swedish relatives and withdrew from the view of the funeral pyre he had helped to build.

Suddenly, piercing through walls and doors, a dismal wail burst from the woman next door. It was shockingly out of tune with the sounds of joyous victory celebrations and the strains of "Germany, awaken!" The telegram announcing the heroic death of their son Helmut crushed the parents. A bullet from a Russian fighter had ended his young life. Helmut was the great hope of the petite bourgeois Norra family. He had done splendidly on his *Abitur* (school-leaving exam) and was on the way to surpassing all his relatives on the social ladder. Helmut, not Klaus or Lilo, was their pride and joy. For the Norras, the dream of a

Great German Reich was no longer an issue. They never stopped complaining about their suffering. They were inconsolable.

Like a blow—not really a surprise to anyone by now—the order came to wear the Star of David. This marked the second anniversary of the war; it was a date marking a turning point. Had it been possible up until now to cling to the notion that all measures against the Jews were to be understood as professional, financial, legal, and social restrictions, from this point on it was absolutely clear they intended to totally eliminate the Jews. The first deportations confirmed this assumption; more and more place names were becoming linked to concentration camps or KZs. On October 23, 1941, a new decree prohibited any further Jewish emigration. The trap had snapped shut. Planning the "Final Solution" (that was the phrase that had been gaining in currency for some time) could begin. All Jews had been considered racially inferior and a danger to the *Volk* for years. Every humiliation in German history was blamed on them. Once again the Jews were the scapegoats; and there were many who prided themselves on being part of the great tradition of German intellectual accomplishment who thoughtlessly took part in the condemnation of the Jews. Condemnation is indeed the seed from which evil grows. This is the basis for estrangement, marginalization, and finally mass murder; only by these means did criminal acts take on the color of legal measures needed to save the German people. What a "scientifically" written article calling for euthanasia and for "eugenic measures" actually looks like can be seen in the following excerpts from Konrad Lorenz's article that appeared in 1940 in the *Zeitschrift für angewandte Psychologie und Charakterkunde (Journal for the Science of Applied Psychology and Personality)* entitled "Interferences in Species-Specific Behavior Caused by Domestication."

The essay is the one about the Greylag Geese. In the final sentence of his introduction Lorenz emphasizes the purpose of his work: "I hope in fact to fulfill a much more ambitious goal, *to direct the eyes of those chosen for selection to very specific values, whose cultivation must remain restricted to those so selected because they cannot fundamentally be influenced by education or acquired traits.*"

The following quotations should reveal the full extent to which theoretical speculation can hold humanity in cold contempt and how it distances itself from human suffering. Using the jargon of National Socialism, Lorenz writes of the "parasites of the race," of "those who are ethically inferior," and "socially inferior human material." These must be all unconditionally eradicated, as must be those who are "afflicted with genetic deficiencies"; and eradicated, too, must be those of alien race whose "elimination from breeding" is thus such a simple thing because one can recognize them so much more easily than the others. The opposite to all this is the "unblemished members of the species" in the "body of a healthy race." "Blood traits" and the "best genotypes" must be protected from the slightest deterioration by "eradication," because "nothing can so seriously damage the continued existence and further development of everything for which we live and struggle." You couldn't more vigorously encourage or support the Nazi program of euthanasia and the destruction of the Jews. (The explanation that he "only" meant the criminal elements doesn't wash.) Read and see for yourself:

> If there are factors favorable to mutation, the most important *duty of the one who will preserve the race* is without question to recognize and to eliminate them; the possibility of humans having genetic deficiencies in their species-specific social behavior constitutes a danger for the *Volk* and for the race more seriously than does cross-breeding with an alien species, for this at least can be seen as such, and after eliminating it through breeding, is no longer of concern. If, on the other hand, it should prove that in the course of domestication mutations do not accumulate but the loss of natural selection is responsible for an increased number of mutant forms and the imbalance of stocks, then race preservation must be concerned even more so than is the case at present with the eradication of the ethically inferior; as a consequence, the preservation of the race must literally replace all factors that determine natural selection. This method of improvement, even after genetically deficient mutations have been successfully eradicated, must continually guard against and treat any reappearance of the homologous mutations. . . .
>
> A minor genetic deficiency in any kind of social inhibition, placing at a disadvantage anyone in the bloodline so afflicted in a farming or fishing village, can enable that bloodline to deceive the healthy members of the species under the conditions of urban life as well as to become a dangerous parasite in the body of the *Volk*. Everyone can think of an infinite number of true examples in which socially desirable characteristics of the fully healthy member were "rewarded" in this way with negative selection. Anywhere competition for space

is the only selecting factor of the species, this phenomenon leads to socially inferior human material being able precisely by means of its inferiority to permeate the healthy body of the *Volk* and ultimately to destroy it. By a very broad biological analogy, the cells of malignant tumors do exactly the same thing in the cells of higher organisms. . . .

By broad biological analogy, namely, the relationship between a body and a cancer tumor on the one hand and that of the *Volk* and its members who have become antisocial because of genetic deficiencies on the other hand, a substantial number of parallel measures exists with respect to what is necessary. Just as with cancer—except for a few inconsequential partial successes with radiation treatment— nothing can be recommended to those who suffer the disease other than the earliest possible diagnosis and its eradication. Likewise, defending racial hygiene against those elements with genetic deficiencies is limited to quite similarly primitive measures. . . .

Every attempt to reconstruct elements that have ceased to have a connection to the whole is therefore futile. Fortunately their eradication is easier for the physician of the species and less dangerous for the entire organism of all individuals than the surgeon's operations are for a single body. The greatest technical difficulty lies in its *diagnosis*. In this respect, cultivating our own inborn patterns, that is to say our intuitive reaction to manifested deficiencies, can be of great help to us. A good person in his deepest instincts can very well tell if someone is a scoundrel or not. . . .

Nonetheless, this role must be given to some kind of human institution if humanity is not to perish because of the failure to select factors in manifesting deterioration caused by its domestication. The racial theory as the basis of our state has already realized enormous achievements in this regard. The Nordic movement has always intuitively been against turning humans "into pets," all their ideals are such that they would be destroyed by the biological consequences of civilization and domestication set forth here, the movement fights for a direction of development that is just the opposite of where the civilized urban man of today finds himself. There can be no doubt for the biologically sensitive person which of these two paths is the path of real evolution, which is the "upward" path! . . .

Therefore, the most effective measure of the scientist who works to preserve the race, at least for now, is of course supporting the possible natural elements of defense, we must—and may—rely on the healthy sentiments of the best among us and entrust them with the selection that determines whether our race thrives or decays. Should this selection be faulty and the extermination of deficient elements fail, these will permeate the body of society, biologically speaking, in entirely the same way as cells invading a malignant tumor permeate the healthy body, eventually destroying itself along with it. . . .

Let me conclude this treatise with a warning: we consider the full presence of all species and race-specific characteristics of our fellow man both emotionally and inevitably as one of the highest values that we know. The word "beautiful" indicates, when applied to a person, that this is present in a physical sense, "good" indicates its presence in inherited, species-specific behavior, the words "ugly" and "bad" indicate its absence. The highest appreciation of the "good," which is by far superior to that of the beautiful, is completely and totally justified, biological superiority acknowledges what we know to the depths of our feelings: the racial health and strength for future higher evolution of the racial stock is directly rooted in nothing, not even in beauty, so much as it is in its inherited, species-specific social behavior. Nothing can so endanger the continued existence and further development of all we live for and struggle for as does each of the smallest deviations from these blood traits. This assessment of the highest values must not, however, hinder us from fully recognizing their deep and indissoluble bonds with nature. No obscure belief in any kind of special laws of nature unique to mankind may prevent us from climbing down, in modest self knowledge, to our simpler and therefore more easily understood fellow creatures in order to learn from them knowledge of facts required to preserve and to cultivate our highest genotype!

What a verbose edifice of notions, whose wobbly foundations are concepts, nowhere logically analyzed, such as "unblemished" or "the ethically inferior person" or the human being who exhibits "manifestation of deficiency characteristics." These are concepts that provided justification in a brutal dictatorship for unscrupulous murderers. Moreover, Lorenz writes as if one could speak of the unity of some sort of European race, whereby he even divides humans into those that are "beautiful" and "good," or into their opposites, "ugly" and "bad."

Again and again he emphasizes the necessity of "extermination," conjuring up the specter of a body attacked by cancer cells in order to underline this demand as emphatically as possible. For those who wish to know how you recognize which cancer cells aren't foreign—that is, those who manifest deficient characteristics—he has ready a sentence that is remarkable for a scientist: "A good person in his deepest instincts can very well tell if someone is a scoundrel or not." And selection and "extermination" he wants to leave to the "best." Of course, he assumes it is clear who that was in the Third Reich.

In 1940, Lorenz surely must have known what flames he was fanning. In no uncertain terms, he was praising the race policies as practiced up to that point, demanding an "*even* more rigorous extermination of ethically inferior people." Also, the profound symbolism of the ruins of Königsberg's synagogue couldn't have escaped him of all people, a professor holding a chair of human psychology here in this city. In those days, every child in Königsberg knew the race policies he considered worthy were directed against Jews, gypsies, blacks, Slavs, enemies of the people (political opponents), the handicapped, and anyone who was antisocial.

Just think how many have struggled to understand how it was possible that thousands of so-called normal people let themselves be persuaded into maintaining this murderous machinery. Surely they must have stumbled onto articles of this sort. With the aid of such cancer-tumor arguments people could finally, on a vast scale, turn off their consciences and justify the inconceivable. For me the question remains why those who advocated criminal acts not only weren't touched afterwards or called to account, but were even showered with the highest honors, while those whom they had led astray were executed or punished. Is it really that different to want "to exterminate" human beings, to call for it, and to rationalize it than it is to carry it out? These thoughts did not just first occur to me when the city of Vienna decided to name the Nobel laureate Lorenz an honorary citizen!

Among the many human "mortal sins" later criticized by Konrad Lorenz, he unfortunately forgot to name one of the worst—opportunism that walks over dead bodies.

The moment I picked up the frayed yellow material printed with the Star of David from the Jewish synagogue and paid for it, a period began when it was no longer possible to act as if I belonged, or in other words, to forget from time to time I didn't belong. Up until then there were still moments when Ruth and I could rent a boat and spend a care-free hour during nice weather on the castle pond. We rowed through the drooping branches of willows, past ducks and swans, and no one would know we weren't allowed. On very rare occasions we would, with pounding hearts, go to a movie, or take a train out to the suburbs to the lake to go swimming. But now a yellow Star of David had to be sewn to every piece of outer clothing and had to be visible above the heart. A violation could mean immediate deportation to some con-centration camp.

It took quite a bit to gather up the courage to step out onto the street as a marked person and to be exposed to people's glances that were astonished, curious, snubbing, but also sympathetic. Since people were sympathetic, another decree was issued only one month after the introduction of the Star of David (RSHA [*Reichssicherheitshauptamt* (Reich Security Main Office)] IV 84b-1027/41, Oct. 24, 1941), which said "All persons of German blood who exhibit a friendly demeanor in public to Jews ... are to be taken into protective custody, or, in serious cases, are to be sent to a concentration camp for a period of up to three months. The Jewish party is in all instances to be taken into temporary protective custody until transferred to a concentration camp." Sympa-thy was against the law. You don't protect 'cancer cells' and in no case do you communicate with Jews. Frightened by this, most people who had been skeptical no longer dared to show any sort of sympathy.

How can you describe the state of affairs and the state of mind when you go around with a mark that generates loathing? As a thirteen-year-old boy I would be described as having a typical German appearance. My schoolmates had just as few of the absurd characteristics Nazi propaganda attributed to the "inferior Jewish race": long black hair, a hunchback, and a hooked nose. Sort of the way the splendid philoso-pher Moses Mendelssohn looked, a man admired by his contempo-raries, including Lessing and Lavater. Now that there was the Star of David, one didn't need a curved nose anymore. The yellow blot sufficed to precipitate hateful reactions, even though those marked looked like their own children or parents. At that time seven church leaders of the National Church, including the president of the regional church of Saxony and the Bishop of Mecklenburg, proclaimed:

As members of the German national community, the undersigned German Protestant Regional Churches and church leaders stand at the forefront of this historical defensive struggle that the Reich-Police decree, among other things, has made necessary, which decree is that the Jews are born enemies of the world and of the Reich; so too, after bitter experience did Dr. Martin Luther demand that the strictest measures be taken against the Jews and that they be banished from German lands. . . . The racial character of a Jew, his national identity, and his biological essence are not changed by means of Christian baptism. The German Protestant Church must care for and promote the lives of the German people. Christians who are Jews by race have no place and no rights here.

So completely were the Jews stripped of their rights that you could, without fear of punishment, order them from the sidewalk onto the street, hit them, spit on them, and, if you wanted to, kill them.

Of course the literal words of the decree were that the Star of David must always be visible, but a left arm raised by chance to the nose can't be controlled all the time, and for a passing moment it was possible to conceal the Star of David.

At first people were mainly curious, but gradually this changed. Aside from other children's unpleasant but comparatively harmless taunts and jeers, I recall some incomprehensible behavior on the part of adults I'd like to recount here.

I've already mentioned the heavy blow to my head from behind. That was the most galling incident. How intense the hatred must be to do that! That the perpetrator bolted was evidence of a bad conscience if not cowardice.

Another time, a few months later, I was going to work as usual when a civilian came up to me. Bellowing as if giving an order, he demanded that I, a "Jewish pig," should have the decency to walk in the street and not use the sidewalk that was there for "decent" citizens. I had to walk in the gutter of the street along with the horse carts, automobiles, and bicyclists until I was out of sight of this gentleman. Refusal to do so—especially if this was someone who held office—meant resistance to the authority of the state and could have led immediately to deportation. There were no longer such things as court trials for Jews. The state police had special guidelines for just these sorts of matters.

It was no less shocking to be spat on. It happened a few times: mostly it was young men who suddenly spit in my face without warning. To avoid them I was soon exclusively using my bicycle to get around. In contrast to the behavior of people in other cities toward their "labeled" inhabitants—for example, Hamburg, Berlin, or Cologne—it seems to me they succeeded in stirring up the population of East Prussia particularly well, probably the result of many diatribes by the ambitious and pathologically anti-Semitic Gauleiter Erich Koch. I base this on some of the accounts by others who wore the Star of David.

Equally unforgettable are the positive things, which also happened of course. A friendly word or a piece of cake hastily slipped to me during an unobserved moment, a glance, a gesture. The fact that this happened only seldom was no doubt because it required a great deal of courage to defy an edict prohibiting this sort of sympathy, punishable with a sentence in a concentration camp.

Once a young woman stopped me. I was going to work on my bicycle. Hurriedly in broken German she told me she wanted to speak to me and that she had noticed me several times. She named a distant street as the suitable place for a rendezvous and a time—half past six, it couldn't be later on account of my curfew. She gave me a sack of wonderful cookies, then quickly and nervously disappeared. (This and the following story happened only toward the end of the war.) When I showed up at the appointed place the next day two women were waiting. They belonged to the thousands of women who had been snatched from the streets of their Russian homeland and shipped to Germany as slave labor. They told me that they were housekeepers for highly placed functionaries and that I just reminded them of a brother at home in Russia. They indicated they had something to do with Jews. Then they gave me another bag of cookies and we made another appointment to meet.

I told my parents this story, greatly alarming my father, who tended to be nervous. He was afraid it might be an attempt to enlist spies and absolutely forbade me to go to another appointment. Today I am almost certain that these pitiful women were Jews who had saved their lives by smuggling themselves into a convoy of transports leaving for Germany. The sight of my Star of David reminded them of their relatives back home, of whose fate they were totally ignorant. In me they saw a substitute brother through whom they hoped to ameliorate their overwhelming homesickness. When the Russians overran Königsberg, they tortured and raped Russian as well as German women. The Russian women were even suspected of having collaborated with the Germans and in many cases they were sentenced to long years in prison.

Toward the end of the war a curious thing happened: I was fifteen or just barely sixteen and received, certainly out of some bureaucratic error, an induction notice. Under the threat of the most dire punishment in the event I defied the order I was to present myself to be inducted on such and such a day at eight in the morning. The place of induction was a building near the zoo. Now, it wasn't at all easy to get time off from my job at the chemical factory. But an induction notice was an order of the highest authority. To disobey meant risking a sentence for desertion. That meant death by firing squad.

When I arrive a bit late at the induction venue an assorted group of sixteen-year-olds are already standing in formation. With my Star of David, I pass by those assembled and go up to a startled, older captain, who jerks back in fear when I hand him my induction notice. Disconcerted, he snaps at me first for being tardy, then checks the "J" in my identity papers, and asks me my name. I say in a loud voice, "Michael Israel Wieck." At that, he orders me, as if he doesn't see the Star of David, to one of the assembled squads.

I, a Jew with the Star of David, am standing in contact, skin to skin, with Hitler Youths who are assembled to replace the legions of the fallen. Everyone is looking at me in amazement. Some are whispering among themselves. However, the boys all trained for blind obedience and no less so the officers in charge here act only on the instructions of their superior. I had received the induction notice, therefore I was to be inducted. After an endless wait I too have to strip and go from one room to another. Here they check our eyes, there they check our ears, heart, and lungs, our height and weight. Then suddenly a doctor sends me into a side room and conducts the stream of examinees in such a way that I am alone for a short time. In the next moment three doctors in white coats enter and warmly shake my hand, asking me about my job and how I'm doing. They assure me of their contempt for the existing state of affairs and tell me to bravely stick it out. Then they swiftly disappear back to their places, open the door, and release me to the others.

Stark naked, I step before a semicircular table where the doctors and officers are sitting. There, like everyone else, I have to stand at attention, turn, and bend over. They don't ask me the questions asked of everyone else, such as "What do you want to be? What type of weapon do you prefer?" Completely at a loss, they whisper at the table. I sense their

feelings of helplessness. After all, they aren't party bosses and their task
is to muster those who show up. Finally, like everyone else, I receive my
service record book, but with the notation "Replacement Reserve—
Unsuitable." Then I'm released.

Only those who know the situation at this time at all knows how
absurd this story is; as if the devil himself had infiltrated a group of
aspirants for the heavenly hosts. At some point I had to hand in my
service record book when they realized the mistake. I was already
secretly thinking of going underground and thought the service record
book might help. How unrealistic that was. Every serviceman who
wasn't at the front had to have a flood of papers that explained his
absence. Desertion was made next to impossible. Later, as everything
was collapsing, they built gallows at the North Train Station, where
they hanged captured deserters as a warning, leaving them swinging
there for several hours. Cardboard signs were hung around their necks
with the words "I had to die because I was a coward."

    With the introduction of the Star of David, the active phase of exter-
minating all the Jews began. Whoever remained an optimist had to
shut his eyes to the unambiguous evidence. With the "badge of shame"
on my breast my childhood was over once and for all. The struggle to
survive began.

My School Days Are Over

One morning as I looked down on our courtyard from the kitchen window, I saw desperate Russian prisoners of war grubbing though the garbage cans, frantically looking for anything edible. Armed guards were cursing at them to stop. Two young fellows had bound their wounds with toilet paper. Everything pointed to the fact that their abject misery was deliberate; nothing at all had been done to alleviate their condition. When I pointed out the poor wretches to Father, he spoke of the hundreds of thousands of starving Russians detained without care and dying in fortress-like camps. Since these Russians worked as trash collectors, we decided to put bread and potato skins in the garbage cans—by this time we scarcely had anything else ourselves. Unfortunately, this was discovered and triggered an investigation that came to nothing. We were immediately threatened with the death penalty, and from then on the overseer opened the garbage cans before the Russians emptied them. I was so shocked by such brutality toward human beings that the courtyard could no longer be a happy and idyllic playground for me. And that was just a foretaste of what was to come.

The circle of people we saw regularly continued to shrink. Most of my parents' friends had either emigrated or were afraid to visit us. I saw Aunt Rebekka and Fanny only seldom. The classes at the Jewish school had fewer and fewer pupils; everything was happening at an accelerated pace. Scarcely a week went by when there weren't worrisome new edicts placing more restrictions on Jews. What follows is a short chronology of some of these decrees from the latter part of 1941 to the middle of 1942, which can be found in the collection of legal measures and guidelines *Das Sonderrecht für die Juden im NS-Staat (The Special Laws for Jews in the NS State)*.

12/12/41 (RSHA [*Reichssicherheitshauptamt* (Reich Security Main Office)] IV B 4b-1244/41)

The use of public telephones is forbidden to Jews required to wear the Star of David in public. Employees of the Reich Association and of *Kultusvereinigungen* (Jewish Associations) may be granted special permission on work-related grounds.

1/3/42 (RFSSuCdDP [*Reichsführer SS und Chef der Deutschen Polizei* (Reichsführer SS and Head of the German Police)] IV B 4a-50/52)

In consideration of the impending anticipated final solution of the Jewish question, the emigration of Jews of German nationality and of stateless Jews of the Reich is prohibited. In special instances, the *Reichssicherheitshauptamt* may approve of individual applications for emigration if the emigration is in the interest of the Reich.

1/3/42 (LeiPK [*Leiter der Parteikanzlei* (Head of the Party Office)] I. 48/648)

The assets of Jewish Associations and of the Reich Association of Jews does not qualify as Jewish, but as property that serves for the benefit of the Reich. The Central Office for Emigration of Jews shall use these assets to carry out its mission (particularly for the "Final Solution"); therefore all relevant agencies and offices are directed to place their applications to the supervisory authorities and the agencies for Jewish emigration prior to identification of these assets. (The order mentions the forfeiture of assets of Jews who have emigrated pursuant to 11.VO [decree] of the Reich Civil Law Code and the restrictions on the authority over movable assets of those Jews still living in Germany pursuant to the order of 11/27/41 Vfg / AnO [*Anordnung* (Order)] II, p. 135–43 (T).)

1/5/42 (RSHA IV B 4-7/42)

Jews required to wear the Star of David in public must surrender all fur and woolen clothing in their possession as well as skis, ski boots, and hiking boots by 1/16/42. Delivery will be made through local Jewish agents of the Jewish Associations to the police authorities: no compensation will be granted.

1/8/42 (RStH [*Reichsstatthalter* (Reich Governor)] Hesse II 5-16930)

Supplement to the Directive dated 9/18/41 from the Traffic Minister. Heavy restrictions on the use of public transportation by Jews.

2/14/42 (LeiPK I 13/151)

Signs are to be posted in bakeries, pastry shops, et cetera, that give notice that cakes may not be sold to Jews or Poles.

2/15/42 (AnO [*Anordnung* (Order)])

Jews are no longer permitted to possess house pets.

2/17/42 (RSHA)

Jews are excluded from delivery service of newspapers, magazines, circulars of laws and edicts by the post office, publishing houses, or street dealers; permission may be granted only in special cases.

3/3/42 (RMI [*Reichsminister des Innern* (Reich Minister for Internal Affairs)]
    I e 30/42-517)

Processing applications from Jews of mixed race to receive permission to marry has been discontinued for the duration of the war.

3/16/42 (Gestapo Dresden)

In Dresden the sale of flowers to Jews is prohibited.

3/27/42 (Gestapo Karlsruhe)

In consideration of the impending anticipated deportation, Jews are no longer to receive permission from the police to leave their place of residence.

4/5/42 (RSHA II B 4/7104)

The police presidents, county administrators, and mayors of the Lower Rhine are directed not to enter the final destination of the transports into the resident registry, but to enter only the notice "moved, address unknown" or "emigrated."

4/42 (AnO)

Visits by Aryans to Jews and to those living in mixed marriages in their homes are prohibited.

4/24/42 (AnO)

In Dresden Jews are ordered to surrender all shaving apparatuses, new combs, and hair scissors at the designated places.

5/12/42 (RSHA IV B 4b-859/412)

Non-Jewish barbers may not serve Jews who are required to wear the Star of David in public.

5/13/42 (Ob [*Oberbürgermeister* (Lord Mayor)] Berlin HErn V 4b-2310)

Gypsies have recently been made subject to the same labor laws as Jews. This parity is to be applied to matters of food allocation. I therefore request, effective immediately, that neither supplemental cards for heavy laborers nor additional cards for agricultural and night shift workers be issued.

6/12/42 (RSHA IV B 4b-1375/42-20)

Jews are required to surrender immediately all electrical appliances, bicycles, photo equipment, binoculars, etc. This does not apply to Jews living in privileged mixed marriages or Jews of foreign nationality. Violations are to be punished in strict accordance with measures of the State Police.

7/7/42 (RMWiss [*Reichsminister der Wissenschaften* (Reich Minister for the Sciences)] E II e No. 1598)

In view of the developments resulting from recent resettlement of the Jews, the RMI *(Reichsminister des Innern)* has, with my agreement, ordered the Reich Association of Jews in Germany to close all Jewish schools by June 30, 1942, and to give notice to its members that effective as of July 1, 1942, any schooling of Jewish children by paid or unpaid teachers is prohibited. I hereby give notice. This decree is not to be published.

I often have to think of the beautiful Schubert *Lied:* "O gracious Art, in how many gray hours . . ." The Kreutzer Sonata I played with Mother in those days after a fashion and the undisturbed moments with paint and brush became indispensable counterweights of increasing importance to me. The sound of the violin bewitched and intoxicated me. We were no longer allowed to listen to the radio or go to concerts, so every bit of music that drifted in through an open window or door was like a greeting from a lost paradise. Every now and then I also painted large pictures to express my view of the world. A fit of creative passion would seize me, suppressing both desire and time to eat or drink.

A number of my school friends were able to leave Germany before the ban on emigration became final—Herr Kaelter, the head of our school, and the teacher Nussbaum among them. Fräulein Wolff was now the head of the school. A woman of sensibility, she turned her classes into quite special moments for us to slip into a better world. Opinions might vary whether the great classics were the right curriculum for young people who would very soon have preferred to know which plants and mushrooms are edible and what is more nutritious, grains of wheat or half decomposed animal cadavers. How you treat wounds, illnesses, skin rashes without medicine and how you protect yourself from dive bombers and shrapnel. My experience is that intellectual nourishment is just as much a source of strength for overcoming difficulties as is eating and drinking. Of course, it would have been nice to learn the other things, too. But that would have required teachers who had already lived through what lay before us. There weren't any.

At that time, before some of the laws went into effect, all those hours in the company of the classmates still there seemed to me to be moments of real happiness. It is entirely possible that we were more generous-hearted with each other and the bonds of our friendships were more intense than what I found later in life in my relationships with others. Moreover, I liked our pretty girls and the splendid dancing lessons Herr Weinberg continued to grace us with. Ruth Marwilski became more slender and delicate. She was gracious and a person of character, but a little stiff. When we danced we tripped over each other's toes. The affectionate Hella Markowsky was small and plump; to dance with her was lovely but confusing, especially because you could draw her warm body so easily into your arms. Even such innocent pastimes seemed a bit sinful to us, for pious Jews are prudes.

Manfred Echt was my closest friend. But now we saw each other only in school. Erwin Pätzold, the most gifted student, who could already be called a scholar, was always amazing everyone with his pages and pages of treatises about some topic or other—usually a religious one. The dramatic readings I mentioned before, with a different person taking each role, continued to be a particularly pleasant pastime. We read all the brilliant phrases as if they came from our own hearts, no longer feeling despised or insignificant. It would have delighted Lessing to see what *Nathan the Wise* meant to us, how it was a source of comfort to us because it affirmed who we were. But it was Shakespeare's keen insight exposing human baseness that enabled us to confront the present— and we desperately needed that.

We played sports in the small school yard and cultivated a tiny garden where we sometimes had our botany lessons. A tall board fence separated us from the rubble of the synagogue, which had since been blown up. German boys played war on these ruins by throwing stones from positions they had built. There were injuries that drew blood. Our school yard, needless to say, was not spared from the stone bombardments. But no one was ever hit.

Once we started wearing the Star of David we quickly were forced to become ever more cautious. My swift bicycle certainly helped me outrun dangers, but there were those who lay in wait for us in front of the school, and some of us got beat up. More and more, instead of having lessons, we had orders to carry out for the Gestapo. Employees of the Jewish Association would come into the school to organize collection drives. Each of us were given lists with names and addresses. One time we picked up house pets, another time it was fur and woolen clothing, electric appliances or skis from Jews, who for one reason or another had been prevented from surrendering these items to comply with the deadlines of those decrees.

One time I had to take the beloved canary from Dr. Klein, who had been my pediatrician for many years and who already had been badly treated before. I took the canary to the zoo, where it was simply let go. School children as assistant bailiffs for the Gestapo. Then, after such drives, we would have German lessons again as if nothing had happened, writing long essays, for example about the quotation of Goethe's "*Selig, wer sich vor der Welt / Ohne Hass verschliesst, / Einen Freund am Busen hält / Und mit dem geniesst . . .*" (Blessed is he who spurns / the world without hate, / holds a friend to his breast / and with him enjoys . . .). Fräulein Wolff taught Hebrew five hours a week in addition to German. Fräulein Hiller taught English, taking bitter offense at our unruliness. A somewhat younger teacher, Fräulein Treuherz, taught us biology and Jewish history. There were rumors of a love affair between the sports teacher Weinberg and Fräulein Treuherz, who bore a child a year later. As she was being deported, she showed me this baby on the grounds of the Königsberg fortress near the main train station used as a collection point. She was gushing over it and said something about its hiccups. It was clear that late motherhood was her desperate attempt to counter an inescapable doom with a shred of happiness. Just as if it were only yesterday, I see her still disappearing into the fortress, pushing the pram ahead of her with a lot of baggage piled on top. A few minutes later a starving, yellowish face, wraithlike, portending something ominous, appeared at a window. It was a Russian prisoner of war, staring at me through the iron bars of one of the rooms of the fortress. This picture, too, indelibly etched itself in my memory and evoked even then associations and visions of the fate in store for Fräulein Treuherz and her baby. Herr Weinberg, who wasn't there that evening to say farewell, belonged to the category of the "rejects" on account of his distinguished war decorations; until the end, "rejects" were those Jews held back from the deportations. Nonetheless, he was killed as a former *Freikorps* fighter when the Russians conquered Königsberg—the story got out somehow.

At first only small groups of elderly Jews received notices for "resettlement." Then it was the turn of families where no one worked in jobs considered essential to the war effort. Those affected were told something about work details in the East. The names of the destinations weren't mentioned. Since no one heard anything from the deportees again, their fate remained unknown. Depending on the mindset of those at home, either one assumed that the deportees were doing tolerably well or one feared the worst.

One day it happened that Aunt Rebekka, too, was "resettled." Her transport was supposed to be going to Theresienstadt. It all happened so swiftly we were completely dazed. Everything happened so quickly that to this day I cannot recall if I said goodbye. All of a sudden, she just wasn't there anymore and we never heard from her again. My hand balks, after writing this three-sentence account, from going on to the next event. It's the account, after all, of my Aunt Rebekka's "extermination"—the gentle, totally unpretentious sister of my grandmother.

Then there was the Sabbath on which the full burden of grief and worry of the Jews burst every protective defense erected until then. I can still see the moment of shock:

As usual I'm meeting my friends in front of the sanctuary and, as is customary, we are sitting next to each other wrapped in our white talliths, paying attention to the Torah passage being read. I can't recall which Sabbath it is. Today, the mood seems to us to be particularly tense. The Star of David, the official decrees legalizing discrimination, the edicts, the orders, as well as the total hopelessness of the situation press heavily on us all. On this Sabbath each of us is more aware of our despair than ever before. There is an especially large number of empty places. Everyone has relatives, friends, acquaintances among those deported, and those who are gathered here surely sense that they have departed forever. I suppose that a sudden death would be less awful than what we all faced.

It is beyond description how this sense of foreboding takes hold, choking the breath in our throats. Every word of the Torah, all the prayers seem to refer directly to what is going on outside.

And then, with a heavy step, the rabbi walks to his place. In an extemporaneous speech he remembers those who had been transported to an unknown destination. He powerfully puts everyone's worries into just the right words. Everyone is listening, breathlessly, without making a sound. And then—shattering the painful silence—a heartbreaking sob reverberates, triggering a chain reaction of sobs from countless others. Now almost the entire congregation is weeping, and indescribably doleful sounds of lamentation, misery, sniffling, and sobbing swell into a chorus of lamentation of apocalyptic proportions. This snaps the nerves of us young boys. We look at each other quizzically. At that point, we lose our self-control; however, instead of bursting into tears, we burst out laughing. Helpless laughter: that's our reaction to the harrowing atmosphere. We are powerless to suppress our spasms of laughter. We struggle desperately to regain control, tears rolling down our cheeks from our efforts. It's as if we've been seized by the devil who's using us to sneer and taunt. All efforts to resist him are paralyzed as if by magic— not just for an instant, but so it seems to us, for an eternity. Totally miserable about our helplessness, we try to crawl into our talliths. Only when we are totally enveloped in them and shielded by the prayer book can we banish the devil haunting us; at that moment, as if delivered into the empty space of an infinite room, I am no longer capable of understanding anything, nor can I think or feel. Fortunately the cantor begins to sing in a loud voice, drowning out everyone with a passionate prayer. Gradually, he calms us all down again.

Only many years later I learned that such attacks of laughter are the expression of overwrought nerves. But at that point it was such a bitter experience that I ceased going to services. Aside from the fact that shortly thereafter my entry into the work world left me no free Saturdays, I was appalled by my lack of maturity; and I was ashamed.

We children still resisted thinking the unthinkable. A little while later, after what happened to Aunt Fanny, nothing could suppress the ever thickening sinister clouds of foreboding. Not one of us, however,

ever knew anything definite about what was happening in the extermination camps.

I was beginning to have more serious doubts about whether God
existed or acted as humans imagined. The "countenance" of God had
changed. Only some years later, when I was reading Spinoza's *Ethics*,
could I connect my feelings and ideas with an awareness of God as
expressed by someone else. But now I was defining God less and less
through religious rituals. Without tallith or tefillin, I felt His presence
far more keenly. It was just the opposite of what my rabbi had so
urgently warned me about. The "cloak" of Judaism that one easily shed,
according to the rabbi, when the fates give us warm and sunny weather,
is the "cloak" I took off just as the weather was turning bitter cold.
Today I know that Judaism isn't a "cloak" that one puts on and takes
off at will.

The well-known and highly regarded orthopedist Dr. Kiewe was
supposed to be with the same transport that took Fräulein Treuherz
from us. When he wasn't there as they were checking off names from
the list, I was peremptorily ordered to see why he hadn't showed up.
(This order was the reason why from then on I never accompanied
Jews to the gathering points or bid them farewell, or helped carry their
baggage.) When I rang the doorbell at Dr. Kiewe's, his very affable wife
answered and led me to the white-haired doctor, whom Königsbergers
called "the good Lord of Steindamm." When I told him that I had been
sent to remind him of his order to go to the gathering point he remained unperturbed, asking me to tell them that he wasn't up to being
transported. From his constant work with X-rays, he looked bad and
his hands were cancerous—in those days people didn't take adequate
precautions. Amazingly, the officials accepted his excuse. But this I
know: shortly thereafter Dr. Kiewe took his own life. (Since Dr. Kiewe's
wife was a gentile, I don't know why his name was on the transport
list. It's possible that he wanted to protect his wife, having divorced his
wife before he carried out his planned suicide.)

These incidents, the transport of Jews who didn't work at jobs considered essential to the war effort, and that we school children were
used as messengers for the Gestapo, made me decide (along with my
mother) to leave the Jewish school much earlier than required to find
a position in a job essential to the war effort. My schoolmate Bernd
Lewi had already done this and reported that he was happy with his
work in a mirror factory. He thought it was better to be learning

something than to be coerced into a job at the chemical factory. So I reported as a worker's assistant at Lembke Cabinetmakers. This was not an easy decision. I loved my school and I was leaving my friends, whom I would only get to see now and then. A few months later the Jewish schools were closed down all over Germany by official order. I was thirteen years old when my school days were over.

Cabinetmaking

Without anyone noticing, we Germans were about to conquer ourselves to death. Leningrad was under siege, we were marching on Moscow. The number of Russian prisoners of war was running into the millions. Japan attacked the Americans at Pearl Harbor. Germany and Italy declared war on America. Rommel was victorious in Africa. Obsessed with power, the Germans organized, deported, and looted. The concentration camps were being fitted out for exterminating humans, and more and more displaced foreigners and prisoners of war were working as slave labor in shops and factories. Only the increasing numbers of fallen German soldiers and the first bombing raids on German cities demonstrated that the enemy wasn't totally defenseless.

Air raid sirens began to howl more frequently in Königsberg too, driving anxious people scurrying into air raid shelters. No bombs were falling yet, but no one remained unfazed with up to three alarms a night. Every wail of the sirens meant immediately pulling on your clothes, grabbing your suitcase, and running to the cellar. Waiting for the all-clear to sound could take forever or only a while. Scarcely had you fallen asleep, the alarm would sound again, and then again, and sometimes once more. At first, there we sat, decorated with our Stars of David, in the same cellar with all the other residents of the building. Later we had to use our own coal cellar, which hadn't been reinforced with extra support. The building supervisor, who was entrusted with the task of making sure everyone had left their apartments, was also responsible for seeing that blackout measures had been fully carried out. Every window had black roller blinds for this purpose. However, when the heavy raids began two years later, the bomber pilots found Königsberg straightaway. Darkened windows helped not one whit.

Klaus, the Hitler Youth neighbor my age, and I, the bearer of the Star of David, remained friends. Politics, laws, and prohibitions were taken as a given. They weren't a topic of conversation, but they did force us to be careful. The doorbell would ring announcing a visit from Klaus. My visits to him tapered off; I sensed his mother's mounting fear that someone might see me at their place. Klaus would tell me what was going on in his life. He often brought things with him of interest to young boys: mechanical toys such as artillery pieces or tanks that showered sparks. He also had a chemistry kit, which could be used for lots of nonsense. We learned how to make gunpowder and ignite it with a drop of nitric acid. This was, by the way, the basis for making explosives. We managed to explode rifle bullets clamped into a bench vise and did a whole lot of other things too. Such moments disproved on a small scale all race theories and race propaganda. Our fondness for each other and our amiable times together exposed the total absurdity of that ideology.

With horror I recall two instances when our being together might have ended in tragedy. I was helping Klaus clear out the attic. As a safety precaution all flammable materials still under the tiled roof had to be removed. We were up on a ladder and using an axe to knock out the boards that partitioned the attic into as many divisions as there were apartments in the building. With a particularly heavy blow of the ax, the sharpened head flew off the handle, whizzing so close to Klaus's head he could feel the rush of air. "Jewish Boy Murders Hitler Youth" would have been the headline, and the consequence would have been my immediate arrest followed by deportation to a concentration camp—quite apart from the tragedy that the loss of their second son would have meant for the Norra family. This episode repeated itself a second time in a more serious form. Like most boys in those days, Klaus loved to play with anything that could shoot. Slingshots, air rifles, and homemade muzzle-loaders. One day he came over with an old pistol, what's called a lady's pistol, I believe. It wasn't very large, and you had to draw back the cock to put in a bullet and fire. The cock spring was apparently very weak, and Klaus said it couldn't be fired. He had tried countless times. With that, he snapped the cock onto the bullet several times, then handed me the pistol. I tried it out on our balcony and likewise couldn't get it to fire. After cocking it a number of times and trying to fire it, I held it out to hand it over, pressing the trigger one last time as a lark. This time there was an ear-splitting noise and Klaus collapsed. Klaus clutching his stomach in a heap on the floor and me with the pistol in my hand, pale as a ghost—that was the tableau we presented to my bewildered mother, who was scared to death when she burst into our room on hearing the bang. On closer examination, we discovered that the lead bullet had ricocheted off his *Jungvolk* belt buckle. We found the flattened bullet. Having only felt the blow, Klaus thought he had been injured. Even after the three of us realized we had gotten off lightly, we still took a long time to calm down. In his mind Klaus thought he had been shot, and I thought I had shot someone—it would have been unthinkable had it really happened. We really should consider these incidents as having been blessed by good fortune. But it gets spooky if good fortune keeps repeating itself. Neither incident hurt our friendship; on the contrary. The pistol shot, of course, remained a closely guarded secret.

Also kept secret were the occasional bicycle trips I made on my own—wearing a partially covered Star of David. I went to the Hammer Ponds, where I had learned to swim, and further on, to Juditten and Metgethen. I loved the stands of forest there. Of course it was forbidden to go there, as this counted as leaving one's place of residence. But actually—so it seemed to me—the fact that Mother and I were alive was prohibited; compared to that, one more infraction of the rules was unimportant. The trips along the banks of the Pregel were especially lovely. Along the riverbanks were storage sheds, picturesque old ones and monstrous huge new ones. Barge after barge floated by on the Pregel. Most of them were so heavily laden and deep in the water it wasn't necessary to open the bridges, which were quite low themselves. They were always being opened and closed anyway. There were plenty of other kinds of ships. Just three years later I had to unload a barge. There were five of us tossing boxes of laundry detergent to each other. It seemed an endless task to us, as if the belly of such a ship were an entire coal mine. What made it particularly dangerous was that the approaching Russians were shooting at us and shrapnel fragments were hitting all around us. But at this moment, I was still enjoying the illusion of having a free human existence on this bicycle trip.

It must have been three months before Ruth was deported that we spoke about our hopes and dreams. Since both of us belonged to the Zionist sports club Bar Kochba, which had once been quite active, we were wearing our blue gym pants with white stripes and white gym shirts with a blue Mogen David (Star of David). Sports activities were

limited to track and field and ball games; our playing fields were the
Jewish cemetery and our school yard. We all cherished the hope of
being able to begin a new life in Palestine; it was the only thing that
we could still hope for. Such conversations quickly became charged by
the strong feelings we had for each other. A squeeze of the hand, a
glance, or an affectionate gesture occupied our time together.

Even in the darkest days of persecution, with her love of literature
and music Mother was a better German than many of the *Volksgenossen* (racial comrades) ill with the "German delusion." My father withdrew from Christianity by studying Goethe, Lao Tze, and Confucius.
Aunt Rebekka reposed imperturbably in the tradition of the liberal
Jewish tradition, while at school a Zionist attitude reigned. My bar
mitzvah lessons at first contained a lot of Polish-Hasidic elements, later
Jewish Orthodox ones. I've already described how Herr Benjamin, out
of pure trust in God, failed to save himself and his family from the
criminals. He probably could have done so. Last but not least, the press,
kiosk posters, flags, and banners spread the gospel of the Thousand-
Year Reich. People blithered on about the role of the "essential German
character" in saving the world; they believed in the superiority of the
Aryan race, which never existed at all in any pure form. Hitler, who
knew well not only Wagner's operas but his political writings as well,
turned Wagner's thought into terrible reality. His successes and victories must have seemed evidence that he had been correct. In addition
to all this, there were monarchies, democracies, and communism. All
these currents and countercurrents were sources of political struggles
of which I was becoming aware.

I was constantly holding conversations deep in my soul with the
God as He existed at whatever level of maturity I had at the moment.
Meanwhile, I believed there was an elementary power responsible for
everything that happened. Only I had begun to doubt more and more
that this power was what Christians or Jews imagined to be God. My
bar mitzvah was certainly the expression of my love and my respect
for this elementary power that I, like everyone else, feared. I no longer
could imagine that there was supposed to be only one form of showing respect. My father called his God "Tao," I called Him "Adonai," and
my mother didn't call Him anything at all. Allah and Jesus weren't foreign to me, and Hitler always spoke of Providence. With such a prolific
but nonetheless unsatisfactory array to choose from, I simply had to
form my own image of God.

Among my courageous friends in those days were Ilse Rose, Gerti Weschollek (later my father's wife), and Doro Georgesohn. They slipped bread ration cards into our mailbox from time to time. There were also those among our music-loving friends who frequently made declarations of sympathy to my parents. They too added to our ever diminishing supplies of food now and then. The Jews were always having their food rations cut. I can't recall all the names of our benefactors anymore, but I'm still grateful.

Great was our joy when once a month the twenty-five-word letter from my sister arrived. The Red Cross arranged these exchanges between people in enemy countries. Miriam lived at a pious Christian college in Scotland. We thought she was doing fine. She, of course, never wrote just how lonely she really was.

One day Father took me to Master Lembke, the cabinetmaker. He had been recommended to us. His shop was certified as essential to the war effort; in this way I hoped to be spared forced labor or deportation. As a worker essential to the war effort, I wouldn't be stuck in the chemical factory where the work was mind numbing and unhealthy. Mother talked enough about that. We went by bicycle for at least half an hour towards Königsberg-South, crossing the Pregel on the Reich Railroad bridge at the Holländer-Baum Train Station. We went through streets and alleys, arriving in Oberhaberberg at a large extended inner courtyard with several workshops on the left—woodturning, upholstering, metalworking, cabinetmaking, and plasterer's workshops. Each one had a sign above the door with the emblem of its trade. On one side of the courtyard there were storerooms for the larger firms and way in the back there was a workshop that packaged butter.

Like almost all the streets in Königsberg, the courtyard here was paved with cobblestones and had lots of atmosphere. The workshops were one- to three-man operations and the rooms were low and tiny. We knocked on the door, and the cabinetmaker Herr Lembke emerged. He was rather fat and unhealthy looking. My father introduced us. Herr Lembke inspected me, my Star of David, and then my muscles without a word or comment. He decided on the spot to take me, but the work wasn't easy. There was a lot of piecework and for unloading boards you had to be strong. We agreed on everything; I was to start the next day. We spoke about work clothes and that he would see to getting me ration cards for a "blue outfit," something like a pair of mechanic's overalls. Only he didn't like my name; on my first day at

work he announced I would be called Max, not Michael, and proceeded to introduce me as Max to the three people in his shop.

The first one was an older journeyman, quiet and reserved. Then
there was Franz, even older, gaunt, with plaited hair, flashing eyes, and
so busy with his work that he scarcely looked at me. He was building coffins as piecework. The seventeen-year-old apprentice Heinz had
a nervous look. Three steps led down to the cabinetmaking shop.
Directly on the right there was a high shelf full of various planes. On
the left next to the entrance underneath a wide glass protective shield,
was the joiner's bench of the master. The coffin maker used the joiner's
bench along the long wall on the left and the journeyman used the
one along the back wall. The interior was mostly filled with coffins
set up on sawhorses and coffin lids. On the right wall was a door leading into the shop with woodworking tools. Here were the circular saws,
a molding cutter, and a band saw. Along the opposite wall there was
a planing table. The room was full of shavings, scraps of wood, and
sawdust. Boards and all kinds of wood were stored outside in the
courtyard, across the way against the warehouse wall, and under the
workshop roof.

On the first day, Master Lembke took me outside, put two blocks of
wood down, then laid specially selected boards on top, measured them
carefully, and marked them with a pencil. When no one could hear us,
he said to me, "Max, for me you're a human being just like anyone else.
You're hired as a worker's assistant, but I'll teach you everything. Only
be careful about saying anything political. My journeyman is a party
member and is probably spying on me. Franz is an ex-con who's been
pardoned. He murdered his wife in a fit of rage. Now he works like
crazy, hardly says a word. He makes coffins and he's paid by the piece
so he earns a lot. Certain tasks will be your job." He didn't say anything about Heinz other than he was weak in the head. Then he gave
me a piece of wood, wrapping sandpaper around it, and showed me
the globs of glue that needed sanding. That was the first thing I did as
a worker. I threw myself into the job, and quickly became aware how
exhausting it was. Every section of a coffin had clumps of dried glue
as hard as stone over each of the thirty-two recessed nails. You had to
exert a lot of pressure while scrubbing hard. Then we took the coffins
and the lids outside into the courtyard, where they were washed down
with a stain dissolved in thinned liquid ammonia. The master applied
the varnish himself. I soon discovered why. He diverted a large part of

the alcohol rationed to him for the varnish. This he mixed with anise drops I had to fetch for him from the pharmacy shop. Many a day he drank this high-proof schnapps after hours. Even though this alcohol was denatured, it apparently agreed with him.

Unloading boards, cutting them with a hand saw, sweeping out the workshop and courtyard, holding on to something here, climbing up there, these were my first tasks. I liked the smell of wood; actually, it wasn't bad at all. The master took me along whenever he went to customers to put up a shelf in a cellar or to put in a window frame or to build pantry storage bins. He simply ordered me to remove that "crazy" Star of David whenever we were out on a job. You just couldn't expect people to put up with that, was how he put it. So Mother put snaps on the Star of David and my overalls. To my great good fortune, the Nazis among the craftsmen in the neighboring workshops were probably all away at the front. The old master craftsmen of the other shops who remained behind—many couldn't carry on because of the labor shortage—showed a warmth toward me that revealed what they really thought. The visit from the son-in-law of our party comrade, the senior journeyman, was truly grotesque. One day, he entered the workshop in his SA uniform, saying he finally wanted to see a Jew. His father-in-law had told him about me. He was very disappointed. He was hoping to meet someone who matched his mental image of a Jew from the *Stürmer*. After he had looked at me for some time, directing me to turn my head to the right, then to the left, he said that he could recognize definite Jewish characteristics. But you had to be, he said, specially trained to recognize them. Indicating that he possessed this special knowledge, he obviously wanted to impress his father-in-law, who, even with the greatest effort, couldn't recognize any exceptional features. Afterwards I was quite concerned that I had some sort of unusual characteristics after all.

To everyone's astonishment, even the ex-con Franz spoke with me from time to time. He soon invited me to go to a certain restaurant with him during the midday break, where they occasionally had smelt soup. Smelts are small fish that apparently consist only of a head, eyes, and fins. But they are wonderfully tasty, and Franz gave me the necessary ration card coupons. We didn't say much to each other; the companionable presence of each other did us both good. The master brought a food package his wife fixed for him every day. His sandwiches and chicken legs were a rarity in those days, filling all of us with envy. Every now and then he slipped me what was left over. Wonderful cold cuts and cheese sandwiches. I had no idea how he managed to improve so bountifully on the worsening shortage in the food supply. I then discovered when we were out on jobs he also stole, each time giving me precise instructions at what moment I should make which cans of food, bottles, or sacks disappear into his large briefcase. He noisily diverted the owners while I did as instructed. It was astonishing how filled to bursting the storage cellars of most of his customers were. If anything had gone wrong, I would have been literally left holding the bag, but things always went well. I had no way of knowing that this was a very important lesson in survival. Without stealing, we would have starved to death under the Russian occupation.

The master's jokes were coarse, and it wasn't only the beloved cat who suffered from them. This cat lived in the workshop, most of the time asleep. The master would say, "Let's see how far Little Peter can jump today." He would then dip a cotton ball into ammonia and drop it in front of the nose of the sleeping cat. The entire crew would cheer no matter which direction Little Peter leaped.

It would be wrong if I didn't mention I found it very hard to get used to a long workday, and there were plenty of days when the work was more than I handle. Those were the times I couldn't sleep at night. When I finally did fall asleep, I continued to work in my dream.

One thing soured the climate at work that had started out so well. The apprentice Heinz became jealous and turned out to be sneaky. He began to bully and torment me. Since we worked relatively independently on most things, no one else saw how he always managed to make me be the one walking backwards to carry the coffins. Whenever he shoved the coffin forward—just as I started up the steps backwards—I would stumble or fall and the heavy coffin would slip and crush me.

Even more dangerous was his habit of shoving me in the shop when the woodworking tools were running. All the tools were relatively unprotected back then, particularly the circular and the band saws. But so too was the planing table: when the lathe was set open, the sharp edges for planing the boards were turned upwards. If I complained, he cursed horribly, ending with "Shut your trap, Jewish pig." It was useless to appeal to the master for help. I was thirteen, Heinz was seventeen. It would've only made matters worse. But the situation was becoming more and more untenable; finally, it was a living hell. I was miserably unhappy. Although I liked cabinetmaking, every day was now a nightmare. Desperate, I managed to do something that even today I look back on with satisfaction: Heinz was a random bully. When he wasn't bullying, I was the one he talked to. He was the kind of person who is always cursing everything without stopping for breath. That was how I learned a bit about his life and mental state. He really wanted to go into the navy but had been rejected. He couldn't keep up at school. His parents were divorced and his father had made him become a cabinetmaker. Probably due to various deficiencies, he had been rejected elsewhere. He was also out of place as a cabinetmaker. In the direst of straits I hit upon an idea. I cursed with him. I constantly fired up his disappointment and brought his desperation to the boiling point. I had noticed a building that housed an office of the merchant marine. That's what inspired me with the notion that was my salvation. I persuaded him to sign up and volunteer his services to the merchant marine. I figured with the shortage of personnel they wouldn't be so choosy. I expansively elaborated a paradise of a dream life on the merchant ships. That was, after all, what he had originally wanted. I almost had to take him by the hand and drag him to the merchant marine office before he decided to follow my advice. And lo! It didn't take long; one day Heinz disappeared forever. The merchant marine had accepted him and liberated me. I hope he found happiness.

A completely new era with Bernhard commenced. Bernhard was Heinz's successor, a sixteen-year-old gypsy boy with a sunny nature. He had black hair and was strong, lively, musical, good-natured, and willing to help. We got along dazzlingly. It should not go unmentioned that I was amazed to discover a gypsy entirely different from what I had imagined. So then I, too, was a victim of the prevailing prejudices. Even though I was ostracized myself, I had unconsciously accepted the Nazi slogans about stealing, dirty, dishonest gypsies. How else can I explain how pleasantly surprised I was.

From one day to the next my life at work became quite pleasant. Rarely have I met such an imaginative person as Bernhard. Unfortunately, he whistled and sang hit tunes the whole day; even to this day the melody of "For One Night Filled With Delight" causes me to become slightly nauseous. He was full of practical jokes. He was always up to something, jeopardizing life and limb. For example, removing or hiding the screw clamps when Franz was gluing the coffins. At the very moment when he had to squeeze the boards smeared with hot glue with the clamps. Delay could ruin the whole process. Franz always discovered the prank just as he was gluing something quickly and a clamp that had been laid out was missing; a hot-tempered person, he was rabid. I saw how he hurled one of the long iron clamps at Bernhard with such force that he could have killed him had Bernhard not nimbly ducked.

During the midday break we went exploring and discovered a place where we found buttered paper lying about—paper from which we could scrape off little bits of butter, a valuable find in those days.

As a gypsy, Bernhard was subject to restrictions similar to those imposed on Jews. As a result of one particular order, gypsies were given parity with the Jews. So he had no prejudices toward me. We were really friends, fellow victims, and we felt at home in the cabinetmaker's shop until one critical mistake ruined it all. We exposed the journeyman, whom the master had warned us about, by asking about politics and the war, and then doubting his answers. Bernhard even ridiculed him. Even though we were good workers—I could now operate the tools and even tenon the side pieces of five hundred first aid boxes with the molding cutter (an experienced cabinetmaker knows what I am talking about)—the official order came that I was to leave the cabinetmaker's shop, and upon reaching my fourteenth year I was to transfer to the chemical factory of Gamm & Son. This factory was the one I had wanted to avoid by voluntarily leaving school. The master, Bernhard, and I were very sad, and we suspected someone had denounced us. We suspected the journeyman.

So you see that the time I spent with the cabinetmaker had its difficult moments as well as its good ones. My transfer into the factory marked the end of another brief chapter in my life.

The Chemical Factory
of Gamm & Son

The events I felt compelled to relate earlier in the first chapter took place during this period. With a transport of several hundred Königsberg Jews I lost my school friends and also my Aunt Fanny. Almost every person dear to me was crammed into a freight car and "eradicated" in the truest sense of the word. Losing them was a terrible thing, an irreplaceable loss. The acute pain of this separation is beyond any words to describe. It was traumatic. My reaction paled to insignificance compared to the fate of these people, for whom there is no account and for whom no one can speak. Nary a sign, by word of mouth or in writing, indicates what happened to them or how they died.

To remember these people is one of the reasons for writing the story of my life. There's a difference, though, whether some are remembered by name or remain only an impersonal number buried in statistics of millions. To this day it remains incomprehensible to me why these people had to die, while I, of all people, survived. Of course back then everyone quietly clung to the hope that those who were deported somehow were allowed to go on living. But the first rumors reached my ears and everyone could see that Nazi cruelty escalated as their losses became heavier. There wasn't anyone who didn't have a dark premonition. Thoughts of gentle Ruth being abused and my friends tortured haunted my imagination. Then there was the farewell that wasn't a farewell from Aunt Fanny—I felt I was suffocating. Guilt plagued me, my spirit darkened. It was a rare day indeed when there was an occasion for joy. It was the same for my parents. But they had been spared the sad sight of Fanny, exhausted, sitting on the curb.

It isn't by happenstance I began my memoirs with these events. I couldn't delay telling the tale. It was the first thing to pour forth. I waited anxiously for some sort of effect. Relief. After all, I had read that talking about a trauma or writing about it could bring a sense of closure and that this method was often used in psychoanalysis. But nothing, not even time itself, will lessen my grief over the fate of these people.

It mustn't be overlooked that the conqueror had to make extreme sacrifices in other countries, especially in Russia in 1942 and 1943. Victories, medals, and promotions whitewashed, but with ever less effect, the sufferings of families of those who fell or were mutilated for the rest of their lives. Many people now began to question things, too late, of course. There were also embittered reactions "until the bitter end." The game of "all or nothing" officially began; it was played by those who had always wanted everything from the beginning. Death didn't care if slaves, soldiers, prisoners, or heroes died; and behind the dying and destruction, forces that seemed to have a life of their own were unleashed. Woe to the person who lets them loose.

The factory of Gamm & Son was located in the middle of the city of Königsberg, on a side street off Steindamm, directly behind the large movie house Alhambra. The factory had a high chimney and consisted of two bleak four-storied buildings with barred windows, a tiny court-yard surrounded by a high wall entered by an iron gate. Everything that "Little Fritz" thinks of when he hears the word 'factory' was there: barrels, boxes, foul odors, dirt, and people bustling about. By the exit there was a something like a time clock everyone had to punch. If a red light went on, they searched pockets and clothing for stolen goods. The factory produced laundry detergent, soap, liquid butterfat, skin cream, cleaning fluids, glycerin products, and similar things.

In one building there were huge cauldrons heated with steam as well as drying machines for the soap flakes and storage rooms filled with tin drums. In another room they made and packaged the laundry detergent. A smaller administration building housed bookkeeping and management. The head supervisor and business manager were combined in one person who was *Gausiedemeister* (District Boiling Master) Täuber. He looked like Göring, but his paunch was a lot bigger. Always smoking big cigars with his hands folded behind him, he played the big boss—almost like a Charlie Chaplin film. Everybody trembled when he made his rounds. He would bellow loudly and season his criticism with rages. Sometimes even worse things happened. Herr Täuber once saw an elderly Jewish worker smoking while he worked. He immediately called the Gestapo, which hauled the man off as I was standing next to him. Not long after, the urn of this amiable man was delivered to his gentile wife.

The workers in the factory were people whom an arrogant, insolent regime deemed inferior: prostitutes, deported Russian girls, French prisoners of war, Poles, gypsies, and Jews. Jews were considered *Untermenschen* and ranked the lowest. We were all guarded by older foremen and supervisors who were, for one reason or another, ineligible for duty at the front.

On the first day, after I had been to personnel, I went to Herr Täuber, who took me to Herr Altenburg (or some such name) in the factory. Herr Altenburg supervised a floor where laundry detergent was taken from silos, put into little packages, packed into cartons, wrapped in wire, stamped, and stored away. Mother worked at a table with seven other Jewish women. Most of the time I saw her with a gauze cloth protecting her nose and mouth, shrouded in a cloud of washing powder, filling cardboard boxes at high speed. On other days she weighed them or glued them shut according to what production required. It was my job to see that there was enough laundry powder in the rolling bins, that there were cardboard boxes and cartons on hand, and that the full cartons were moved. I wrapped these cartons with wire using a gadget that didn't always work, stamped them with sequential numbers, then piled them up to the ceiling in the next room. This exhausts the description of my work for the first few months, leaving it to the reader to imagine how long, achingly long, every day became after ten hours of mind-numbing work. Only fourteen years old, I was seized with an immense longing for knowledge and meaningful work. The routine of the factory was appallingly boring, time lost, time without end.

When the women at the tables quarreled, it provided a change of pace. For example, "Madame President of the Court" made an arrogant remark to Frau Lehmann, or Frau Levy thought Madame Dr. So-and-so was taking it easy at her expense. Even conversations about news of the day could degenerate into such squabbling that I sometimes urged peace; otherwise Herr Altenburg would have done so in his insulting fashion. He sat in a little partitioned-off office and was basically concerned with filling production quotas. As the only male in the room, I soon enjoyed a certain respect. Not entirely appropriate for someone my age, I made my first study about the behavior of women of varying educational backgrounds and social lineage in stressful circumstances.

Little by little, more and more women with the Star of David were deported and one day there simply weren't any more. A fate that became a fact of daily life for us. The thought obsessed each one of us: when would it be our turn to go?

Registered prostitutes and, somewhat later, Russian girls seized from the streets where they lived replaced the Jewish women. I lost my prejudice against prostitutes. Friendly and willing to help, they adjusted to the new situation. The sentimental Russian girls had a much harder time. Unsurprisingly, one or another would break down in tears, which always made us feel very sorry for them. They were beset by homesickness and worried terribly about their families, about whom they generally heard nothing. No one could do anything for them.

The two work breaks were held in separate rooms. Outside the work areas (and if possible, inside, too), contact was prohibited among the different groups. Men and women even ate their meager meals separately. I ardently desired to work either in shipping or production because the monotony of my existence was becoming harder to bear. If I was a little bit ahead in my work I would dash upstairs—Altenburg mustn't see me—and would help with the production of laundry detergent that was going on there. In this way I was successful, after exerting some pressure, in having the foreman ask for me. When one of the Jewish men departed, I got into his department. It was at least less monotonous work, even if it was more physically demanding. The sacks of soda weighed more than the cartons of detergent. The detergent mush had to be hauled by wheelbarrow from the mixers to the drying racks. The next day, the dried mass had to be hacked into pieces and shoveled into a mill. But the men I was with had interesting conversations I could join. So the workday was richer in content, my thoughts more stimulated. I am particularly grateful to Dr. Heller, who worked quietly and knew how to say a lot in a few words. He brought books for me, explained things, and at the same time organized our work.

I no longer remember how many days off we had. It was only a few, and after ten hours working in the factory there were still many daily needs to attend to: standing in line to buy food at the special shops for Jews, obtaining fuel, and so on. Today we no longer know how difficult it was to take care of a household. For example, the heavy wash day with the wash trough, washboard, kettle of hot water, wringing out the clothes in the laundry room in the cellar, hanging them up in the attic, and ironing in the kitchen. In accordance with the practice of the day, Father didn't lift a finger; I had to help. Father was, after all, learning Chinese. That was his escape from a reality he couldn't bear. I had only a few moments for my violin. Nonetheless, I practiced daily and made progress. Mother accompanied me on the piano and tried to encourage me as much as she could, but we were both exhausted after work. I even produced some art works in this period and, every now and then, a poem. I would think about these during boring days at the factory. As much as I tried not to think all the time of my schoolmates, I was haunted by worry about how they were doing. I longed for them because I really missed them.

Soon only Jews from mixed marriages remained working at the factory. A Herr Mendelsohn and his slender, somewhat cheeky daughter were working in shipping. They too belonged to the "rejects." Herr Mendelsohn was talkative, telling me things about his life that no one quite believed. His daughter knew how to engage Herr Täuber's favor to advantage. Both of them livened up the dreary atmosphere of the factory, spreading good cheer. When I was a little bit older and stronger and the shortage of workers more severe, Mendelsohn occasionally helped me in shipping. I had to carry hundred-weight sacks, roll barrels, haul cartons, and was even permitted to go by truck to the harbor. But that was two years later.

These two years were long years. Daily servitude, the daily wait for possible salvation or the end. Everybody's nerves were raw. Time cared not one iota about our desire for something to happen quickly. Although the war raged with ever greater desperation, time stood still, as if paralyzed by fear—or so it seemed to us.

Even a mere summary of the major events clearly shows that the high point of military expansion had been reached. At the same time, the intensifying anti-Jewish decrees testify to the existence of secret orders that accelerated carrying out the "Final Solution" of the Jewish question.

In Africa General Montgomery achieves his first major victories at El Alamein when American and British troops land in North Africa on October 23 and November 7, 1942. At the same time the Soviets begin an offensive that encircles the Sixth Army at Stalingrad. On February 1, 1943, the Sixth Army surrenders. Just a few days later Goebbels announces "total war," which means more serious restrictions for everyone. Thousands of bombers carrying out air raids on German cities become part of the enemy's strategy. On July 10 the Allies land in Sicily and on

September 3, in Italy; the Italian dictator Mussolini falls. Hitler's military good fortune begins to turn against him.

Some of the many hundreds of anti-Jewish decrees from this period (from *Das Sonderrecht für die Juden im NS-Staat* [*The Special Laws for Jews in the NS State*]):

8/7/42 (RSHA)

It is not permissible for Jews to use their former titles or professional titles on documents or other written correspondence with the authorities. In the event this regulation is disregarded, those affected may expect further measures. This order also applies to Jews living in "privileged mixed marriages."

8/14/42 (RMF [*Reichsminister der Finanzen* (Reich Minister of Finance)] 0 5400-217 VI)

Appraisal of furniture the Reich has received through forfeiture of Jewish assets are to be for the benefit of designated wounded pilots, resettlers, and Germans exiled from foreign territories.

8/21/42 (RFSSuCdDP)

Persons who harbor Jews not legally registered shall be subject to measures of the Security Police.

8/22/42 (HK 80/42)

All Jews in Dresden wearing the Star of David are forbidden to purchase ice cream.

9/1/42 (RMI)

The estate of KZ [concentration camp] prisoners is to be seized for the benefit of the Reich.

9/18/42 (RMFLand [Reich Minister for Finance: Agriculture] II B I-3530)

Provision of meat, meat products, eggs, milk, and other distributed foodstuffs to Jews is to cease. Food rationing for Jewish children shall be specially marked. Food packages are not to be distributed.

11/5/42 (RFSSuCDP)

All concentration camps located within the Reich are to be made *judenfrei* [free of Jews], and all Jews are to be deported to Auschwitz and Lublin.

3/11/43 (RSHA) II A 2 No. 100/43-176)

Jews are to be directed to the concentration camps of Auschwitz or Lublin after serving a sentence.

7/11/43 (RdErl LeiPK [*Runderlass v. Leiter der Parteikanzlei* (Distributed Directive from the Director of the Party Office)] 33/43)

Secret! With the approval of the Führer it is so ordered that whenever the Jewish question is discussed in public, one is to avoid mentioning the Final Solution: Jews are being sent to work, en bloc and in an appropriate manner.

Every book I liked to read in those days had the special effect of transporting the reader completely into another world. *The Mendelssohn Family*, written by the composer's nephew, described the lofty human and artistic caliber of this family. I was no less affected by Vasari's *Lives of the Artists*. *The Posthumous Writings of a Genius Who Died Young* by Otto Braun showed what a source of strength and comfort the creative spirit could be. Adalbert Stifter's idyllic world must have had a similar compensating effect. In addition there was the wisdom of Lao Tze and Confucius, which made my father happy, and which provided topics for conversation every now and then. Engagement with significant works of the human intellect, such as music, provided tranquility and consolation. It allowed us to ignore the catastrophe inexorably creeping closer to presenting its bill for the megalomaniacal delusions of grandeur and hatred. Bombs reduced one German city after another to rubble. Every hard-won military position began to crumble. After steady advances, the retreats began. *Frontbegradigung* (straightening the front) as retreat was coyly called, while the numbers of dead ranged into the millions.

It was only a matter of time before the fighting would reach Königsberg as well, and in August 1944 it came to pass: two air raids with over eight hundred heavy British bombers smashed once and for all everything that had been arduously built and acquired over the centuries. The incomparably beautiful, old, honorable city turned into a city of ruins engulfed in a sea of flames. In two short nights, one after another, a bloody, blazing thunderbolt announced to the shattered people of Königsberg the approaching end.

Air Raids over Königsberg

I was having trouble again grasping the nature of justice. It was all too obvious that fate or chance, the justice of God, or human justice made no apparent sense or had any discernible logic. My workmates told me about some Poles who'd been hanged down by the harbor. Supposedly they had stolen packets going to field soldiers. Hans and Sophie Scholl were betrayed as they were spreading leaflets calling for resistance. Freisler, the president of the *Volksgerichtshof* (People's Court) had them beheaded. Kurt, the son of a family known to us as a courageous opponent of Hitler, bled to death between the frontlines from a gut shot. At the same time we witnessed arrests, transports, and suicides of Jewish relatives, friends, and acquaintances. And then came the events of July 20, 1944. We were stunned. Another attempt to assassinate Hitler failed, and we knew this was the last chance to end the insanity ourselves. They buried our hopes when they hanged or shot the members of the resistance. Now Hitler could eliminate even his enemies among the generals and tighten the already draconian security measures.

It seemed as though unknown forces were protecting the powers of destruction, as if people had to go on slaughtering each other as long as possible and destroying their cities, towns, and countries. What other explanation could there be when fate so damned those who sought peace? I quarreled with God. I became angrier than ever with Him. It looked to me as if the heavenly director needed a dramatic climax for the tragedy in which we were the human players, as if after such an excess of hubris only a catastrophe of apocalyptic proportions would do as a finale. An ending that required many people to die, as many people as possible. And however many that happened to be was a matter of complete indifference to Him, as long as it wasn't those who had set this cataclysm in motion. My thoughts at the time were filled with deep reproach. "Because, Michael, you do not know Me, you have false expectations, you are disillusioned," were the words I heard, indeed, I felt in my mind. I could understand that. But what does God's mercy, God's wisdom, God's goodness look like? I had no doubt that everything that existed, everything that happened, happened due to a power that acts. I had experienced this power and felt it. It filled me with awe; I was ready to bow down before it at any time to revere its omnipotence. Only—what was His purpose with all this wretchedness?

More and more the thought took hold that it was false to force God into human categories. I discovered that the biblical stories didn't lead to God. They merely humanized Him. I now saw the bible—be it the Old Testament or New—as an obstacle; it was something that shaped our taboos over hundreds of years and prevented us from knowing God in any other way. I thought we had to be able to conceive an ele-mental force, one and the same for life or death, one that is the source of all being. Its infinitely numerous modes cause everything to exist and everything to die; it certainly doesn't need or share our judgments or ways of understanding. This immanent elemental force is a God of earthbound nature, including the smallest as well as largest creatures; equally so it is a God of the stars and of the entire cosmos. A person of reason loves this God certainly no more than any other. There's no reason to. Human reverence is unworthy of it. But whoever knows it can know Him. And feel Him.

Such reflections brought me into conflict with my father. I became more openly critical of him. Father retreated behind aphorisms about "good" and "evil," about justice and injustice. But he could see, just as I could, that what was happening reduced these arguments *ad absurdum.*

But it was true: only because perfect justice doesn't exist on earth, people relocate it to heaven, postponing it beyond death. Not only because it's convenient but also because no further proof is necessary. Slowly and inexorably, Father and I became estranged and soon we were bitter opponents—further complicating an already enormously complicated situation. Bound together by fate, we depended on each other to survive, but at the same time we were trying to attack, hurt, and destroy each other. Later, Mother's straightforward, simple max-ims defused the tension and neutralized the rancor. Once, when it really was about to explode, she merely said, "It'll all work out some-how." That was all. Our hot tempers cooled down at once. Her other saying I've always liked was "Sometimes one just can!" which ended

our arguments over the nature of justice that cost us the energy we so
desperately needed during the Russian occupation. With this somewhat mysterious saying, she created a certain ongoing diversion. Her
maxim gave no clue as to how much one just could or under what
circumstances one shouldn't any longer. That is, it certainly was a liberating maxim, but not completely unproblematic. I've often felt I've
somehow been left stranded in my life. I have to admit, though, that
"sometimes one just can" has influenced many an important decision.

Klaus and I had laid a line made of cheap doorbell wire and trans-
formers stretching from his bed to mine across our adjoining bal-
conies. Using Morse code tables and little blinking lamps, we could
send messages to each other. It was fun but robbed us of needed sleep.
Air raids took place mostly at night. We had grown quite accustomed
to the eternal wail of sirens, but now the flak started. We learned what
the Allies were preparing to do on August 26, 1944:

> Some time after Klaus and I had blinked "good night" to each other the
> sirens begin to wail. This howling scourge stood on the roof of one of
> the houses catty-corner across the street from us. We've fallen into the
> habit of responding slowly; all too often it's a false alarm. Until now, no
> bombs had fallen, aside from the paltry few at the beginning of the
> Russian campaign, which had taken us by surprise. Even as we are
> sleepily pulling on our clothes I hear the anti-aircraft guns starting up.
> This anti-aircraft artillery emits a hellish noise. The shell bursts are
> exploding all around with a nasty cracking sound.
>
> Today the guns seem more nervous, firing more rapidly than usual.
> The fireworks tell me this time it's definitely dangerous. Out of curiosity
> I go out on the balcony. That's strictly forbidden. For one thing, someone
> could signal to the planes; for another, there's the danger of flak shrapnel.
> The night sky proffers an impressive sight. As if painted on a ceiling
> against a black background, bright white beams of the searchlights sweep
> nervously back and forth across the sky. Intermittently the exploding
> shells flare up, and just then flares quietly floating down on parachutes
> in the sky begin to light up the city. They look like huge Christmas trees
> decorated with miraculously burning candles. The bomber pilots use
> them to find their targets. Soon I hear the low, ominous rumbling of the
> planes. It sounds different from the engine noise of the German planes
> I'm familiar with. I know it's high time to go to the cellar where Mother,
> Father, and the other tenants have already sought safety. Everyone in

one cellar room: Mother and I with our Stars of David, air warden
Wolf with his helmet and arm band, and the block warden Rogalli in
his SA uniform. Thick wooden beams shore up the ceiling of the cellar
and are meant to protect us from being crushed by the weight of the
building in the event of collapse. The two windows in the ceiling are
protected from bomb fragments by diverted concrete air shafts. The iron
cellar door could simply be double-bolted. We sit on wooden benches
arranged around the support beams. By now, we each have our
accustomed seats. In this motley community, we've become the alien
element, which makes us and everyone else very uncomfortable. Each
time Rogalli makes a point of demonstrating his annoyance and total
contempt. Everyone is afraid of him because he can cause trouble. No
one dares breathe a word to us. Not even the Norras. Mother and I
are limited to listening silently to what the others are saying among
themselves. (Eventually, this state of affairs would be ended by decree.
We would no longer be permitted to go into the cellar fitted with its
extra measure of protection, but would have to go to our tiny coal cellar,
right next to the laundry room.)

Today everyone's nervous. The air warden passes on the announcement
that a large number of British planes is approaching Königsberg. The
mounting tempo of the flak tells us this is true. And then it begins. The
earth begins to quake, and a rumbling, thundering sound we've never
heard before petrifies us. Herr Rogalli turns white, which I note with
secret glee. All the time the rumbling and wailing is getting louder and
louder—the bombs whizzing down must have sound devices—I strain to
see if I can tell by the sound when it will be our street's turn and how
far away the bombs are hitting. It's impossible since the bombs are
different sizes. I wonder what would happen if our building took a direct
hit. The floor shakes, the walls wobble, and our faith in the building's
strength evaporates. The deathly fear that seizes the others doesn't grip
me. The possibility of suddenly dying is something I'm used to,
something that I've long made my peace with. Since I can determine
neither when nor how I'll die, my belief that "dying is in God's hands"
has become part and parcel of me—my protective skin.

Mother is probably of the same mind although we never speak about
it. The bombardment lasts an eternity, or so it seems to us in the cellar.
Every time we think it's over it begins again. During a pause in the
bombing when it's quiet for a moment, the air warden musters up
enough courage to peek outside, reporting he can see fires, but all the

nearby buildings are unharmed. Then, at last, the air raid is over; the sirens sound the all-clear, discharging us from the cellars and giving us the feeling that everything—at least for us—once more turned out all right.

The sky to the north of the city glows red. How many has the raid killed or injured? There's the smell of fire, there's a whiff of phosphorus or magnesium. But the relief, not to have been hit, outweighs every other thought.

Just three nights later, on August 29, we were driven into the cellar again, and this time the inferno is almost beyond description. The raid and explosions never stopped. Several times we thought our building was hit, but it wasn't. The Hufen—an outlying district of Königsberg—was only partially destroyed. This time the bombers systematically and thoroughly carpeted the entire center city from the North Train Station to the Main Station. They were using napalm for the first time. They also used a variety of bombs, high explosives, and incendiary devices, so that within a short time every part of the city was set ablaze. The civilians living in the narrow streets had no hope of escaping the heat or firestorm. They were incinerated in front of their houses as effectively as in their cellars. The only ones who survived were those who saw the danger in time and during the raid itself—before the fire broke out—escaped the center of the city. Many jumped into the Pregel. Every one knows about the fire bombing of Dresden because it's often been described in all its horror; it happened to the people of Königsberg six months earlier.

As thousands were desperately trying to escape the inferno, I stood on the balcony again, watching the flames blaze to the skies as they licked the city. It was too late for any sort of rescue. At dawn, the column of smoke could be seen more clearly. It was as broad and tall as the mountain of smoke from later atomic bomb explosions. Half-charred pieces of paper, scraps of cloth, and bits of wood sucked up by the winds floated down on our heads from the towering clouds. A half-burnt exercise book, scraps of curtains, bedclothes, packing paper, cartons, every conceivable item rained down from the heavens blanketing our untouched neighborhood. The crackling and popping noises were deafening. The fire department couldn't even think of fighting the flames. The murderous heat prevented any approach closer than twenty yards. Rescue operations were concentrated on the occasional house burning in the outlying districts. Historic Königsberg was to be left to its fate. Helplessly, we watched it burn.

As I made my way around the burning city a few hours later—I had to at least attempt to get to my job—the misery was beyond words. Hundreds of thousands of homeless people were moving their things by handcart, wheelbarrow, baby carriages, pushcart, anything with wheels, into city parks. Everywhere suitcases, sacks and baggage, the remnants of saved possessions. As could be expected, the sight reminded me of Jews gathered for transport. Still, this was completely different; these people had survived and could count on others helping them. Many were covered in soot, wearing burnt clothing, and were weeping for the missing. Full of compassion for mothers, children, and helpless old men and women, I covered my Star of David and went back home. For almost three days no one could enter the city. Even after the flames died down, the stones and ground were incandescent, cooling off only gradually. All that was left were charred ruins with black holes for windows; they looked like rows of skulls.

Special troops gathered the incinerated corpses lying in the streets or suffocated in their cellars, shriveled by the heat; there were thousands upon thousands of them. Each fate was an individual one, including, as we found out later, the fate of Jews living in mixed marriages. Who will bear witness to the last minutes of these poor wretches? How hot must it be before you lose consciousness? Everybody was stunned by the reality of war, by a dimension no one had thought possible. Party organizations represented themselves as heroes in the hour of need, dispensing blankets, coffee, and words of comfort, an hour of need that they themselves had provoked. The Allies must have known that such air raids killed civilians, women, and children while scarcely influencing the outcome of the war. These acts of revenge were neither heroic nor reasonable; they were manifestations of a mentality equally corrupt. This was not the way to stop Hitler's war machine—on the contrary. It bred bitterness and desperate acts.

In his book *Das Kampf um Ostpreussen (The Battle for East Prussia)*, Major Dieckert writes:

A very heavy air raid with approximately six hundred bombers, passing over Swedish territory according to the report of the *Wehrmacht*, hit the densely built center city with devastating results in the night of August 29/30. New incendiary bombs were tested with the most gruesome success; firestorms, which sacrificed the lives of thousands of people trying to escape, raged through the streets. The fire departments and air defense were helpless.

This time only residential areas with the usual scattering of shops and administrative buildings were hit, justifiably permitting one to speak of a terror attack. Almost all culturally valuable buildings with their irreplaceable contents, such as the cathedral, the castle church, the university, and the old warehouse district, fell victim to the flames. The damage to buildings in these two air raids amounted to over 50 percent, the number of the dead, mostly civilians, is estimated to be about thirty-five hundred [it was far more], and over one hundred fifty thousand were made homeless.... The fire raged for days in Königsberg. Even most of those left unscathed precipitously fled the city, finding mostly quite primitive shelter either nearby or further away. The people of Königsberg shall never expunge these nights of terror from their memory.

1. Grandmother Clara Wieck, née Palme, was the great-aunt of the Swedish Prime Minister Olof Palme, who was assassinated.

2. Grandfather Bernhard Wieck, born in 1844, was an engineer, then an architect, and later the mayor of Berlin-Grunewald.

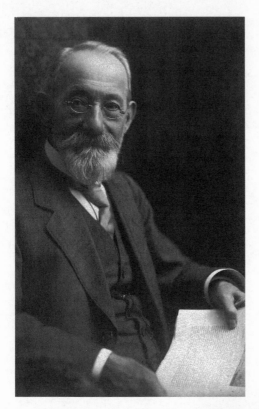

3. My grandfather Arnold Hulisch was the first academically trained Jewish construction engineer. Later he was the City Construction Engineer for Königsberg.

4. Grandmother Jenny Hulisch, née Eisenstadt, played the piano and was fluent in many foreign languages.

5. May 1935: Miriam Wieck (9¼ years old) and Michael Wieck (6¼ years old).

6. My parents' music careers left them little time for us children. We were brought up primarily by our unmarried Aunt Fanny, who was later murdered.

7. Nidden: The old-style fishermen's cottages with thatched roofs on the Courland Spit looked like this.

8. The banks of the lagoon with *Keitel-* and *Kurenkähnen* (broad boats without keels equipped with lea boards for shallow water).

DAS KÖNIGSBERGER STREICHQUARTETT

August Hewers   Kurt Wieck   Hermann Hoenes   Hedwig Wieck-Halisch

9. The Königsberg String Quartet, in which my father played second violin and my mother played the viola, was one of the first quartets that was performing Hindemith and Schoenberg as early as the 1920s.

10. My father always seemed to me to look like men found in the paintings of Manet.

11. My mother Hedwig Wieck, née Hulisch (born in 1888, shown here at the age of 20), was always quick to show enthusiasm; she loved the great classics of music and literature, played the violin and viola, and taught, among many other pupils, Hannah Arendt, who remembers her warmly and with gratitude in her memoirs.

12. This photograph was taken in 1941, about the time of my bar mitzvah. (It was the style of the day to smear pomade on your hair.)

13. My teachers from the Jewish School: David Franz Kaelter, L. Nussbaum, Hermann Erlebacher, Frau Wolff and Frau Hiller. Wolff, Hiller, and Erlebacher were murdered by the Nazis; Kaelter and Nussbaum escaped to Palestine.

14. The synagogue of the Orthodox congregation Adas-Israel (exterior view; see photo 16 for an interior view).

15. I wore this Star of David on a jacket. My mother kept it.

16. When I was bar mitzvahed in the small synagogue of the Adas-Israel congregation (note photo 14 above), the interior as shown here was no longer intact. It had been completely destroyed during *Kristallnacht.* The last services of the Jews of Königsberg were held in the provisionally repaired synagogue.

17. Königsberg: North Train Station. From here we took the train to the coast and from there we went by ship to Nidden on the Courland Spit. From the same train station (actually the freight station located on one side) Aunt Fanny and my schoolmates were later deported to the death camps.

18. This photograph shows the Paradeplatz bounded on the northwest side by Albertus University, which was founded in 1544. In 1945 the underground bunkers of the Festungskommandant Lasch were here. From these bunkers, he continued to direct the losing battle to defend the city, incurring heavy casualties, up until the moment the first Russian soldiers reached these grounds. Only then did he capitulate.

19. The Königsberg Cathedral was considered one of the most beautiful examples of *Backsteingotik* (Gothic architecture built in brick); it was completed as a three-nave *Hallenkirche* (hall church) at the end of the fourteenth century.

Königsberg I. Pr.,
Blick vom Schlossturm.

20. In this picture of Königsberg the beautiful large synagogue of the liberal congregation, rich in tradition, can still be seen at the upper left edge. To the right is the island in the Pregel River, known as the Kneiphof, with the Cathedral.

21. This photograph must have been taken shortly after the second major bombing raid over Königsberg (during the night of August 29–30, 1944). The canister in the foreground was one of thousand such canisters filled with a new type of phosphorus mixture (napalm) that was used for the first time—that is, months before they were used to burn Dresden.

22. View of the warehouse district next to the Königsberg harbor just after it was destroyed, August 1944.

23. The warehouse district before it was destroyed; Königsberg was considered to have one of the most modern harbors on the Baltic.

24. The banks of the Pregel were always picturesque and busy. The temperamental East Prussian fishwives could be argumentative, earthy, and quick-witted.

25. The same scene, emptied of life, was like a ghost town after it was destroyed in 1945.

26. Here is a especially lovely picture of the Kaiser-Wilhelm-Platz: at one time the center of Königsberg, which lay at the foot of the castle.

27. A burnt-out side street with a view of the destroyed castle tower before Königsberg was captured by the Russians.

28. Here is the southeast side of the Paradeplatz (cf. photo 18). In one of the
buildings in the background was the bookstore Gräfe & Unzer, one of
the largest in Europe at the time.

29. The destroyed Französische Strasse in the center of the city.

30. Soviet troops make their way through the burning city. In the chapter "The Russians," I describe this armored track vehicle. The Russians used these heavy cannon, which were transported on track vehicles, but were armored only in front and left completely open in back, as support for their tanks.

31. / 32. When the Russians introduced identity cards for German civilians, they took these pictures of my mother and me. The lower right corner was left blank for a stamp. My clothes had been stolen, so I had to buy two shirts and a coat from a Russian soldier.

33. In 1948, we were allowed to "emigrate." The arrival in West Berlin was a
second birth. In this picture, I am playing the "Gypsy Melodies" by Pablo
Sarasate in a live broadcast of the RIAS (Radio in the American Sector).
This was my debut as a soloist.

34. Reunion in 1949 with my sister in Edinburgh after a ten-year separation.

35. The first violins of the Berlin RIAS Symphony Orchestra, which was conducted by Ferenc Fricsay. I was its youngest member (1954).

36. Thirty years later as member of the Radio Symphony Orchestra of Stuttgart.

37. The official photograph of the Stuttgart Chamber Orchestra (in the Stuttgart Castle) under the baton of its conductor Karl Münchinger. Concertmaster: Michael Wieck.

Winter Storms

We watched helplessly as flames greedily devoured venerable old Königsberg. The fire burned for days. Like an evil spirit, a giant cloud of smoke squatted over the city, barring the way to booty. In the first two days, this image barely changed. Then, the blaze began to die down. Black clouds of smoke glowed with touches of orange, then dark red. The smoke and stench permeating everything were inescapable reminders of the relentless course of events. Many Königsbergers were so terrified by the air raids they fled the countryside as well as the city. Heartsore, everyone was choked with grief. Although I longed for Hitler's defeat—for only the surrender of Hitler could bring me freedom and an end to the war—we mourned the fate of Königsberg from the depths of our souls. A fate, it must be noted, Polish, Russian, and French cities had already experienced—not only cities such as Warsaw, but also Coventry in England and Rotterdam in Holland. We had once assumed that cities would always outlive us—as they had outlived generations before us—that they would continue to prosper, that they were immortal. But that moment was the beginning of the end of 690 years of Königsberg history; and so began the death of a city that lost forever what had made it what it was.

The fortress of Königsberg was founded in 1255 by the German Knights of the Teutonic Order in honor of King Ottokar of Bohemia. The fortress, later the city, and the surrounding countryside often had to go to war to survive. Against the Lithuanians in 1370, then against the Poles. In 1525, Ducal Prussia was a principality under Polish feudal rule. History books written before 1933 describe this period as a golden age. In 1544, Duke Albrecht founded the university that bore his name. Only the university in Cracow founded in 1364 by Kasimir III (the Great) was older. A period of peace ended when Lithuania, Poland,

and Prussia formed an alliance to defend themselves against the Grand Duchy of Moscow, which was pushing westward and against the Tartars. There were four defensive wars with heavy losses. The brutal Tartars are said to have seized eleven thousand men and women to sell into slavery. The Swedish-Polish War (1655–1660), also inflicted great misery on Königsberg. After the Swedes had advanced to the walls of Königsberg, the Grand Elector succeeded in freeing East Prussia in a winter battle when he crossed the frozen lagoon. In 1701, Friedrich I was crowned King of the Prussians in Königsberg. Shortly thereafter the plague broke out. A few decades later, the Russians defeated the Prussians near the village of Gross-Jaegersdorf, and the Czarina started to dream of absorbing East Prussia as well as the Memel region and the Baltic ports into her empire. It is said that the misery during the period of Russian rule during the Seven Years' War was so great that in the capital city, parents sold their children to Russians for eighteen silver pennies apiece to save themselves from plague and poverty. Fear of pillage forced them to pay ever larger tributes to the Russians again and again. Despite these burdens, they scraped together whatever they could to aid Friedrich's armies.

The years between 1762 and 1806 were years of peace and, aside from a devastating fire, it was a period of quiet progress. Trade prospered and intellectual life flourished, to which the name of Kant added everlasting glory. Then the Napoleonic Wars and three armies—those of France, Russia, and Prussia—laid waste to the land, which provided them with supplies for months at a time. It is said they even fed the straw from the roofs to their horses. No part of the Prussian monarchy suffered as much as did East Prussia. Tributes could only be paid with loans that mortgaged Königsberg until after 1900.

In the book *Königsberg in Preussen (Königsberg in Prussia),* published by the city of Königsberg in 1924, we find:

After the Wars of Liberation in the nineteenth century, Königsberg recovered only very slowly. Even by mid-century, when the best minds were concerned with the great questions of the day regarding the unification of Germany and participation of the people in legislation, Königsberg was at the forefront with men such as Theodor von Schön, Dr. Johann Jacoby, Simson, and a host of other thriving talents who lived within its walls such as Wilhelm Jordan, Gottschall, Gregorovius, Hoverbeck, Hobrecht, and Rupp. Königsberg's son and later honorary citizen Simson was the spokesman of the deputation that offered Friedrich Wilhelm IV the Kaiser's crown in the year 1849. [Two of the acclaimed names mentioned here were Jews or of Jewish descent: Dr. Johann Jacoby and Eduard von Simson.]

Nor did the First World War spare East Prussia; battles against the Russians took place near the Great Masurian Lakes at Gumbinnen and Tannenburg. In a referendum in 1920, 98 percent of East Prussia (92 percent of West Prussia) voted for Germany. And then there was Hitler, who wanted to create his Thousand-Year Reich. Driven by his ideology that only a member of the Germanic race was good and therefore had the right to enslave everyone else, Hitler decided to launch his treacherous attack on Russia from East Prussia. Ever since Napoleon, just about everybody agreed that Russia couldn't be conquered. It was also well known that every failed attack on Russia had brought territorial gains. But Hitler believed he could accomplish the impossible with modern weaponry, so he broke the treaty with Russia with a surprise attack. For this reason—and only for this reason—the Red Army was now advancing on East Prussia, on a nation that had fanned out to conquer the world and had to be brought to heel. What we most feared at this point was that, after the defeat of Hitler, there would be no more history of Prussia in the area surrounding Königsberg.

The air raid on Königsberg served as notice of its impending destruction. The refusal to bring a war already lost to a timely end and to destroy a dictatorship—whatever it took to do so—squandered away the last chance for East Prussia. The great accomplishments of countless people, a beautiful homeland, the entire intellectual and physical patrimony of courageous forefathers simply became part of the bankrupt's estate, the assets of world conquerors who had failed.

Before it finally came to that, however, soot and ashes first turned all shades of black and silver gray. For a long time, incandescent traces of red-orange lingered and, later, the rusty red of the bare bricks continued to glow. Only two days later—after the heat had cooled off a bit—was it possible to walk through the broad streets of the city now lying in ruin. The entire city was a danger zone, everywhere buildings were on the brink of collapse. I had to pass the blockades posted to keep out unauthorized persons. We workers at factories designated essential to the war effort, of course, had passes. When I got to the factory, I saw that even though the walls, stairs, and upper floors had

been badly damaged they were still standing and usable. It was immediately apparent that things could be repaired. On the very first day we
started cleaning up and repairing production equipment with a group
of French prisoners of war to assist us. We were given the hardest
work, and our Russian girls, all of whom had survived, had to work
around the clock. They had fled to the outlying districts before the fire
had fully spread. Even their living quarters in the rooms in the cellar
were unharmed, aside from some slight heat damage, and their bunks
could still be used. The factory wasn't located in the center of town, of
course, and there were some houses in this district that hadn't been
destroyed. There were a few undamaged basements, and some street
corners were still intact. Administrative offices and all sorts of workshops were immediately set up.

We soon had the factory up and running full swing. The workers
were at their places once again, producing mostly laundry powder and
"war soap." I was always doing something different at work. I became
the "wild card," a jack-of-all-trades. Sometimes I had to stand at the
drying apparatus, shoveling the soap flakes spewing forth in a steady
stream into the boxes, which I then stacked up. It was conveyor belt
work I hated, for this apparatus set the tempo all day long without
letup. Sometimes I was taken along on a truck to help unload train
cars or barges. The strongest men were needed to carry sacks on their
backs—many of which weighed up to two hundred pounds. At that
time I was still strong enough and didn't actually dislike this work.
Driving back and forth gave me more a feeling of freedom than I had
at the factory, where I was locked in a room with barred windows.

One day Voss, who handled the job assignments, ordered me to
delouse the beds where the Russian girls slept. The task turned out to
be one not without consequences. After the beds had been taken apart,
I washed the pieces with caustic soda used in soap production, slaughtering the bugs and their eggs by the millions. Despite taking every
precaution, I brought these nasty little creatures home with me. It was
a while before I noticed, but by then it was too late. From the point of
view of exterminating bedbugs, it was stroke of good fortune when our
house burned down.

The number of workers with the Star of David dwindled. Little
by little, most of them were deported and probably had already been
killed. I remember Olaf Boenheim and Bernd Levy, who were a little
older than I. Their gentile mothers protected them and their fathers

from immediate deportation. Even Herr Weinberg was working somewhere and came to visit us from time to time. He would have me play
the violin for him and then he would play our beautiful Blüthner
grand piano. His visits are the only ones I remember from this period.
Father's friends and acquaintances, of course, hadn't dared to visit a
home where Jews lived in a long time. The party and the Gestapo
inspired such terror that everyone was gripped by fear. There was no
lack of phrases to turn an innocent act into treason: undermining the
will to fight, collaboration with enemies of the people, *Rassenschande*
(having sexual relations with a non-Aryan), spying, and so on. The
penalty for each of these was death. And there were many people
only too glad to take advantage of the fact that nothing stood in the
way of their nasty little intrigues. Only just before the total collapse
did this change. But at this point even my father nervously gave the
"Heil Hitler" for fear someone might cause him harm. Besides, the
Hitler salute was obligatory. This eternal anxiety made me furious. I
sometimes hated my father for this. Our relationship badly deterio-
rated. He certainly gave me no advice or encouragement in my efforts
to progress on the violin. He had been a renowned teacher in this
regard. Father isolated himself and increasingly ignored day-to-day
events, as well as any opinion I had of them. I was angry and we exchanged bitter words.

One problem was getting enough food. At this point, we couldn't
live on the rations allotted to Jews. Whatever my Father obtained with
his ration cards had to be divided three ways. We were beginning to
starve and were losing weight. One day Klaus brought me a baby rabbit; I built a little hutch for it on the balcony and zealously foraged
greens for it. We planned to have a genuine festive roast for Christmas.
But I quickly became attached to the animal and loved it dearly. It was
allowed to run around in the apartment, where it liked to pee on the
beds—it couldn't be trained not to. So we had to lock it up again.

My friend Klaus also gave me earphones and a radio rectifier. Without electricity, using an indoor aerial and a crystal that looked like
pyrite, it was possible, with fine tuning, to listen to the radio. The sound
wasn't bad. I installed the set, hiding it behind my bed as, of course,
it too was something forbidden. For the first time I could listen to
the radio in peace and quiet, mostly at night. The music I heard overwhelmed me. I quickly figured out the schedule for the good programs.
My favorite was "The Little Treasure Chest" on Sunday mornings.

There was poetry, read by Mathias Wiemann, and the most splendid chamber music. I can still recall the names of two musicians, Michael Raucheisen at the piano and the violinist Rudolph Schulz, whom fate decreed I would meet one day. The joy I had listening to Bach, Mozart, and Beethoven in those days is as difficult to describe as is the taste of a slice of bread eaten by a starving man. I ardently wished always to be surrounded by music. Nothing seemed to be as unsullied as music; nothing could be a starker contrast to politics, to the factory, to the war. That it was possible to terrorize with music I only learned much later. We humans bring our compulsions to everything we do. Our craving for admiration, our tendency to dominate, our capacity for hatred, joy, sorrow, and love. Alas! In those days, the good and the noble were clearly distinguishable from bad and evil; and music, as far as I was concerned, unquestionably belonged to the good and noble.

Painting was another avenue of escape for me. The praise my efforts earned here inspired me to try harder. My painting, so I believe, was the only thing I did that my father admired. I drew portraits and painted pictures with philosophical ideas. But I never believed I had real talent. I definitely felt I lacked the necessary spark of artistic creativity. My one desire was music. I chafed at having so little time for it. Even during work breaks, I practiced bow movements with a twig or a pencil; a sort of violin gymnastics, which was really quite effective.

Incessant propaganda kept hope for victory alive, but also postponed what had to be done for a long time. Every hour of blind obedience—by generals or civil authorities, soldiers or civilians—was costing thousands of lives and guaranteeing the destruction of more and more German cities. The fact that now every German had to fear for his life did not increase the chances of survival for anyone with the Star of David—on the contrary. Not only did the Nazi extermination program threaten our existence, but so did the fortunes of war. What's going to happen to us, we kept asking ourselves, if East Prussia becomes a battlefield? The attack on the Russians had been launched, after all, from East Prussian soil. They'll make no distinction between the degrees of guilt. Shells and bullets certainly didn't. But before it even came to that, everyone with the Star of David would surely have been "exterminated." The decrees to carry this out had already been drawn up.

In October 1944 the Russians occupied the Memel region, encircling the divisions stationed in Courland. The situation was becoming more critical, with one city after another lost despite heavy resistance.

Königsberg resembled more and more a city on the frontline; it was an armed camp. An army report dated October 19, 1944, reads:

> The battle on the border of East Prussia between Sudauen and Schirwindt continues with increasing intensity. Eydtkau has been lost, but our troops are fighting bravely, delaying the breakthrough the Russians are hoping for. In the three-day battle, 250 enemy tanks have been destroyed so far.

And on October 23:

> The Bolshevists have penetrated fairly deep between Sudauen and Goldap. Goldap fell into enemy hands after heavy street fighting. South of Gumbinnen, the Grenadiers cut the supply line of the advancing Soviets. When the Bolshevists' attempts to encircle Eben-rode failed, they sustained heavy casualties. In the seven-day battle in this arena of fighting, 616 enemy tanks have been disabled or captured. Soviet attacks on the bridgehead of the Memel have been repelled.

These reports unambiguously show that the campaign against East Prussia was well under way. Many people were obsessed by dark forebodings, and the rumor mill provided an extra measure of nervousness.

> At the end of October or the beginning of November, Herr Mendelsohn is very secretive. Taking me by the arm, he says, "You've got a good ear, come upstairs with me, I want to show you something." We go up to the top floor. He opens a window to the east. His eyes sparkling, he whispers, "Now just try to listen in the distance. What do you hear?" I have to concentrate very hard, then I hear it clearly. Like an endless thunderstorm, it is rumbling and roaring without a pause far in the distance. Although very faint, it's sinister and threatening. I strain to figure out what it could be. Such a thunderstorm with such blue skies, it couldn't be. Besides, the thunder never ceases. "That's the sound of battle, still very far away, but you can hear it without a doubt. Hurrah, the Russians are coming."

I shall always bitterly think back on this hurrah. Later no one would utter a hurrah, and Herr Mendelsohn wouldn't live to see the Russians.

It was only natural at that point that we pinned our hopes on the arrival of the Russians. It seemed the only way to get rid of Hitler. I would run to the window and listen to the ominous rumbling whenever I had a moment. I kept wanting to reassure myself I wasn't mistaken. I strained to pick up every change in the sound roaring on the distant horizon. It was exciting. Sometimes I thought I heard the battle sounds closer, then farther away. Then, not at all. I was buoyed up with new courage.

The attitude of our torturers unmistakably altered too, at least the demeanor of some of them. Herr Täuber became friendlier; the block warden Rogalli, more unsure of himself. Their increasing anxiety was palpable. The Russians advanced to Gumbinnen, even to Insterburg, and the fighting was bitter. The war had moved onto German soil. The contrast of the present situation to the previous arrogance and victory slogans couldn't have been more stark. Confusion grew, doubt stalled action, collapse was imminent.

It was at this time that the revolt of the National Polish Home Army took place in Warsaw. The English and Americans, having landed in France, reached the German border and occupied Aachen. Italy was now fighting against Germany, too. Even Romania and Bulgaria declared war. Finland surrendered, and Hungary announced a cease-fire, and both countries continued to fight the war on the side of the Allies. Only a few believed Goebbels's drivel about a wonder weapon that would win the war. The power and superiority of so many opponents could no longer be ignored.

Although Hitler had set up the *Volkssturm,* which turned children and old men into soldiers, they certainly couldn't halt the impending doom. In the face of impending collapse, Hitler's criminal orders were still carried out. The only explanation could be pervasive fear. Fear because most people had cooperated in some way and bore some responsibility. Fear of the power of the party and the police, whose tentacles infiltrated the tiniest detail and ruthlessly controlled everything. Fear of a judicial system that executed without mercy and sentenced as treasonous even those who merely expressed doubts. Fear of the enemies' revenge. For generals who surrendered, the members of their family were held liable; with their wives and children they faced the death penalty. To save their troops, they were forced to sacrifice themselves. And there were such generals. Nonetheless, one must conclude that the failure of courage that would have been necessary to resist in 1933 made it possible for Hitler to bend the law; even now there was failure to protest as the senseless killing and destruction continued to rage. It's true such courage is seldom shown when it carries so high a risk. Even more seldom when one's own life or the life of one's family is at stake. The attempt to liberate Germany on July 20— Count Stauffenberg's assassination attempt—and other brave acts of individuals cannot now serve as an alibi for everyone else to claim that such courage existed. There were simply too many officers and officials who, although they disagreed with Hitler and his machinery of extermination, nonetheless did his handiwork directly or indirectly for such a claim to be credible.

The Siege of Königsberg

The Stock family got in touch with us. There were even cautious visits. The prospect that everything would be over soon gave us all a feeling of hope and even a bit of courage. I listened to Ute practicing the piano. In my free time, I played my violin. It was in marked contrast to the constant rumble of battle, now closer and louder. It must have taken thousands of large and small explosions to produce this constant roar, which meant countless dead and wounded, day after day and hour after hour. At work, everyone's nerves were increasingly on edge since no one really knew what was going to happen. Up to this point there were no orders or preparations for evacuating civilians. Quite the reverse, we had the impression they would press weapons into our hands so we could fight to prolong the lives of those who had brought this all about in the first place.

Physically, I was growing weaker, especially after our balcony bunny was slaughtered for our Christmas dinner at the end of 1944. I had been feeding him the whole time for this very purpose. Our neighbor Norra killed him. I then had to watch him be hung by his rear legs, skinned, and gutted. I really had to force myself to watch. Ultimately, I knew we had to eat him to survive, but I had no idea that I would become sick as a result. Our high hopes for a savory Christmas roast were dashed as far as I was concerned. After I'd eaten my beloved rabbit, I became nauseated. I threw up and, strangely, never really got better. Everything was upset, my stomach as well as my soul. Strength I badly needed alarmingly ebbed away; just now when it was a matter of jumping what might be the last hurdles. A doctor we knew examined me at this time. He was very worried about my general condition. His diagnosis was malnourishment, lungs and heart affected, urgently in need of rest. Not the best condition for facing the most difficult time yet to come.

On my way to the factory I saw more and more refugees from the East Prussian districts that now were directly in the path of the fighting. We saw the soldiers in the streets marching in staggered step exactly ten paces apart. To match the winter landscape, they wore white camouflage. We began to see more and more horse-drawn wagons used as means of transport. Due to the shortage of fuel, trucks ran on wood gasifiers. Heavy war equipment was seldom seen. The "tongue telegraph" was working at full speed, and not a day went by without more rumors. Unbelievable stories were told of atrocities by Russian soldiers as they took the first German cities. Soon we, too, would feel the worst.

Rumors flew in all directions. By the end of January 1945 Königsberg had been sealed off. There were no more air raid alarms. Russian planes flew unchallenged over the city any time of day or night. Not a German plane was to be seen. Fear mounted among civilians. Everyone was drafted to construct tank traps, which, when actually put to the test, were totally ineffective. Outside the city, endless trenches were dug under armed guard, one-man bunkers were built, and crossroads were fortified. Sentries stood on every corner, looking for deserters. Although many people continued to stay in their apartments, we moved into permanent quarters in the cellar. The Russian artillery now began to bombard Königsberg at irregular intervals. Without warning, shells would explode anywhere. Their fragments were even more dangerous. I remember how Herr Norra once came into our cellar saying a shell had exploded not far from him. He was stunned and shaken. After a while, when for some reason or another he took his wallet out of his jacket, he discovered a small, jagged shell fragment had half penetrated it. The wallet had saved his life. Without it, the fragment would have pierced his heart.

Bombs dropping from planes, artillery shells, party discipline. Any of these things could have brought the war to an end. But it went on and on. Festungskommandant General Lasch describes in his idiosyncratic way the dramatically worsening situation in his book *So fiel Königsberg (How Königsberg Fell)*. Major Dieckert and General Grossman also describe the last days of destruction in *Der Kampf um Ostpreussen (The Battle for East Prussia)*. From here on, the excerpts from these books are quoted as a contrast to my experiences. General Otto Lasch writes:

> We sent repeated and urgent warnings that when the fighting began, and it was expected to begin shortly, the population would be forced to remain in East Prussia in order to avoid an unimaginable chaos, since all roads are occupied by troops. The stereotypical response came once more: "East Prussia will be held, an evacuation is out of the question." ...
>
> By proclamation to the population of Königsberg, now filled to overflowing with refugees who had trekked on foot from countless points in East Prussia, it was announced that should Russian tanks break through from the direction of Tapiau, the news would be reported by telegraph. In such an event, the population of Königsberg was to immediately take to the streets—in other words, flee—towards Pillau. This announcement came on January 27. It can well be imagined what then happened in Königsberg and on the road to Pillau on this and subsequent days. I myself drove to Pillau that day to discuss with the navy commander the need for ships to be ready to evacuate civilians from East Prussia. On my return from Pillau to Königsberg, it was almost impossible for the car to get through. As a consequence of ill-considered party measures, unbelievable masses of humanity choked the roads. By foot, by bicycle, and by cart, women with baby carriages, convoys of support troops being transferred to the Samland, all were moving forward in three and four columns.
>
> In the Königsberg harbor, there were a few ships already loaded with refugees, but whose capacity was completely inadequate for the thousands of people trying to squeeze into the harbor.

A new and particularly nerve-wracking danger were Russian fighter planes that, unimpeded by any defense, flew low over the buildings, hunting down anything that moved. If they saw someone, they fired their machine guns. If they noticed a vehicle, they dropped small bombs right on target. It was particularly bad whenever the sky was clear. I remember:

> Every morning when I wake up in the cellar, my first thought is the weather. Bright blue skies mean the fighters will be lurking. Mother and I

already are familiar with the lethal game, played as follows: before you step out into the street, you look for a place that provides cover thirty to fifty yards away. That can be a doorway, archway, or stone wall. Then you listen for the planes. If everything is quiet, you go by bicycle or run as fast as you can. Once you reach cover, you can give yourself a breather. Since the planes fly so very low, you have, once you see or hear them, only a few seconds to reach the next spot to take cover. On such days, the trip to the factory takes forever and these cat-and-mouse games can be repeated over and over again. Today it's really bad. Scarcely have we pedaled halfway through the Schrötterstrasse when we see a plane diving directly at us from the Hammerweg. It's beginning to shoot just as we dive into the next doorway. The feeling this time is that it's only a split second's difference between being hit and not being hit and our nerves are jittery. Scarcely drawing a breath, we wait a moment before beginning the next lap, and pick up the bicycles we had hurriedly cast aside. On the Hammerweg, we encounter two soldiers on a horse-drawn wagon. Of course we know you make a big detour around anything military. But our paths cross since we have to go up the Hammerweg a bit, past the Luisenkirche to the Hufenallee. Moreover, we only notice the wagon when we enter the intersection. Barely do we reach the Hammerweg when the two drivers leap from the wagon and lunge toward a doorway. We hadn't heard any engine noise, but assume the soldiers know what they're doing. We too make a beeline for the same doorway. When we reach cover, I see two planes, this time coming from another direction, and after a brief pause, there's quite a nasty burst of fire. We're all completely dazed, then I hear one of them who's peering at our Stars of David with irritation say, "Goddammit, Ernst, sonofabitch." As we leave, we see the remains of the horse-drawn cart. Everything is scattered about nearby. Boxes broken open with engine parts between the broken wheels and pieces of wagon. One horse is lying on the ground blown apart, his limbs still twitching in all directions. Overcome, one of the soldiers shoots the poor creature in the head. Immediately it stretches out its legs and we have the impression that it is now completely at peace. This act impresses me enormously, and I imagine how it would be if everything suddenly came to an end without drawn-out suffering or a painful transition.

We have to duck for cover two more times before reaching the factory. But even there we aren't safe. It's only a matter of time before the well-informed Russians will bomb the factory we've just repaired to smithereens. Especially since artillery shells are now manufactured on the ground floor. Almost overnight part of the soap factory had been turned into a munitions factory. Mother works on the third floor, I work on the fourth floor and also in the courtyard when there's loading or unloading to be done.

We had long since figured out that bombs of a certain size had to be dropped from a certain height, and therefore we could see, if the weather was clear, whether the planes were flying directly toward the factory before releasing their bombs. They did this long before they reached their target. When warned immediately—right after the bombs were released—you had time to whip from the third floor to the first or even into the cellar. We took turns watching on the roof to share this heavy responsibility. Management agreed to our alarm system. Only watch out if it was a false alarm; then we had to work without a break to make up for the lost time.

During my shifts at the factory, it was only bombed once; and that was when we were all on our midday break, the very moment when the roof post wasn't on duty. But we had taken our break in the storeroom in the basement on account of the heavy air traffic. To make use of the time, Mother had gone to one of the stores temporarily set up right around the corner on the Steindamm—she could use my father's food ration cards there—when all of a sudden there was an ear-deafening explosion, followed by several explosions one after another, then it became quiet. Our fourth floor was hit and partially destroyed. Fortunately, it was only a small bomb. I immediately started to worry about where the other bombs had landed when someone, all upset, told me that bombs had fallen on the Steindamm, directly in front of the store where my mother had said she was going. There were, he said, dead and injured still lying there. My heart skipped a beat. I was convinced my poor mother had surely been hit this time. Bleakly assuming the worst, I went to check. Meanwhile, air wardens and Red Cross people had already arrived on the scene to take care of the wounded. As far as I could tell, Mother wasn't among them. I asked what the people who had already been carted away looked like. Someone confirmed that a white-haired lady had been among them. Mother had white hair. Completely crushed, I went back to the factory. There someone told me Mother had returned without a scratch and was looking for me. We fell into each other's arms. Mother told how she was in the store when the bomb hit in front of it. She had been standing way in the back and hadn't been hit, either by the shrapnel or the glass fragments as had most of the people next to her.

As a countermeasure the walls around Königsberg were blown up. By the end of February, a corridor to the harbor of Pillau had been opened. This had resulted in retaking the suburb of Metgethen, which was about five and a half miles from our house. Civilians had been cruelly tortured and murdered there. With the cry "Remember Metgethen!" these most pitiable of creatures were used to inspire fighting on for a cause long since lost. General Lasch writes:

> The Russians had wreaked singularly terrible havoc in Metgethen, where, among other actions, thirty-two civilians had been gathered in a fenced-in tennis court and blown up by an electrically triggered mine.
>
> The commandant of the Grenadier Regiment describes what he saw after retaking of the towns that had been occupied by the Russians:
>
> "The sights we saw in retaken territory were terrible. The Russians had mass-murdered the Germans in these towns. I saw women who were still wearing a noose around their necks that had been used to drag them to death. Often there were several tied together. I saw women whose heads were buried in the mire of a grave or in manure pits whose genitals bore the obvious marks of bestial cruelty. All women and girls between the ages of fourteen and sixty-five had been raped, older and younger ones as well. Obedient to Stalin's order, 'Take the blond German women, they are yours!' the Russians fell on German women like wild animals, no, much, much worse. A girl barely sixteen was raped eighteen times in one night."

Thousands upon thousands of young lives were heedlessly sacrificed during the next few weeks. Never has the cry for revenge boded well, and certainly not the slogan "Avenge the vengeance"—the Russians were taking vengeance too. It was already criminal and crazy to begin the war, crazier and more criminal still to prolong it with slogans of vengeance. It is true that the corridor to Pillau that had been retaken had given a small portion of the civilian population the opportunity to escape by ship to North Germany, but they had to struggle all the way to Pillau under bombardment. On roads that were jammed with troop transports. Finally, they risked going down with the ship as did those on the *Wilhelm Gustloff* and the *Steuben* when they were torpedoed by Russian submarines.

We too had the impression that refugees were trekking into Königsberg. Many of them were certainly breaking out of the encirclement at Heiligenbeil. The Russians had encircled Hitler's Fourth Army here, and they were in the process of annihilating it. Only later did I hear about the fate of those who had tried to flee over the Frisch Lagoon. They were shelled and shot as they went. The ice broke in many places. Their agony must have been beyond all possible imagination. General Lasch describes in great detail the situation of the civilians and their chances of success:

> Thanks to the courageous efforts of the troops stationed in Königsberg, rail and roads to Pillau were liberated. Once again, Königsberg had a link to the outside world. The possibility arose to make good the unforgivable failure of the party authorities and to evacuate large numbers of Königsbergers from the battle arena. How very soon were these hopes to be dashed once more! At my tenacious insistence, the attempt was made to move masses of civilians out. Since the required number of places on ships could not be provided on short notice in Pillau, and the swelling population unable to move elsewhere was making only gradual headway, a provisional camp was quickly set up in Peyse on the Königsberg maritime canal for the people streaming out of the city. There was no planning and things were badly organized. Hunger and sickness soon plagued the barracks that were the camps. Before long, women with children and baby carriages in these camps came to me in Königsberg, desperately imploring me to allow them back into their homes and houses in the city, where at least there was something to eat. Moreover, they were quite understandably afraid of entrusting themselves to large transports across the sea to the Reich: the news had circulated about two of the ships—the *Wilhelm Gustloff* and the *Steuben*—torpedoed by the Russians and going down with all aboard. Over the objections of the party, which demanded I forcibly prevent the people from flooding back, I did not hesitate to grant what these poor people wanted, thereby giving them the chance to remain in Königsberg and escaping, for a while at least, the worst misery....

During this hard winter, people dragged themselves along on icy roads, trying to escape over the frozen lagoon to the west. Thousands—especially women, old men, and children—found only death. Wagons and sleighs often had to be left behind; only the strong managed to escape with nothing but their lives, assuming they were not overtaken and crushed by the Russian tanks or sacrificed to enemy strafing and bombing over the lagoon. Some of the refugees reached Königsberg just before it was sealed off and there they met with a dreadful fate.

Our neighbors, the Norras, were so terrified by what had happened in Metgethen they took their suitcases one evening and fled. They managed to make their way to Denmark. Later, I met Klaus near Cologne, but Father Norra hadn't survived the rigors of the flight.

Ute now came over more often to play music. On Sundays, when there was less shooting and bombing—yes, that did happen—we would go to the apartment and practice Beethoven's *Frühlingssonate*. This was unmitigated joy for me. Not only because the music was so heavenly but also because my feelings of love could be expressed, if not communicated, in our musical companionship. It sufficed that she took me seriously. With music one listens, after all, more carefully to each other than is usually the case in conversation.

Many people were no longer afraid to talk to us or even come by for a visit. For the first time, Concertmeister Hewers came by; he had once been first chair in my parent's quartet. I was allowed to play for him. He was very encouraging and gave me some pointers. Shortly thereafter, he fell in the final inane battle for Königsberg.

But we couldn't delude ourselves. Herr Weinberg told us the party and Gestapo had strict orders to prevent anyone with the Star of David from falling into the hands of the enemy. He claimed he knew this firsthand. What that meant in the hopeless case of Königsberg was only too clear. Indeed, there was a decree from the RSHA (Reich Security Main Office) dated January 13, 1945: "All citizens capable of work living in a mixed marriage and stateless Jews (including certified Jews) are to be transferred to Theresienstadt as a closed work detail."

Mother and I looked for a hiding place and found an air raid shelter in the burnt-out center of town. We planned to disappear there until the Russians took Königsberg. The trouble was we didn't know how long that would be, and someone could come any day to fetch us for liquidation. Since I was firmly convinced that the person fetching us would be our SA-man Rogalli, I hid our ax—normally used to chop wood—right behind the cellar door. I was determined to use this ax if Rogalli asked us to come along. But he appeared more and more infrequently: anxiety about his own life preoccupied him more than party orders. The struggle to survive had become everyone's most pressing concern and the march of events was turning us all into what we really are: creatures like every other one in God's creation. No more, no less. The meaning of such concepts as superior or inferior, rich or poor, educated or ignorant became irrelevant. In our struggle to survive we're all alike. General Lasch writes:

The ratio of fighting forces on our side and on the enemy's side was especially absurd with respect to air power. At this point about a third of the entire Russian air force had been consolidated under the command of an air marshal, and there not one single German fighter plane arrayed in defense. Our own flak batteries lacked ammunition and therefore were compelled by necessity to focus on the ground battle. The superiority of the enemy's artillery was particularly overwhelming, especially with respect to the availability of ammunition. There was enough only for one day of heavy fighting, and for that day we had been hoarding ammunition since the beginning of the siege. Compared to the approximately thirty Russian infantry divisions, we had only four newly assembled divisions and the *Volkssturm*. In other words, there were about 35,000 defensive forces facing 250,000 offensive forces. After subtracting the Fifth Tank Division, the ratio of tanks was 1 to 100. The fortified city had only one assault company remaining. The enemy's superiority in matériel stemmed in part from weapons delivered from the U.S.A. Sherman tanks and American planes appeared, not to mention other equipment of every description. It was discovered when the tenth anniversary of the victory over Königsberg was celebrated that even a French air squadron had taken part in the final battle for Königsberg....

About thirty army divisions and two air fleets completely blanketed the fortified city day and night with an ongoing barrage from thousands of guns of every size, including "Stalin pipe organs." In wave upon wave, enemy bomber and fighter squadrons rained annihilation on the city, which soon lay in flames and ruins. The artillery of the fortified city, short on ammunition, had nothing to counter this fire, and not one German pursuit plane appeared in the sky. The flak batteries, squeezed together into one small area, were powerless. Moreover, they were stretched to the limit just to defend their own position against enemy tanks. All lines of communication were quickly destroyed. Only runners attempted to find their way through the heaps of rubble to their combat positions or troops. Under the hail of fire, soldiers and civilians huddled together in the cellars of buildings.

Life became more and more precarious. Not only did every clear day turn into a nightmare whenever the planes strafed us, but also more and more artillery were firing shells into the city. They appeared to be firing into distinct districts; and I managed to differentiate among the different sounds of the artillery, especially the one that came from the gun with its barrel trained on our neighborhood. Whenever I heard its distinctive noise—it sounded like a tongue clicking the note of G—I would sound the alarm. We had enough time to find cover, even to leave the apartment quickly and go to the cellar. The impact came only seconds later. At this point they were only firing irregularly on the city. The terrible barrage came later. How our nerves held out I do not know, especially as both our food supply and our health were deteriorating.

It was one of those clear days again that made our lives hell. As a rule, we would take the shortest way through the city to reach the factory. Sick of always being hunted down, we decided to go home by another route on this day, which was once again so dangerous. We wanted to cross southwest of the city. This was a big detour, which took us through parks, past cemeteries, past the Veilchenberg and the Neue Bleiche, toward Luisenwahl.

Mother and I are going by foot. We can take cover more quickly and, most importantly, hear the planes sooner. This time we avoid the streets and are going along some earthworks from which we have an unobstructed view of the entire sky. To our left are the gas storage tanks for Königsberg, completely full and undestroyed. We have to go past them just as do a small troop of soldiers going in the same direction a hundred yards in front of us. Just as we're very close to the storage tanks—about three hundred yards separate us from them—we hear the drone of planes again. They are flying higher and there are a lot of them.

Before we can figure out what they are aiming at, we see the soldiers looking for cover and signaling us to do the same. They had seen the bombs being released. There is nothing nearby but a pile of railroad ties and we press ourselves flat on the ground against them. Then all hell breaks lose. Heavy bombs are dropped on the storage tanks, but miss. Our thoughts are fixed on the fact that if the storage tanks right next to us explode, we will be annihilated. We stay pressed against the ground. We hold our mouths wide open to relieve the pressure from the explosion. The dirt kicked up as the bombs hit the ground rains down on us; then it's all over. The storage tanks remain untouched. We can see what would've happened.... The soldiers are also relieved. They ask us where we're going and give us friendly advice.

Enemy planes attacked day after day virtually without respite. With a clear view, they bombed tactically important targets, particularly those parts of the city not yet destroyed, such as the Ober- and Unter-haberberg. There was no air defense worth noting. Many parts of the city were already in flames by the evening of April 6, including the Ober- and Unterhaberberg. The brave people of Königsberg— as I recall approximately one hundred thirty thousand inhabitants had been counted in the city shortly before the attack—stoically attempted to save what could be saved. One saw old men, women, and children carrying furniture or household goods from burning buildings and extinguishing the flames with inadequate equipment. They didn't seem to fear the bombs or shells falling on them. The combat positions, the temporary infirmaries for the wounded, the main dressing stations, and the hospitals were filled with wounded soldiers and civilians. Königsberg was the very image of terror. The air was filled with smoke and haze, and at night the sky was brightly lit by the spreading conflagration as well as by flying sparks. The combat posts and cellars were jammed with civilians seeking refuge. (Otto Lasch)

How much longer was this supposed to continue? We had been under Russian siege for almost four months without the Russians launching a major attack. One might have assumed they were hoping the *Festungskommandant* would be reasonable, for the conquest of any city costs a ghastly number of lives on both sides. Meanwhile, April had arrived and the authorities continued to fortify the city; tank traps and bunkers were placed on just about every corner. The North Station was the worst. Only one route passed through the railroad junction here. This was where I saw the young soldiers hanged who had wanted to do the one rational thing: end this senseless war. They did what the army commanders—Hitler at the top—were too cowardly to do. There were signs around the soldier's necks: "I had to die because I am a coward."

Reports were coming in more frequently about the flagging morale of the soldiers crammed together in cellars with civilians. In some instances, desperate women tried to tear the rifles from the soldier's hands and hang white sheets out the windows to bring the horror to an end. (Otto Lasch)

But all demands to surrender were ignored.

The Russians

On April 5 we had difficulty getting home. The artillery continued to pound without respite. On the Hammerweg and in the neighborhood of Luisenwahl, the infantry had taken up their positions. Rifle and machine gun fire indicated the fighting was very close. I felt as if I were crossing the frontline. Every few yards, I had to show my worker's pass, then throw myself flat to take cover from incoming shells whistling in with their typical high-pitched whine. No doubt about it: the Russians were beginning their final push we'd long been expecting. All of us recognized the Russian superiority: it was hopeless even to think of resistance. General Lasch himself estimated the attack forces to be 250,000 compared to the defense forces of 35,000. A third of the entire Russian air force was deployed over Königsberg, without a single German plane to be seen. The ratio of tanks was 100 to 1. No one could comprehend why the civilian population was being subjected to this murderous bombardment. Lord knows, everyone had suffered enough. We choked with impotent rage at the commanders who were squandering their troops. Everyone cursed and grumbled, openly and loudly.

Only with enormous effort, we manage to reach Steinmetzstrasse 26, and we know we won't be leaving it again until the Russians come or we're buried under the rubble. Once more, we enter the air raid shelter, which by now has fallen in. Rogalli's been missing for a few days. The Norras and two other families have fled, so we can spread out. It's natural that we chat with each other now. The Nazi regime is finished and they're all suddenly very polite. They must be quietly entertaining the hope we can protect them from the Russians.

April 6: A hellish din fills the hallway outside. Shells are hitting the building. Even so, we can tell we aren't in the midst of the battle yet.

Soldiers in full battle gear with bazookas, machine guns, and radio gear are going through the cellars, which have passages from one to the next. All the buildings are connected by narrow passages through the walls. But this means the Russians can also pass through whole blocks of buildings without leaving the cellars. This makes the street fighting even more insidious, with both sides not only pressing forward against the enemy on the streets but also through the maze of passageways in the cellars.

German soldiers, now passing through our cellars, were being urged by the civilian population to stop fighting, to take pity on us at last. With regret they always refused, saying they were under orders. The necessity of obeying orders for soldiers; the necessity of obeying orders for the General. Whoever has pledged obedience apparently is relieved of any further responsibility for thinking—no matter how many more people die or what more will be destroyed. Dieckert and Grossman write in their book:

On April 6 the death struggle began for the *Festung* Königsberg. At half past seven in the morning a particularly strong heavy drum-fire began against the southern front and at half past eight it began against the northern front. With thousands of cannons, mortars, and rocket launchers, the enemy began to hammer the defending forces. Squadrons of bombers in terrifying numbers circled endlessly above Königsberg and dropped their bombs by the ton destroying every-thing they hit in that wretched city. Fighters zoomed in again and again, strafing the roads and our positions, every gun blazing. The city sank into burning ruins. The German positions were crushed, the trenches plowed under, the foxholes leveled, entire companies buried, communications destroyed, and ammo dumps blown up. Clouds of smoke hung over the ruins of the heart of the city. Chunks of buildings, cars riddled with bullets, horse cadavers, and corpses littered the streets. Terrified civilians fled from their bombed and burning homes and sought shelter anywhere they could find. Others remained where they were, stunned, indifferent, and apathetic.

After this firestorm, behind a tidal wave of fire, the Russian in-fantry and tank corps began to attack in waves. The enemy began to focus its attack in a pincer movement from the north to the south through the pine forests, and from the south to the north through

Ponarth. Our artillery, having only limited ordnance, could do nothing against this superior power. The flak was powerless against the swarms of fighters. It had to fight against enemy tanks. The infantry, consisting mostly of inexperienced troops and new recruits, was helpless. . . .

The same eerie picture the next day! Again the Russians rained down a hail of bombs and shells of every size on the German positions. Again the enemy fighters strafed the defending forces, spitting bullets. Buildings collapsed and trees exploded. Just getting around the city was the most serious difficulty for the couriers.

In the southern part of the city, the enemy pressed forward and in the area near the harbor and wharves they encountered less and less resistance. The enemy reached Amalienau from the north just west of Luisenwahl. The attack by the Fifth Tank Brigade to take back the position held by the 548th Division was not carried out; at the request of General Lasch the Brigade had been detached from the 561st Division and approved for April 7. During the drive to connect up with the Fifth Tank Brigade, there was a heavy Russian attack on the 1st Division north of Seerappen. Again and again, the enemy attacked the Division. In this melee fifteen enemy tanks annihilated it. . . .

The troops, now rapidly melting away, defended their position bravely despite the overwhelming hail of bombs. The Russians smoked out one nest of resistance after another using flamethrowers. The number of wounded grew alarmingly. There were no field hospitals in the ruins of the collapsing city, and medical supplies could not keep up with the demands of the wounded. . . . In this dire state, General Lasch requested approval to break out of the *Festung* toward the west in order to save the population from the Russians. [Lasch knew perfectly well that there wasn't the slightest chance of approval!] The army command brusquely refused the request.

On April 7 the sound of battle was at its height. We sat in the cellar, holding our ears. A sergeant and four men came to take up a position in the corner window of our cellar and the adjacent one—just what we needed. Our building was on a corner, and corner buildings were exactly the ones typically flattened in street fighting. My father asked the sergeant, who looked like a reasonable man, how he could possibly answer for what he was about to do. Surely it must be obvious to him that at the slightest hint of resistance we would be blasted to smithereens. Since the cellar was full of civilians, the residents of the building forbade him to fire one shot. The sergeant listened quietly, then reassured him, "Don't worry, we'll disappear at the right moment." That calmed us down. We gathered from this they had no intention of putting up a fight. They stayed in their cellar, paying close attention to the sounds of battle, which raged first in one place and then in another. Toward the afternoon the shelling became heavier. They were definitely fighting now in our immediate neighborhood. It was our street's turn now. Shells crashed in by the bushel along with salvos from the so-called Stalin pipe organs. These are rocket launchers mounted on the backs of trucks; they could rapidly fire off quick-fused shells. Airplanes buzzed endlessly above, dropping large bombs, one of which hit the courtyard and another the intersection in front of our building. The floor shook, holes appeared in the walls, dust filled the cellar, things came crashing down, and the increasing air pressure threatened to explode our heads. Compared with that, artillery shells seemed harmless. We had bolted the cellar door and hoped the thick beams would be enough to support the ceiling of the cellar if the building collapsed.

At this moment on April 7 our section of the city became the war zone, bombarded with constant shelling. It was unbearable. It was hard to imagine that people had to live through this in an open field. Pity the building if someone tried to resist there now. Fortunately for us, our soldiers had disappeared without our noticing. Toward evening things quieted down. Shelling was concentrated on other streets. Then the quiet became menacing. We expected someone to throw a hand grenade into the cellar or Russians to appear. We were in no-man's-land; tensions grew and I kept going to one of the unprotected windows to see what was happening. I saw that all the buildings were heavily damaged. They had huge holes in the walls and the partially destroyed floors gaped open. There wasn't a single window intact. The façades with countless fragments and shell holes looked as if they were covered with freckles. Dot next to dot; hole next to hole. But nothing seemed to be burning in our immediate neighborhood.

As a sign of local surrender, I saw a white bed sheet hanging on the door across the street, which I reported to our cellar residents. We immediately decided to do the same thing: a deed that just a few hours before would have counted as treason was now the signal for a long-desired peace. I hung a white bed sheet on the front door of the building as well as on the door to the courtyard. I thought I saw gray-brown figures in a doorway on the other side of the courtyard disappearing. I couldn't see more clearly because it was dark. Now we sat and waited to see what would happen—and absolutely nothing happened until dawn. Dieckert and Grossman write:

> Without having first spoken with the *Festungskommandant* about organizing and protecting the civilian population, the party gave the order for civilians to come to the main road to the west at 0030 hours. They noisily arrived in motor vehicles. The enemy immediately observed this advance and covered the entire area with heavy artillery fire, causing a horrible bloodbath among those gathered there. After initial success, the attack foundered, General Sudau fell. General Sperl was badly wounded, even Grossherr perished. Everyone fled back to Königsberg. It took great effort to throw up a weak barrier toward the west.

Today is April 8, Father's birthday. I wake up because I've been hearing the clanking of the tank tracks again, still in the distance, but coming closer. The horrible sound of fighting moves off. Our street is relatively quiet compared with the noisy hell of yesterday. Consumed by curiosity, I run to the next cellar where I have a good view of Steinmetzstrasse. I'm confronted with the sight of a Russian soldier in the middle of the street on a bicycle, totally without cover or protection, machine pistol at the ready—guiding his bike with one hand. He pedals slowly down the street from the right toward Schrötterstrasse. He rides by my cellar window and I duck out of sight. When I look again, I see him swerve to avoid a bomb crater and then he disappears from sight. I admire the soldier's courage. I cannot fathom how anyone dares to ride into enemy territory so utterly unprotected. Surely he expects to be ambushed at any moment. To explore a no-man's-land like this is surreal. I wonder if this is an order or a test, a punishment or a wager that the Russian must carry out. We're all very excited. Finally, the moment is really here: the one we couldn't imagine, the one we've hoped for so long.

Again we hear tank tracks clanking, this time coming closer and closer. I run back and forth between my lookout and my hiding place in the cellar. I don't dare look out again until the din of the tank tracks suddenly stops. Even the engine is turned off and everything is quiet. I'm careful because I might be seen and be taken for a sniper. There in front of me is a tank, armored in front, near the intersection, right next to one of the larger bomb craters. It is a self-propelled cannon. I can see everything in the part that's open in the rear, where four or five Russians unwrap something and begin to eat. They're calmly taking a breakfast break. Their helmets are the helmets of tank drivers. Everything has the air of being on maneuvers until I hear my first *"davei!"* and the artillery-men quickly take their positions, start up the engine and rattle away. It probably was a radio command that had cut their breakfast short. At the same time a hellish racket begins and shells whistle over our building, it seems to me, in both directions. The battlefront has moved on and we are now in Russian occupied territory. German artillery is shooting back from center city into the parts of the city held by the Russians. True, these are only random volleys, but we can't believe our artillerymen are firing their shells—blindly it seems—onto buildings occupied by women and children. Meanwhile, fully armored tanks are rolling through our streets, making the ground shake. (Later, when I was in New Zealand, I would dream one morning when an earthquake shook the city of Auckland that Russian tanks were driving through the streets.) Then it's quiet again. Somehow, we pictured everything differently. I wasn't at all expecting that in fact so little would be happening.

It isn't until about noon when the first Russian enters the cellar. Visibly tipsy, he asks if there are any German soldiers and waves his machine pistol about. My father and I try to get him to be friendly, but can barely understand him. It would have been nice to have learned some Russian. It certainly would have made this first day easier. All over Germany public air raid shelters were marked with "LSR" *(Luftschützraum)*. A popular joke said this meant *"Lernt schnell Russich"* (Learn Russian quickly). Well, that was true enough. For now, the unmistakable *"Uri, Uri"* (watch, watch) is heard, and my father gives him his silver pocket watch. The Russian proudly shows off his pockets stuffed full with watches.

That was our first contact, so long desired, with one of our liberators. It was immediately clear that frontline troops couldn't make everything right all at once. So we had to wait some more and keep on hoping. We had no notion that we were now in the second circle of Hell and the third circle awaited us.

More and more Russians entered our cellar during the day. They were searching for soldiers and wristwatches and alcohol. Many were out and out mean, threatening us with the MP (machine pistol) after we had run out of watches. No one took any notice of the Star of David. Toward evening another drunken soldier stumbled in—probably looking for a woman. He threatened Mother, but probably wanted something else. At the time, Father was at the back of the cellar. After a difficult discussion in sign language, we persuaded him to retreat up the cellar steps. Then Mother made a mistake. She whistled our family theme, which was from the second movement (allegretto) of the Beethoven quartet, opus 59/1. She was frightened and wanted Father to come. Instead of Father, the Russian stormed back into the cellar, this time with a drawn pistol. He yelled and screamed in rage and looked as if he were about to pull the trigger. We had no idea what had made him so mad, but figured out it had something to do with the whistling. We explained with gestures. The Russians spoke without pause of *"nemezki Soldat"* (German soldier) and suddenly fired his pistol next to me. It was so close the blast hurt my ear. He had aimed at the ceiling so no one was hurt. With that dramatic gesture, he left just as my Father, terrified, came forward. His sixty-fifth birthday wasn't exactly a holiday, but nonetheless the birthday of a new era.

We soon learned that no Russian soldier gave a damn whether someone was a Nazi or a Jew. They were looking for soldiers in hiding and for plunder. They simply despised all of us and cursed us all. Contempt and scorn were audible in their voices.

Evening came and we were still in our cellar. Every apartment was destroyed and windowless. Several times during the night, Russians came in and suspected me of being a German soldier. They couldn't read our identity cards; the Russian alphabet is written with Cyrillic letters. But we soon figured out that the search for soldiers was really a search for women. In our cellar there was no woman under the age of fifty and they quickly made themselves even older with scarves and clothes. Cries for help from other cellars indicated the Russians had found what they were looking for. The cries cut me to the quick. I didn't know exactly how to imagine a rape. Without the slightest sexual experience on my part, I thought it something that killed the soul. I thought the poor girls and women must be suffering horribly. My Jewish upbringing had been extremely prudish; it embedded sexuality in an aura of something special. With so much whispering, the childish imagination placed the act of procreation in a kingdom of fear ... how is it possible, I anxiously wondered, that an act of love can also be an act of hate?

Their cries for help preyed on me, cries that brought no help. I thought of Ute and my sister, who, thank God, was elsewhere. We had heard the reports of the atrocities in Metgethen, which we had partly dismissed as propaganda or at least as exaggerated. Now we wondered who would be the next victim.

By the evening of April 8, the sense of elation and relief at the end of the Nazi era had already given way to new worries and a sense of foreboding. The cries for help, the pistol shot, the uncurbed animus of most of the Russian soldiers did not augur well. Our hearts would pound every time a Russian appeared and we would fear the worst. There were, of course, a few friendly faces in response to a friendly greeting. But as a rule there was icy rejection, even mean, bitter rage at anything German; and there was the desire for revenge. Our worries returned.

My own health worsened, the feeling of weakness increased. I had never heard someone in agony cry out for help. It haunted me. We strained to listen into the night, and what we heard did not allay our fears: Russian commands, shots, horrible battle sounds in the distance where the next morning everything would be engulfed in flames. It was obvious that the defenses in the center of town had been reinforced where soldiers continued to mount a resistance and that Festungskommandant Lasch still hadn't surrendered. This only further enraged the Russians, who vented their anger at such monumental stupidity at civilians. If you're going to prove you're going to go on killing Russians in a lost cause, you shouldn't be surprised if Russians want to kill as many of you as they can.

I ask again: If you really were concerned, General Lasch, about civilians and saving human lives, as you later claimed to be, wouldn't you have long since surrendered? Not when the Russians were already in the square in front of your bunker, or almost there. We suffered not only horrible bombardment but also ghastly excesses fed by a hatred continuously reborn in this endless fighting to the last man. I saw with my own eyes the flyers on the street demanding surrender. They appealed to logic and reason and urged you to prevent further bloodshed. The authors of these appeals weren't "bad Germans who were in the pay of the enemy," as you write, my dear General Lasch. For me, you are the bad German, who was in the pay of a criminal. Surely you didn't surrender because you feared at first for your own head. But it was the very same fear that made you surrender at the end!

The next day, April 9, I went to the cellar where the Stocks were. I was very worried, but someone there could speak a little Russian and had spoken so adroitly to anyone coming in that they calmed down and went away. Only once did someone want to haul off Ute, but they were able to distract him with a bottle of schnapps. But what about the next one? We considered what we could do. We were even more disturbed by the reports of rapes and someone being shot in the neighboring cellar. Outside, troops of captured soldiers were being marched by, whom we almost envied. They weren't scattered throughout various cellars the way we were and didn't have to deal with the whims of drunken Russians. They shared a common fate. We civilians, on the other hand, were unprotected game, especially the poor girls and women. General Lasch wrote in his book *So fiel Königsberg (How Königsberg Fell)*:

From the point of view of operations, further defense of Königsberg was of no importance now for the end of the war. Since the beginning of April, heavy Russian contingents were already deep in Pomerania, Brandenburg, and Silesia; and English and American forces had already crossed the Rhine and were standing before the gates of Hanover.

On April 9, the tactical situation in Königsberg was hopeless. At the time the decision was made to surrender . . . only the northern section of the inner city was held by exhausted and decimated units with no heavy weapons.

For the decision I had to make at this point, the most significant consideration was the realization that by continuing to fight, I would only be senselessly sacrificing thousands of my troops and civilians. I could no longer answer to God and my conscience for such a decision. Therefore, I decided to end the fighting and to bring the horror to an end.

I knew I would be handing over the *Festung* to a brutal enemy that knew no mercy. But there was at least the hope of saving the lives of most of the people as opposed to the certainty all would be destroyed if the fighting continued. Events proved me correct. If this decision meant I could no longer halt the loss of the East Prussian homeland I could at least have the satisfaction of knowing I saved many human lives from certain destruction. . . .

After the negotiations were completed, just as the Russians were leaving the command post with us, a Russian company reached the Paradeplatz. . . .

From the numerous accounts of the battle for the *Festung* Königsberg, it can be seen that every single soul had done his duty in exemplary fashion to the last. The final battle for East Prussian soil shall remain for evermore a glorious chapter in the history of the German military tradition and in the history of the people of East Prussia.

I have made an effort to show with the quotations I have selected what was happening militarily as well as the personal problems of the army commander. Even in all fairness I cannot read these memoirs without a shudder. How many officers fought a battle already lost simply on the basis of having received an order?

They generally surrendered when the situation was hopeless, after most of the solders entrusted to them had been sacrificed. General Lasch surrendered as the enemy was standing at his bunker door. You can't help but think he capitulated to save his own neck. Lasch writes he acted to answer to God and his conscience. But before that, it was he who organized and sent to the slaughter the very young in a battle he himself calls hopeless. And this he calls "a glorious chapter in the history of the German military tradition," which he and others cannot glorify enough.

The last pockets of resistance in the inner city were now totally destroyed. Civilians had long since ceased to live there (although possibly a few fled back at the last minute). The resistance surrendered only when the Russians set fire to the sector of the city they had already conquered and where there were still some civilians. In quite a few cases, they burned civilians locked in cellars in the process. Later I had to bury some of these victims. Under the pretext that conditions of war still prevailed, the Russians abused civilians brutally indeed. With the senseless resistance in the days after April 6—that is, after the beginning of the major assault—Königsberg's civilians were mercilessly delivered up to the fate of battle. Thousands of human lives could have been saved had surrender come just three days earlier.

Hitler sentenced General Lasch to death, of course; he actually should have rewarded him for faithfully carrying out his duty. One way or another on April 9, Königsberg would have capitulated to Soviet superiority. Had the *Kommandant* been killed in battle, the "heroic epic" of Königsberg, in Hitler's sense of the word, would have been preserved untainted. Taking this into consideration, General Lasch's claim that he had saved human lives before God and his conscience is poppycock. Well, he certainly saved his own life.

War memoirs of generals such as Lasch may be historically illuminating. They can even inspire admiration for what humans are capable of in terms of energy and organization for the sake of battle. Still, there is much that is incomprehensible. For example, the rage over the catastrophic defeat was mainly directed at local cowardly party bigwigs, such as Gauleiter Koch, who ruthlessly saw to their own safety, while goading their troops on to the last droop of blood. But the generals' memoirs spare those who enmeshed the peoples of Europe in this murderous war with their arrogant ideology and their systematic military preparations. Not a single sentence acknowledges the consequences of their megalomania: a fragmented Germany, a destroyed Europe, and suffering multiplied into the millions. Not a single word acknowledges any awareness of their own complicity. They all justify what they did, but they do not produce a single word of regret for what the Germans did: in the invasion of Russia; the destruction of Russian, Polish, and French cities; the attacks on these countries; the deportation of civilians into forced labor; the murder of German and foreign Jews, Communists, gypsies, political opponents. They can never utter such a sentence that expresses regret without putting their entire heroism into doubt. Hitler's war was, in a word, criminal, and they were his stooges. Their victories were pirates' victories.

The sudden disappearance of all German uniforms brought an enormous sense of liberation. We had suffered long enough under the authority of German uniforms. No one would vilify us as inferior and no one would want to kill us. Maybe they would give us preference. It would be a form of reparations granted to us for our lack of culpability for the National Socialist war. That would only be fair. Most heartening of all, we would receive normal rations, for we were at the end of our strength. But the important thing was the war was over and Hitler was defeated.

We had to decide if we should throw our Jewish Stars of David away now or continue to wear them, as a kind of sign we weren't Nazis, as

a badge that all Russians would immediately respect. We were thinking something along these lines, and even though I hadn't wanted anything more ardently than to finally get rid of this stigma, I kept on
wearing it at first. Who knew what would happen.

Was the feeling of being free at last accompanied by the wish for
revenge? Yes, at first. After I was certain that the Russians had taken
the Hufen, something impelled me to go to the house across the street.
The grocer Dossow lived there. He had constantly bullied us, spied on
us, and had denounced us. With my Jewish Star of David clearly visible, I knocked on the door of his ground floor apartment. When he
opened the door, he cringed at the sight of me. I told him, feeling an
uneasy sense of satisfaction, "Herr Dossow, the Russians are here. The
time for bullying us is over. I just wanted to tell you that." Dossow
looked frightened and confused, slammed the door, and said something I couldn't understand. I went home, completely unsatisfied and
not paying the least attention to the fact that it was way too early to
go outside. Advancing Russian soldiers were shooting anything that
moved on the street—a characteristic peculiar to "follow-up frontline
troops" bringing up the rear.

This was my only act of revenge. However, it left a bad taste in
my mouth. I knew that revenge has nothing at all to do with justice.
Revenge is probably inappropriate for settling any score. And, as a rule,
it's directed against the wrong people.

That afternoon I learned by chance that all civilians were supposed
to gather at the corner of Luisenallee and Hermannallee. They were
planning to set on fire any part of Königsberg still intact. We were
told this warning was an ultimatum to surrender. It would be carried
out the same day if the *Festung* positions in the underground bunkers
in the city center did not surrender. An incomprehensible ultimatum.
When you destroy your own booty, you don't damage the enemy unless
you think the threat of systematic destruction of the city's remains—
on account of the finality of the damage and losses for all civilians—
will make an impression on your commanders. I don't know if there
really was such an ultimatum or such a warning. More likely, Stalin
wanted to erase Königsberg and a German East Prussia forever from
the world. General Lasch doesn't mention the language of the Russian
demands to capitulate that we found in flyers dropped on the streets
and courtyards. This too should have been included in a full account
of the destruction of Königsberg.

It should be obvious that the Russians had a large stake in not caus-ing any more casualties. They had already sacrificed over twenty mil-lion lives to repel the invader who classified them as subhuman and wanted to enslave them. There would be advantages to a German sur-render before there was street fighting with heavy losses. The price for such a surrender would be reasonable if Soviet casualties could be pre-vented. That they didn't want to make concessions for a city they had defeated at such high human cost was, from the Russian point of view, unsurprising. Even given the abominable behavior of the Germans in Russia, especially that of the SS, it is clear that the Russians would have made concessions for a timely surrender. They did so elsewhere. *Der Kampf um Ostpreussen (The Battle for East Prussia)* by Dieckert and Grossman gives an account of such an instance.

It took some persuasion to convince the residents sitting on their last few belongings and food supplies that it would be better to go together to the place indicated than to remain in the cellar and wait for the next intoxicated Russian to stumble in wanting something or stirring up trouble. Besides, if they really burned down the Hufen as announced, the heat alone would make the situation critical. We gathered up our backpacks, carry-alls, violins, and suitcases. And off we marched along Steinmetzstrasse as a little company in the direc-tion of Schillerstrasse. In the center of town, artillery shells were still whizzing past our ears. No one was returning fire anymore from our neighborhood. We went along the streets strewn with stones, debris from buildings and pitted with bomb craters. We passed all the half-destroyed houses that now, after all this, were to be burned down. There was no end to the lunacy. In the first one hundred yards the image of a Mongol soldier driving two young women into a ruin with a drawn pistol is seared into my memory. They didn't resist—what else could they do? I could only fervently hope that he let them go when he was finished, for many women were killed afterwards, something I learned later when I buried bodies. In the neighboring streets we saw them marching groups of German prisoners along in double time.

I think we weren't wearing the Star of David at this point. We real-ized there would be no exceptions and our destiny was to share the fate of all. I didn't want any more special favors that would make me an outsider again. No, we were all without distinction for the Russians; we were all despised Germans. They were even driving along Russian girls who had been seized for forced labor as if these poor creatures had voluntarily collaborated with the Germans. No one could comprehend this. There was no logic in what was happening. No one seemed able to think of the future. Our little company consisted of eighteen people, and we could only make slow progress. Everyone could see the Russian soldiers now on the streets were no longer troops from the front. The frontline troops had moved on about half a mile toward the city center. These soldiers were hungry for booty, taking watches and hand baggage, wandering through abandoned apartments and cellars as they looked for things to send home. The rich supplies of wine and schnapps thoughtlessly left behind obliterated any remaining inhibitions. There was no one for miles around who could have put a halt to their actions. Some tried out bicycles, from which they tumbled off. These soldiers came from regions where there were neither bicycles nor toilets. When I went to a toilet on the second floor of our building that still functioned, I found they had done their business on the floor and had used the towel for what we used paper. It stank horribly. The high rates of losses over the years had forced them to mobilize men from the most distant regions of Russia, so that when they took Königsberg these children of the steppes were probably encountering a modern city for the first time. Incited to a frenzy, wild in their joy of victory, astonished at a civilization full of luxurious items, and drunk, they were beyond any control, they knew no bounds. They indulged every instinct, be it sex, power, greed for possessions, gluttony, or murder. They were without fear of punishment or of any consequence whatsoever. What blinding hatred! But, whosoever attacks and defends as ruthlessly as the Germans did, will be fought and vanquished with an equal absence of mercy.

Even our little company quickly attracted the attentions of soldiers, who eyed our women and baggage. They finally zeroed in on two suitcases that looked good and strong. With cocked pistols they took the suitcases, only to discard the contents, mostly clothes and personal mementos such as photo albums, etc. on the street. Then they took off with the empty suitcases. They only wanted empty containers to send their valuable loot back home. Gradually, we became more and more apathetic about the loss of personal things and were happy if they just left us physically unmolested. Our women had made themselves look as old and as unattractive as possible—including Ute—like bent old hags.

We finally reached the designated place, where civilians from all the neighborhoods of the Hufen had gathered. Here something like discipline had been established, for officers were putting many people into some front yards where, exhausted, we could settle down. We felt much safer close to commissioned officers who were actually being obeyed. I noticed something like a feeling of happiness had returned. This feeling stemmed solely from the fact of not being an outcast anymore, of not having to be afraid anymore, of talking with people, of asking questions. Finally, no more special fate. I enjoyed this state of things although the faces around me were etched with their horrible experiences, with fear and helplessness. I was also struggling with what had just happened and what I heard at night. Incredible tales were told and someone pointed to girls eleven and twelve years old who had been raped, they told of murders when the parents had intervened. Shots through the cheeks—across the mouth—when things were not surrendered at once. Nothing seemed impossible or inconceivable. The most gruesome thing could happen at any moment and certainly as a rule rather than as an exception. Everything that one had heard of the Thirty Years' War, of the raids by the Tartars, robber legends, or other horror stories—overnight, these turned into reality, a reality far worse than anything imaginable or any retelling as a story or tale.

Anyone who fell into the hands of the Russians met with a terrible fate, whether they stayed in their homes for some reason or were caught on their flight from the Soviets. The Russians killed many men, especially if they tried to protect their women or daughters. During the day and especially during the night, they hauled off women, even young girls and women as old as seventy, and these pitiable creatures would be raped by one Russian after the other. In fifty-four towns in the district of Rössel, the Russians murdered at least 524 people. They threw 26 peasants into a root cellar and blew it up. In Gross-Rosen they burned 28 people in a barn where they had been rounded up. Others suffered the same fate in a church. In Kronau, in the district of Lötzen, the Russians murdered 52 people, including 19 French prisoners of war; 97 near Nikolsberg who were on a trek from Lyck; 32 children near Schlagakrug in the district of Insterburg, who had become separated from the column of refugees. The same with any man recognized as being in the *Volkssturm*. (Dieckert and Grossman)

We waited for hours at the assembly point. Sanitation and water were becoming a problem. As for food, it was every man for himself. I think at that point I hadn't had anything to eat or drink for some time. Thirst made itself painfully felt. Toward three o'clock in the afternoon, larger groups were being assembled and marched off with two soldiers. No one knew where. Our little group was going toward Charlottenburg, away from the city and into the neighboring Samland. As we were crossing a stream, I asked the first person handy for a cup or a pot, ran down to the stream, and filled up everything with water. Mother, Father, some others, and I gulped it down. But we were marched on without letup, driven on by the unrelenting *"davei"* of our guards.

We passed German and Russian shot-up equipment, armored vehicles, defense guns, and dead soldiers. I'm sure most of them had been removed, but not all. In the hatch of a Russian tank, probably hit by a bazooka, two Russians had become stuck, both trying to escape at the same time. Their upper bodies were hanging out the opposite sides of the hole. Inside the tank, they must have been incinerated. Not far away, an old man from the *Volkssturm* hung from a tree and at the next tree crouched a man—he was slumped over, shot dead. Not only did the farmsteads show signs of heavy fighting, but everything was peppered with traces of gunfire, strewn with shell holes, the trees all split or exploded. A few yards on, there were two country women sitting— probably mother and daughter—by the side of the road. They sat there as if frozen, with fixed stares and bleeding lips. Having fled the hell of their isolated house, they had sought safety in the fields. On a supply road with more traffic, they probably would have found more pity or their perpetrators might have had more scruples about molesting them over and over again. None of us would ever forget such a pitiable sight. Compared to these women, the mangled and swollen bodies of the dead seemed to me to be released from suffering.

We are taking a short rest on a small hillside, where we are quickly surrounded by more booty-hungry people eying our baggage. Our guards even make an ineffectual effort to shoo them away. More and more of our baggage is taken. It's a miracle that we've managed to hold on to our violins until now. We try to hide them as best we can. You can't even see Mother's viola under her coat. But just as we're leaving, a Russian notices Father's violin strapped to his back. The Russian steps among us and points at the violin to indicate he wants it, but Father refuses. With that, the Russian draws his pistol and presses it against Father's cheek with me in the line of fire since I'm standing right next to him. When Father says, "O.K., shoot," I lean my head back, out of the line fire should he pull the trigger. At the same time I gesture to him not to shoot. He doesn't and leaves us in a huff, but, it seems to me, with something akin to respect.

Although Father, certainly not a heroic man, was acting out of desperation, I was impressed by his demeanor. It would be a terrible thing to have his wisdom teeth shot out. We knew that they broke down resistance this way if they weren't in the mood for murder. Again, we could thank our lucky stars. Luck, this strange, almost insistent attendant of so many who survived.

The Stocks were in our little group, and everyone had successfully managed up until now to protect Ute. It had become dark and we were spending the night on a patch of grass out in the open. We were so shocked by what we had seen during the day that no one could or wanted to say another word. But we were even more profoundly shocked by what we heard at night. What we had seen had already happened; what we heard was happening at that very moment. Screams, cries for help, shots, moans, and more pleas for help conjured up images that overwhelmed us. It became unbearable. As a backdrop to all this was Königsberg, which had just begun to burn more brightly.

The Russians had kept their word: they had set fire to all the unburned houses. It was a good thing we had been evacuated. What must have happened to those who had remained behind in their homes? Now I was watching the suburbs of Königsberg burn from a greater distance than when I watched the fire in center city after the air raid. When the flames blazed up again to the heavens, the relentless stupidity and senselessness of everything that was happening left us numb.

The next day, our progress was marked by the same things as the day before, only this time Father lost his violin in a combined attack that was both a threat and trade offer. He was given the choice of being shot or getting two rolls, which we, starving as we were, craved. He had finally recognized that he would loose his violin sooner or later. So he chose the rolls, whereupon they took his violin, which disappeared never to be seen again. We waited for the rolls in vain. No one took any interest in my violin in its ugly box. Taking away a violin from a violinist is taking away a part of his soul. At this moment, Father seemed tired and broken. We really couldn't take another step, yet we hadn't reached where we were going. The roads were filled with Russian supply vehicles, truck after truck—unmistakably American—with a tank or other track vehicle now and then. Female Russian soldiers directed traffic at the intersections waving little flags. Indeed, the farther we got from the fighting, the more uniformed women appeared. Our guards were friendly Russians, and we made some sort of genuine contact. We finally saw something of the human side of our conquerors. It must have been forbidden to show human feeling or to deal with us in a humane fashion. Lev Kopelev's book *To Be Preserved Forever* talks about this phenomenon, even though he downplays the extent and the duration of the excesses.

We were given a rest break in our march in an abandoned farmyard, where I immediately searched for something to eat. I found a small sack of poppy seeds, which we happily consumed with relish. Someone discovered a box of oatmeal; others, some rotten potatoes; finally we had something to eat. On the whole, this second afternoon was quieter. After a night that was better than the one spent in a cellar, we reached our destination sometime the next morning.

The place was called Quanditten. There was an abandoned, but undamaged farm with several buildings, a park, a lake, and adjacent woods. When we got there, the Russians bathed in the lake while others shot off thick branches from the splendid trees—their way of gathering firewood. Later, they threw hand grenades into the pond to bring masses of dead fish to the surface, a method of fishing unknown to me at the time. Apart from these acts of vandalism, these Russians seemed less dangerous than those in and around Königsberg. They even seemed to look after us a little. Apparently we were under a command with superior officers whose authority could be felt even with these soldiers. We were assigned to a rather large room where we had blankets. We were still suffering from the cold weather. Finally it was quiet, and we could sleep. If they grabbed women away, it was for work in the kitchen, and soon we had some potato soup.—At last, I thought, a little bit of peace.

There was a lieutenant who spoke fluent German. It was a German unmistakably related to Yiddish. Our hope that we might be finally understood by a German-speaking Jewish officer proved to be absolutely in vain. He was merely a translator and could effect nothing.

When we told him we were Jewish, he was rather embarrassed. It was soon clear to us that he was ashamed of being Jewish and was trying to conceal the fact. When we showed him our Jewish identity cards, he brushed these aside in two sentences, "We know that Hitler killed all the Jews. If you are still alive you must have worked for the Nazis." It was that simple and now we had to disprove this charge or we would have been under worse suspicion. We asked the Stocks to vouch for us as the Russians took all of us off, a few at a time, to be interrogated. They were apparently making personnel files, trying to extract military secrets such as where weapons were hidden or information on possible "Werewolf" activities. The Werewolf was an organization that the Nazi party had set up—mostly Hitler Youths—that was supposed to carry out acts of sabotage behind Russian lines. They seemed to fear them, perhaps scattering the civilian population in all directions for this reason.

That evening we heard the Russians singing their folk songs. It was incredibly beautiful. Chorus and solo passages alternated, and I simply couldn't comprehend how humans could sing so beautifully yet be so brutal and heartless.

It was night when the lieutenant came to me ordering me to play my violin. At first, I thought it was the pure love of music and a desire to be entertained. Probably it was, but mostly he seemed interested in the violin and its sound, asking how old it was and who had made it. His questions made us uneasy. Mother could charmingly play some salon pieces by Kreisler and Wieniawski, and immediately attracted a large audience. Her playing noticeably awakened a feeling of good will and even softened some of the stony expressions of the soldiers watching.

Two days later, during which we were interrogated several times, they put together a small group of men, including Stock and me. They told us we had to go to the work detail: that meant separation from our families. Mr. Stock took very close care of his wife and daughter. But no one suspected how worried I was about Ute, whom I was quite fond of. There was some futile comfort that it would only be a limited time. We had to leave our baggage behind, and the lieutenant took my violin for himself. I was furious with him beyond words. Embittered, Father and Mother shook their heads.

Accompanied by a guard, we set out with heavy hearts. Once again, no one knew where we were going, but we soon noticed we had to be going back to Königsberg, which was still smoking. We passed along the main roads, where trucks, tanks, Stalin pipe organs, and, now and then, a formation of infantry, all of which were moving along in such numbers we wouldn't have believed it. If there were this many vehicles and soldiers along the thousand miles of frontline, all of Russia had to be on the move. By now, traffic was being hand-directed at every inter-section and there were direction signs and place names in Cyrillic script. East Prussia had been turned into Russia.

Our little group grew larger. Other groups joined us, some with women, even younger ones. It was already a matter of course that they were taken from their beds at night, with flashlights and pistols waved about. Schooled to misery, they let it happen without putting up any resistance. Despite all this, we fell asleep and found them in their places the next morning. I couldn't stop worrying about Ute.

We approached Königsberg, once more crossing the battlefields. Swollen corpses of soldiers were still stuck in shot-up vehicles. Women were again, or still, sitting on the side of the road. An elderly wounded woman stretched out her hand towards us, and one of the Russians standing nearby gestured to me to take the woman along. I felt much too weak, scarcely able to keep up with our march. I couldn't help but think of Aunt Fanny.

The Königsberg "Cemetery"

We finally reached Königsberg. Most of the structures not destroyed in the fighting had been torched. Even our neighborhood in the backwater of Steinmetzstrasse. Everything had been burned, down to the cellars. A more disconsolate picture of Königsberg cannot be imagined. Ruins, nothing but ruins. Only here and there a half-burned building or—miraculously—one with its interior almost untouched. In the suburbs there were small "command posts." We registered once more with a great deal of red tape. We had to scavenge for food in the cellars. A packet of Dr. Oetker's Pudding Powder or vanilla sugar, a can of vegetables or, if we were really lucky, canned meat or sausages. We devoured anything we found. Very quickly, we realized what we had to do. The city was still littered with unburied corpses. Soldiers had been buried, but the troops hadn't considered themselves responsible for unburied civilians. It was now our task to search buildings, cellars, courtyards, and gardens for corpses and "remove" them. One couldn't really speak of burying them. I have to force myself to describe what we did. Our first removal was a partially naked young woman lying in the basement of a half-burned building with dried rivulets of blood from her vagina and mouth. Her face was sweet and delicate. Wearing the gloves issued to us, we grasped her arms and legs to carry her up to the street; we were ordered to toss her into the nearest bomb crater. Others transported a man who had been shot. They threw him on top of the woman. The corpses were about a week old and were already beginning to decompose. The Russians decided we worked much too slowly and carefully so they devised a new method. We were given ropes with a noose at one end. This noose was slung around the feet or hands, and now even one person could drag a corpse to the closest bomb crater. The work went much more quickly. I can still remember almost all these poor murdered men and women; not only do I see their faces, but the positions of their bodies, and sometimes even the objects around them. Children as well as old men and women; most had been shot, some had been stabbed or strangled. There were also a number of suicides. They had taken poison or hanged themselves in a stairwell. In one instance, an entire family had killed themselves. In the neighborhood of the Hufen there was a street with a particularly large bomb crater—I've forgotten the name of the street. I found people shriveled from the heat of the buildings burning down around them and hauled them to this hole. They had been intentionally locked in the cellar and the iron door had been bolted from the outside with a beam. Sadly, there were cellars without the breach in the walls to save them. These people were easy to "transport" but all the more terrible to look at. Just before everything was shoveled over, some of our work detail dragged over the remains of a horse that had long since met its end. The Russians did the shoveling with a sort of snowplow. They had jerry-rigged a track vehicle to do this, while we civilians used shovels. This grave with a man and a horse imparted a peculiarly eerie feeling to me. It was, after all, in the middle of a street and had to be continually refilled as the subsoil kept sinking.

Hunger and mental stress knotted my stomach. Once a soft-hearted, sympathetic Russian wanting to do us a favor gave us each a slice of cheese smeared with honey. This was such a rarity I couldn't imagine where he had gotten it. It was delicious pleasure, which unfortunately made me throw up and made me sicker than I already was.

Communicating was difficult. We quickly tried to learn some Russian, and many people proved to have remarkable talent. Frequently what took place were "word-salad conversations." If someone reproachfully pointed out to the Russians cruelly murdered people, they shrugged and spoke passionately of mother, father, brother, or sister who had died. Although the words were incomprehensible to us, they probably told of homes destroyed and all the atrocities that had happened there. Whoever uses the phrase "Bolshevist riff-raff" after 1960, as General Lasch does in his book, surely held an even worse opinion under Hitler. The Germans had cruelly murdered Communists, commissars, Jews, and partisans; they had starved Russian prisoners of war as well as obliterated cities and villages. In Leningrad alone almost a million people died during the siege. The Russians had no way of differentiating between the actions of the SS or Gestapo and those of other organizations (such as the *Wehrmacht*); these all belonged to the same occupying power. And why should they? Ultimately, they all participated in the invasion of Russia. For the Russians there was only one enemy, the German invaders. And they all were under one supreme commander, Hitler. I have absolutely no desire to distinguish particularly the different degree of schooling of the German who invaded Russia from that of the Russian who conquered East Prussia. The educated person should be more aware of what he is doing than the uneducated. In retrospect, one must always be careful not to confuse cause with effect. I most deeply regret that because unutterable atrocities were committed—really, acts of vengeance—by the Russians, many Germans deem it unnecessary to reflect on our own guilt or at least to feel some regret about the wrongs inflicted on others. I am thinking here not only of many war memoirs. This "inability to mourn" is the terrible result of the failure to discuss honestly the question of guilt.

Certainly, respect for those who actually opposed the regime and were persecuted or imprisoned precludes speaking of collective guilt. They too were Germans. There wasn't collective guilt but there were unforgivably many who were guilty within the collective. And the knowledge must be engraved deeply upon our consciousness what extreme behaviors people are capable of—the ability to mislead, the capacity to act brutally, and the willingness to remain morally supine. Such knowledge must arouse our attention to the degree to which humanity is imperiled. Lamentably, Theodor Heuss's rejection of the notion of collective guilt—he spoke instead of a collective shame—was taken as a personal acquittal by the very people who had every cause to examine their own guilt. You can feel shame at what someone else has done and what others are responsible for. What you reflect on when accused of guilt is not the same as when you feel shame. People were ashamed of course—often only of having lost the war—and dumped the entire burden of responsibility onto a few main players. They waited, moreover, until they could replace the feeling of shame with new pride. Soccer world cups, economic successes, and above all, the rivalries among the Allies, who were rapidly splitting into enemy camps, made it very easy to overcome feelings of shame quickly without even once having to think hard about what really happened.

Our most recent history offers an enormous opportunity to learn much about human behavior—assuming we do not repress unpleasant facts. Aside from everything else, it is important that young people know about that fatal transformation when frightened people are confronted by the powerful, and the fatal transformation when the powerful are confronted by the powerless. Young people should know what happens when instinctive reactions rule and the fateful consequences that follow. Solzhenitsyn calls this phenomenon the most lethal and dangerous of human diseases. I prefer to call it the most perilous ignorance, for then I can cling to my timid hope that knowledge can cure the disease. However, knowing and repressing are mutually exclusive. Whoever represses things does not wish to know and whoever does not know runs the danger of repeating mistakes of monumental proportions.

The Rothenstein
Concentration Camp

To scour the ruins for something to eat, to carry out work directives, to not always be freezing, to find water, to protect oneself from arbitrary power: all this required every ounce of energy, intelligence, and concentration. There were no limits to my powers of imagination and invention. Even in a completely burnt-out ruin with no stairwell between the floors charred cans of food might be stashed in the corners of kitchen pantries, concealing still edible food beneath the sooty exterior. Using a ladder and defying the danger of a building tottering on the brink of collapse, you could maneuver to within its grasp. I never could manage to cut a hunk of meat from a half-decomposed horse and cook and eat it. Those who did had no problems. Even so, diseases soon appeared, and widespread dysentery preceded a terrible typhus epidemic. Almost everyone who managed to avoid dysentery suffered diarrhea anyway; continuous shitting and cramping robbed many poor souls of their last ounce of strength. I lay stretched out, exhausted, with at least twenty other people on the floor of a room that at least had a roof. It was bitter cold even though the windows were reasonably well insulated with cardboard, tin, and oil paintings. Every night, our sleep was interrupted several times by Russians loudly storming in and shining their flashlights in our eyes. They were of course looking for women and girls who untiringly had to do their bidding. Poor women.

On this particular night I was kicked after the usual light was flashed in my face. A Russian soldier angrily ordered me to come with him at once. I packed my clothes and the precious woolen coat I had found somewhere, which I used as my bed, and followed him outside. There we joined a waiting group of men, all civilians. We were now marched off under heavy guard. One of the Germans already registered with this group had escaped and the guards had seized upon me to fill the required delivery quota. Now the count was in order, but the names weren't. From this one detail dire consequences ensued. The rest of the night we spent in a Russian command post. Escape was impossible. I tried to fall asleep on a table. The next morning, we continued on through Maraunenhof, past the lakes of Oberteichen to the former Rothenstein barracks, now a concentration camp. A high fence, watchtowers, and barbed wire—the eternal symbols of inhuman existence—now penned us in. Here they had gathered all the suspicious civilians, probably to flush out party bosses trying to hide. All my identity papers and proofs of my status as a persecuted Jew had long since been taken from me and I had fallen out of the habit of talking about it. No Russian knew anything or was willing to give credit for anything. It was difficult enough to convince them that I wasn't a Nazi. I was obviously so very young. It was even more difficult to prove that I was neither a soldier nor had I belonged to the "Werewolf." Nothing else interested them. They didn't want to hear about Jews or about the fate of Jews. I had certainly learned that lesson in the meantime. The price of being a full-fledged member of the German people was becoming quite high. I had to pay. There was no choice.

We had to line up on the barracks parade grounds. An officer issued instructions. Every sentence ended, ". . . not obey, you will be shot." Everything was forbidden. We stood silently lined up in formation when a young man, who had gone berserk, ran forward, babbling nonsense and jerking about. He headed for the officer, who quickly drew his pistol. With a cry of horror, the poor young man fled, saving his life. Our group was put into a room on the ground floor, a sort of shed, with rain barrels along the side. We ran over to them and drank thirstily. Once we even got something to eat. The soup, however, was handed out only to those who had some sort of bowl. Only if you had a pot or a pan could you take some soup along for someone else. I had nothing to hold the soup, nor anyone who could fetch my portion. So I got nothing from that first meal. A little while later our group was called and we were led into the "cellar." We didn't know yet that the cellar was the worst category in the prison. It was so crowded as we stood in the entryway, not even enough space for one more person. Then they divided us up. They shoved me and two other men into a pitch-dark hole under the low stairs, which rose upwards in a sharp corner, thus preventing anyone from standing upright. It had been a pigpen—probably a "pig hidey-hole"—where German soldiers, perhaps on the sly, had raised pigs. There were a few wooden poles on the floor, covered with pig feces. No boards. Without in the least being able to see anything and doubled over, we arranged the poles to create the illusion that we didn't have to lie down directly in the muck. At first, we sat uncomfortably on the wood, but soon we stretched ourselves out, exhausted. Because we didn't care about anything anymore, we could mentally relax. Most of the muck was almost dry, but still damp enough to smear nicely. Whatever we touched we came up with hand-fuls, not to mention what clung to our clothing. In this dark cellar I began to dream. Not dreaming in my sleep, but while awake. I thought of my parents and hoped that they were still on that heavenly estate (compared with where I was), outside of Königsberg. I thought of playing music with Ute and wished I were back in some sort of apart-ment or in a bed from an earlier existence. I imagined sunshine and fresh air, somewhere by the sea. I was beginning to enjoy these fan-tasies as if they were actually real. My "stall companions" were friendly older men, who felt sorry for me, the youngest kid, and tried to con-sole me. They were worthy comrades in that brief time.

Toward noon the next day, we are fetched from our muck hole, where we also had answered the call of nature. Again, they are handing out food, this time at the end of the cellar hallway. It's gruel and dried bread, partly green with mold. Again, we must forego the soup as none of us has any sort of bowl. I am concentrating now on how I can get my hands on a bowl. It's obvious I'll starve if I don't. Concentration—would others call it prayer?—helps. As we're being taken today to the barracks fence to do our business, the cellar lights blind me at first as they do every time we emerge from the black darkness. I have to close my eyes at first and slowly become used to the light. At that moment the notion dawns on me that the lights have a globe to protect against moisture. On the way back, I watch for the moment when the guards aren't looking and swiftly unfasten the globe held only by one screw and hide it. Now that we've got a bowl we hope the Russians will accept it instead of punishing us for theft or damages. At the next food line, they recognize the exact origin of the bowl, but I see from a smile they accept it. My ingenuity is rewarded with a scoop from the ladle stirred around the pot a few extra times. In the otherwise watery brew I find some potatoes and even a few bits of meat. I estimate that my bowl holds about a liter. We share and enjoy the food. Profiting from my idea, others immediately remove the remaining globes. The little bit of soup gives me so much strength that I soon begin to complain loudly at the next opportunity, cursing the Russians. Our condition is comparable to torture and is absolutely intolerable. And lo! Something happens. When a new group of men arrives in the cellar, we're moved and put with the others. The cellar is long and branches off. The guards stop at a door, and at least eighty people are put into an empty room where we can stand up. We have so much room that the cellar door, which opens inward, can be closed again. Now we are standing in a cellar with only two windows still covered to protect them from shrapnel. That means the windows just below the cellar roof are walled up and have only two air slits that don't begin to provide enough ventilation for a space crammed with so many people. For a while we stand around helplessly, then some of us begin to sit on the floor, which in turn takes away room from others. Gradually we begin to argue, curse, and swear. Each of us fights, shoves, and pushes to get a spot on the floor. But unless we lie on top of one another, it's impossible. We would come to blows if we weren't exhausted and ultimately paralyzed by resignation. We're like cattle on the way to the slaughterhouse, jammed into cattle cars, brought here to die. Our pigpen is dirty but it's a cabin between the decks compared to this. Anyone who falls asleep now is soon rudely awakened. Arms, legs, heads, and whole bodies are on top of you, and it isn't all that easy to shake off the burden. Anyone sleeping falls to the bottom layer, anyone awake wriggles to the top. The lack of oxygen is becoming more and more acute. Since the cellar is pitch dark, someone who still has matches tries to strike a light. Aside from the match head with the sulphur tip, the match doesn't burn, so severe is the lack of oxygen. And then there is the tin drum, this bucket of yellow marmalade that serves as a toilet. It's impossible to get to it and even if you can, some endurance shitter—so we call them—with dysentery is already there. It's not large enough and overflows on the first day. Next to me there's a sick man who always makes a great effort to turn away from me when he coughs. He is really near the end, but touchingly he takes care of me and patiently bears me lying on top of him most of the time. "Kid, keep away from me!" he says every now and then in broad East Prussian dialect.

We're allowed to leave the cellar once a day, and on occasion, twice a day. We're taken under guard to an area with bushes near the barbed wire. We're supposed "to do it" in shallow depressions in the ground, a skill that must first be learned. We have to step up to the edge of the depression without falling in. We're dizzy from the sudden exposure to oxygen and we don't have any paper, anything to hold on to, or hooks for our clothes.

On the way back, we see a pile of corpses. They're stacked against the barracks walls. The next day they're gone, and on the day after that there's an even larger stack. The Russians have no objection to our dying. On the contrary. Sometime in the morning there's water to drink. It's unboiled water from the Oberteich put out in a pan. The water's so murky you can barely see the bottom of the pan. I won't touch the water, but I do take off my undershirt and dampen it to stretch over my face. It acts like a refreshing air filter. I notice that the air close to the floor is a bit better. Fresh air seeps in under the door. In the afternoon they hand out soup. I bring soup for my two neighbors next to me who have no bowls. The nice man who coughs, whom I lie down on top of most of the time, refuses my offer to share the soup with him. He reveals that he has tuberculosis and is very worried about me. I pour soup into his cupped hands for him to slurp down what he can. Every few minutes, a Russian comes to the cellar door and bellows some names he can neither pronounce nor read correctly. Gans Gohngheim for Hans Hohnheim, and so on. Every now and then one of the people called is in our group. Hoping to be released from this hell, he leaves happily. Hours later, he returns, beaten to a bloody pulp, no longer able to speak; his jaw looks broken, one eye is swollen shut. The next one called leaves with a heavy heart and is never seen again. Another returns untouched. At the whim of the powers that be. It's particularly terrible at night. People are constantly being taken for interrogation. Because many are sleeping, the Russians scream at us and blind us with strong searchlights in the cellar. They want to be sure that everyone's awake and can hear them. And because that doesn't work either, we all have to stand up every time names are read out. We hear the names being read at the other doors in the cellar. It's an additional torture when this is repeated ten or twenty times. Of course, my name can't be read out because my name isn't on anyone's list. I think to myself I'll be stuck in this hellhole forever.

We have our first deaths in the cellar. We drag them out to the mound of corpses during morning exercise. There are many of us close to death. Some become resigned and don't bother to go for their food any more. Others immediately seize their food bowls. My spirits sink day by day.

At one point, a Russian asks if anyone is a painter. I immediately volunteer and am taken to an officer. He smiles skeptically and hands me colored pencils and paper. I draw a profile of his face as best I can. It even resembles him somewhat but it doesn't convince him. Before I'm returned to the cellar, he gives me a piece of bread. But my mood continues to deteriorate and my warm-hearted friend with tuberculosis tries to comfort me. Meanwhile, he's going downhill fast. He's very weak and struggles for breath. This lack of air is really terrible, and we both have already edged closer to the door, through which drifts a little bit of fresh air. I keep my nose pressed to the ground here. Each morning at least one person is found dead and we're all happy about the extra space. In fact, there's gradually more and more space, but we're still lying on top of one another.

I've completely lost count of how many days I've been in this cellar. It seems like an eternity and my name is never called. The more dispirited I become, the more intense are my dreams of trips taken in childhood to the Courland Spit. I yearn for the glorious air and the smoked fish. I even make a vow: if I ever get out of this cellar alive, I'll be happy, thankful, and content my whole life long, especially if fate should allow me to earn my living as a fisherman's helper on the Spit with its sea air. I picture the life of a fisherman on the Spit as the most wonderful thing there is.

Later, my life was filled with increasing demands just as the lives of others were. What I would have given at that moment to be able to see twenty-five years into the future as Russian concert-goers enthusiastically applauded when we played Bach, Haydn, and Mozart in Moscow and Leningrad, when the Minister of Culture Yekaterina Furtseva and the German Ambassador Sahm held glittering receptions honoring the Stuttgart Chamber Orchestra. Pâtés de foie gras, meat pastries, caviar, champagne, and other delicacies were served in such quantities that more than half was untouched. Here the KZ inmate, there the celebrated musician. Can there really be a greater contrast?

However, as far as my vow is concerned, I've kept it by two-thirds. Later in life, I was happy and thankful, although by no means always content.

One morning when we're led to our bush-toilet again, I must have "dreamed off" for a moment. I also did my business a bit hidden to the side. As I'm collecting my thoughts again, I see my squad disappearing into our cellar; the guards with their bayonets drawn behind them. As fast as I can, I race after them. As one of the two Russians sees me running along as a straggler, he must think I was trying to escape, but came back when I saw it was futile. There's no other explanation I can see for his sudden irrational rage, for he takes his rifle with the bayonet and takes a swing to stab me. Whether it is my gesture of defense or my guardian angel that protects me—I don't know—he turns his rifle over, and I use this opportunity to quickly reach the cellar door. At that moment, he shoves me with the butt of his rifle so hard in the back I suffer an internal injury. I definitely feel it as I'm propelled by the blow into the cellar. Something tears and shatters—the desire itself to live. To cap my bad luck, I discover my woolen coat has been stolen. In its place lies a heavy coat that is part of the uniform German soldiers wore while standing guard. Much too heavy for me in my starved condition. Someone has used our "stepping outside" to "exchange" his awful coat for mine.

Now I give up and remain lying down when we're called once a day to pick up our food. Everyone who's died also gave up going for their food just before they expired. I yearn to die, and the thought gives me peace and contentment. But my tubercular friend, still alive, talks to me without pause. He gasps incessantly for breath, but keeps exhorting me not to give up. So the next day I go once again to fetch my food on the very day there's an extra teaspoon of sugar. I lick this sugar slowly and with a pleasure never before experienced. It has the effect of medicine, a wonder drug. Scarcely have I sucked it than it alters my thoughts. Instead of utter despair as before, I suddenly have new courage, fresh hope and feel confidence and certainty returning. It's truly a miracle. A few minutes ago, I had reached my nadir and, with a teaspoon of sugar, from one moment to the next, everything doesn't seem so bad. Shortly after that, I meet by chance the officer in the cellar hallway I'm supposed to do the portrait of, and I try, with great intensity, to make my situation clear. He listens, too—reluctantly of course—but in the end he appears to have understood that I'm not on any list and therefore could wait until I'm dead before any hearing to clarify my identity. When he leaves I have the feeling that he'll try to do something for me. I'm hopeful once more.

The next morning, my friend is dead. He had been suffering more and more and always tried to remain as inconspicuous as possible. This hits me really hard. He too is thrown on the pile.

At one point the forsythia blooms for the first time and I take this as a sign. My heart swells with such delight that I have to compare the glowing yellow bush with Moses' burning thorn bush. It's as if God is speaking to me from this bush. At any rate, it gives me great pleasure and confidence and courage. And, as if it could be only on this day, I'm finally summoned from the cellar and led upstairs with a group of people. After a stay lasting weeks in that cursed cellar I feel the barracks courtyard as deliverance. Again I'm put in the shed with the two rain barrels, and since it always rains they are full to the brim. In the middle of the shed, someone has lit a wood fire to keep us warm. Men are busily boiling off some rain water, which they give to us "cellar lice." The more I drink the greater my thirst, and I drink rain water the whole night through. In my greed, I scald my mouth and lips, but drink I must, and drink, and drink. The men around me can't believe I was in the cellar so long. They all know the "cellar," and believe whoever goes in doesn't come out. I feel scarred for life, having been wounded internally body and soul, but nonetheless I feel the worst is over for now.

This time my tête-à-tête with God brought us, so to speak, closer together. If I ignore what happened to others, what one considers a good or a bad life, and what one wants for oneself, then I'm ready to call Him a merciful God. I would reject the word *kind*. Of course I can only speak for myself, not for people I've seen in situations lacking even a spark of mercy. These words will sound like heresy to many. But I've not the slightest scruple in criticizing God. I know He can take it and seldom leaves me without an answer. We differ, you might say, in our points of view. But among friends—or can I not say even among distant relatives—this should be possible without animosity.

What I've observed of dying men assures me they all have felt their death as deliverance. Therefore, death is for me a reality that is something positive—the open arms embracing each of us in the end. In no case may one misuse this as a threat or debase God to the status of a penal officer or a bailiff of the criminal court in the hereafter. Death should linger in the consciousness of people as a great comfort, as the finality that, with certainty, brings peace and repose.

The Reunion

The next day we were ordered to line up and we were marched under guard back toward Königsberg, away from this appalling concentration camp. I could barely walk. I leaned on the person next to me for support most of the way. Others were in even worse shape. Just as we reached the upper lake and were walking fairly close to a low wall at one point, a man broke free and hurled himself over into the lake below. Shouting curses, one of the guards tore his machine pistol from his shoulder holster and fired a volley of shots after him. I hope the man found the quick end he longed for; we all understood suicide. We continued on. For some reason or other the line came to a halt, whereupon some collapsed on the ground, I among them. My desire never to stand up again was so overwhelming that my unknown partner had to haul me up. And then on we went, back to the rubble of Königsberg. Moving mechanically and freezing without a coat—I had long since left the heavy military coat lying somewhere or other—we reached our goal after what seemed an eternity. The march from Rothenstein to Königsberg took us all afternoon. We even took two wrong turns before we found the command post where they were supposed to hand us over.

Once again all our names were laboriously written down on a list while we rested on the cold ground. But the fellow who had been helping me forbade me to lie down on the ground, warning me against catching a cold. I was feeling deathly ill and was supposed to worry about catching a miserable cold? Although this struck me as absurd, I obeyed. After a long wait, two drunken Russians took us to our quarters for the night. We followed the Russians, who fired wildly at the stray dogs hanging around. They took us to a dormitory that had been hastily set up. Civilians, including women, were there ahead of us. They eyed us suspiciously as we entered. We were taking room away from them. I quickly made a bed out of some old illustrated magazines, curtains that had been torn down, and part of a slashed pillow. I crouched into a corner and was happy to find a quiet spot I wouldn't soon be shooed away from. I was dimly aware that our Russians were forcing two women to go with them—"Woman, come"—when I fell fast asleep.

What I wouldn't give to be left in peace. My corner in this chaotic room had become a piece of heaven, and I was jolted awake by the "*davei, davei*" from a healthy young Russian. There was nothing to do but to stand up and go along—it was difficult to stand upright. We went to the command post where we were piled onto waiting trucks. Shovels and spades had already been loaded. Because only a few streets were passable, we took all sorts of detours, landing on a corner blocked in all directions by a huge bomb crater. We were in a desert of ruins, surrounded by stones and steel girders. Together with other civilians, we were given the task of filling the crater with the shovels under heavy armed guard. I wasn't able to move my spade, much less tip a spade full of stones into the hole. So I stood there helplessly, on the brink of collapse. I must have looked so pathetic that even the guard near me could see what a sorry state I was. He took me aside and guided me into the nearest cellar in a heap of ruins. For a moment I thought he was going to kill me, but he pointed to a rusty, burnt-out bed frame, motioning to me to lie down. This was a humane gesture that made all the difference between life and death. While the others were busy shoveling away, I lay down on this frame, trying to get well by relaxing completely. If the Russian had forced me to work, it would have inevitably meant collapse and that would have been the end. Anyone who succumbed to exhaustion was lost for there was no one to care for him. When someone came to fetch me at the end of the day, I felt a bit better. I no longer know what I ate or drank that day. As I remember, absolutely nothing. The next day the same thing happened. I went to my bed frame and lay down, fervently hoping to get my strength back. On that day, the Russian guard brought me some barley soup in a pot. He had saved some for me. I ate this delicacy in tiny portions, happy and touched. Indeed, there were more and more signs that some Russians began to see us as humans, which in turn allowed us to discover the heart and soul of the Russians. Still the abuse inflicted on the women during the night was terrible. But in the bright light of day, we no longer needed to fear them so much.

In our troop assigned to road work there was someone who knew my parents. During the midday break he came to my cellar and invited me to join him and his troop where they were staying. That was somewhat closer to where we had once lived in the Steinmetzstrasse. I gratefully accepted his offer and went along with him. The Russian guards gave their approval when they understood I was looking for my parents. Compared to other groups who were treated like dangerous convicts, our guards were generous and friendly. My new hosts had better quarters and made me a real place to lie down. They gave me some millet to eat and treated me with sympathy. The women there had probably made arrangements with certain officers for whom they cooked and worked. That's how they diverted food, from which I too profited.

It was sheer heaven to stay in bed the next day. The others here had been spared KZ Rothenstein. However, Rothenstein had brought me to the brink of death and I wasn't able to recover very quickly. No matter how selflessly they helped me, their goodwill didn't last. They complained. I felt I couldn't stay. I asked my roommates to ask around again to see if my parents had turned up anywhere. On the very next day, they came back with the news that my parents were living six streets away in quarters in the Schrötterstrasse. So they had been brought back to Königsberg, too.

Overjoyed, I set out at once. The distance was about a quarter of a mile. Dragging myself along, I stopped every other step to catch my breath and managed to cover two blocks. Then, totally exhausted and close to collapsing, I realized I couldn't make it all the way. After standing there a while indecisive and miserable, I had no other choice but to take the shorter distance back. Only after pushing myself to the point of collapse did I reach my starting point. Where was the strength I once had as a sixteen-year-old when I could carry two hundred-weight sacks? Despite my heartfelt desire to see my parents, I couldn't even manage the quarter mile. I told my roommates I would try again the next day and was sure I would make it. I got my millet soup again. I fell asleep, excited and full of hope about seeing my parents again.

The next day I did indeed have the strength to reach the Schrötterstrasse, but only if I went slowly and stopped every few steps to rest. I asked all along the way until I came to where there were only two half-burned buildings, which was now home for a few Königsbergers. For the first time since our departure from the Steinmetzstrasse, I saw our former neighborhood. All the houses that had been left standing or at least could be repaired after the Russians had taken the area, were now burnt-out ruins down to the cellars—a ghost town.

My parents and I were overjoyed to see each other again, a reunion we had ardently longed for. My parents burst into tears at the sight of me. I found them quite changed. They looked awful. I didn't need to tell them anything—and didn't. In their little room, which they fortunately had to themselves, they made a bed for me. The bed was in fact under my mother's bed frame, so that Russians patrolling would not easily find me. At last I had the peace I craved and I was reunited with my parents. My helplessness gave my mother a shock. With unbelievable perseverance and energy she now set about bartering or begging for food. Some white bread for a tablecloth, some potatoes for a few silver forks, some horse fat for a broken clock. Everything that could be found anywhere could be bartered to the Russians. Their demand for everything and everybody was insatiable. They literally got gold and silver for a piece of bread.

For days I stayed under the bed. Lovingly tended to by my mother, I gradually began to recover. After five days I was beginning to get up and move about again. My ribs, injured by the rifle butt, slowly began to heal. Staying under the bed was critical for my recovery. Russians were always coming in, looking for men and women able to work or simply looking around for things they could use. Rapes had become commonplace. And as before, we heard the piercing screams. At night, the sounds were arias from hell. They pounded on the barricaded doors with something hard. Russians swore in loud voices, yelled, and threatened. Then, pistol shots, howling dogs, wailing, pleas, entreaties, sustained whimpering. It was ghastly, a nightmare; and it was our bitter reality.

As I gradually regained a little bit of my strength, I could see that Mother alone couldn't scrounge enough food for the three of us. The objects that could be bartered were gone; as for procuring new ones, younger neighbors were nimbler and more cunning. Moreover, water had to be hauled from a pump in Luisenwahl, about mile and a half away. Mother walked this stretch every three days carrying a pail of water, first in one hand, then in the other. I observed this excruciating procedure and was eager to be up and about again. About eight days passed with me under the bed before I felt better. At that point we were visited by a Yiddish-German speaking officer, bristling with hatred, to inspect our quarters a bit more closely. He discovered me, slugged me in the face, and dragged me out. Mother, Father, and I explained to him that I was *bolnoish* (sick). He calmed down a bit, but ordered me to get dressed and follow him. We went a few blocks to a damaged building, which was to be fixed up to serve as Russian quarters. The rubble had to be cleared away. Others were already busily at work, and so I began, still a bit wobbly and slow, to work again. I accepted this because everyone who worked got something to eat—four hundred grams (less than a pound) of bread. We also had the chance, if we kept our eyes open, to find something here and there.

The Russians exploded with an indescribable orgy of joy when Admiral Dönitz signed the treaty of surrender. The whole day they fired off everything that could shoot. Everyone was relieved that the madness was finally over, and now we could think about a new beginning. Racial dementia and master race claims had provoked a counter blow that could not have been more devastating. The dream of a Greater Germany ruling the world had achieved a field of rubble in Europe and a Soviet Union with an enormously enlarged sphere of influence.

From this day forth, the task of being the breadwinner for my parents fell more and more to me. Father was completely helpless in the face of the new living conditions, which turned us all into predators crowded into a hunting preserve that was way too small. Now was the time to call on every instinct and to act swiftly. The skills needed to save our lives were a combination of keeping a sharp eye out and being creative—to make yourself indispensable to the Russians, to win their sympathy, to repair something, a clock for example or an oil lamp. For that you got bread or oatmeal, barley, or soup.

Mother had tendovaginitis (an inflamed tendon) from hauling water and was in great pain. In the evenings I worked on a yoke—one that lies across the shoulders—from which a pail of water could be hung on each side. That made hauling water easier. Mother could now carry two half-full buckets of water without pain. Soon I was able to fetch the water we needed from Luisenwahl myself. Father became accustomed to us taking care of him and began to study Chinese again. But even as an old man he should have tried to contribute somehow to our support. The Russians respected distinguished-looking, white-haired men now, giving them administrative and organizational work to do. It soon came to a bitter argument between Father and me. The Russians were trying to somehow master the enormous problems facing them, especially as the first cases of typhus and infectious dysentery were also beginning to affect them. Hospitals for epidemics were set up by Professor Starlinger. There they looked after those who were ill with epidemic diseases; everyone else had to look after himself.

There are Königsbergers wandering about on the streets close to starving. You can still smell unburied corpses. Venereal diseases are rampant among women and scabies spreads. Women can now sometimes avoid being raped by saying they are sick. The majority are infected and there is no physician or medicine to alleviate what ails them. There are only home remedies or the bomb craters.

Stray dogs have turned into wild animals, scared of people, making a wide berth around everyone. All the cats have already landed in the stew pot and somehow the dogs sense what we intend to do. Once a jeep careering along wildly runs over a medium-sized dog. I win the race to the dying animal and bring it home. Now it finally serves me in good stead that I once watched my rabbit being skinned and gutted. I do exactly the same thing with the dog. It tastes good and agrees with everybody. Somewhere I find a can of syrup in a heap of rubble, a great stroke of good fortune!

According to my estimates, of the supposedly 130,000 civilians remaining in Königsberg, at most only half that number was still living in the city at this time. In the course of the next few months, half of those died, then half of those again during the next three years. There were no attempts to supply provisions, and everyone had to look out for himself. Either you worked for the Russians, where you were paid at most four hundred grams of bread for a day's work, or you scrounged in the rubble, bartered, stole, cheated—or you starved. Even the Russians themselves received short provisions and had nothing to give away. Under such conditions, older people scarcely had a chance to survive; but even the younger ones managed only if they developed special cunning. Otherwise they quickly died of typhus or of secondary diseases due to starvation. In the end, there are said to be 20,000 people of the 130,000 who survived and were resettled in Germany. But even that number seems to me too high. All the hardships and misery that reduced the population by more than 80 percent are beyond the power of words to describe. In memory of all these poor people, I shall nonetheless try to do so.

Conflicts and Personal Fates

Dr. Stock was now dead, and mother and daughter struggled on alone to survive. Frau Stock had wisely allied herself with a Russian officer, thereby securing access to food and protection. Ute benefited from this, but the course of events blighted her youth and haunted her for the rest of her life.

As much as learning Chinese satisfied one's intellectual needs, it did not satisfy one's physical needs. No one could take flight from reality without endangering one's life. We had to work to persuade Father at least to try to be useful in some way. It was very difficult for him. I began to despise his beautiful sounding aphorisms. If only a wise saying could have taught us how to live through the next day. But we didn't need wisdom for that: we needed cunning, and that was exactly what my father scorned from the bottom of his heart. Therefore, I embodied wicked and low cunning and he, lofty and venerable wisdom. Of course, low cunning was responsible for taking care of exalted wisdom. Otherwise it would starve. I was unable to make my father see that under altered circumstances different values became valid, so that in addition to all my other worries there were bitter arguments with my father. They upset me terribly and took a great deal of my energy. At the time I came to believe that wisdom was fine for those with full bellies, and cunning was the supreme virtue of the hungry. But we really were starving. To scrounge food for three people was extraordinarily difficult. It was impossible to do so without stealing. What I needed was moral support from my father. But that he refused to give me on high moral grounds. It wasn't the stolen food or objects for barter that he refused, no—only moral absolution. For a sixteen-year-old, it's extremely important what his father thinks of him. I was extremely bitter.

I should mention that by now we had greater freedom of movement. We were no longer under continuous guard; we had to seek work for ourselves. But we could also choose not to do so although only those who worked for the Russians got bread. Four hundred grams were scarcely enough for one person, and I was always wracking my brain to figure out how to get enough food for the three of us. There was word at one point that a wharf was being repaired and there was an abundant supply of food to be had—so abundant that you could bring home soup in pots. I applied at once. The workday was twelve hours long with a one-hour break at midday. The trip there and back was an hour each way. I left the house at seven in the morning and returned home at nine in the evening. This soon became too much for me and after ten days I had to admit defeat. Moreover, the pot of soup was not enough to sate my parents' hunger. I had to find something else. Then I discovered that the Russians had fenced in a comparatively un-destroyed house—now and then there was such a thing. They guarded it, probably intending to house the usual military authorities. Of course, the house had also been looted by the fighting troops, but there was still quite a bit of useful stuff to be found. On either side of the house where the wooden fence ended were collapsed ruins of the neighbor-ing houses. It occurred to me that the breaches in the wall still had to be there, connecting the cellar under the debris with the cellar of the fenced-in house. As all the stairs were buried in rubble, the only way into the cellar that hadn't yet completely collapsed was through a cellar window. I wasn't disappointed; the breach in the wall was still there. This was a one-time opportunity to filch bed linens, crockery, pots and pans, cutlery, and a whole lot more. Mother then offered the goods to the Russians in barter. She would proudly return in the evening with food she had gotten in exchange. The guards at the house noticed the break-in at one point and blocked off the passage. I was lucky that they didn't entice me into a trap. In such cases, they shot on sight. Had they caught me, they would have rid themselves of a thief who inflicted quite a bit of damage on them over the next few years. This break-in was the harmless beginning of my ever more brilliant career as robber and thief. But I'm anticipating events a bit here.

There was no lack of trying to resolve our problems and hardships in an honest and therefore less nerve-wracking way. I was concerned not only about today and the day after but also about my future. It had nothing to do with what I wanted to become or where I could learn something. No, my worry was how are we going to feed ourselves in a few months after all possibilities are exhausted—this was my great worry about the future. The Russians apparently wanted us all to starve, die, or disappear. It was their intention that East Prussia become forever Russian and Polish. German East Prussians who remained alive were simply a hindrance, mischief makers who would only clamor one day for their homeland and want once again to dispossess the new owners of everything. That's probably what they thought.

As a precautionary measure, we decided to grow potatoes in a rather large lot located on the Steinmetzstrasse extension. We bartered for just enough potatoes. These I cut into two or more pieces and planted them in the garden I had prepared. Just as I had seen as a child on the Courland Spit. Only how could I have been so naive as to think that I would also harvest them? When they were the size of marbles or walnuts, someone starving ripped them out one night. Our seed potatoes were gone, our labor in vain, and our hopes dashed.

They were advertising for a carpenter for a bakery; this sounded very promising. The Russians were trying to start up food processing plants to provide for their own population. Experts came from Russia to rebuild what had been wantonly destroyed. Specialists and workmen were needed, and their value was rapidly increasing. Accordingly, I held myself out to be a carpenter. Had I not learned to handle saw and plane? The officer to whom I presented myself as a carpenter didn't believe me. He handed me boards, a handsaw, hammer and nails, pointed to an empty door frame in the ruined part of the bakery, and said, "Go make a door." I managed somehow to put something together, which he allowed as a door. And that's how I became a carpenter in a bakery. There were three other carpenters, who tolerated me and with whom I worked to finish various projects. We were all in the bakery to get to bread or flour, something that proved to be difficult. The Russians had come to know us well enough to protect all foodstuffs like crown jewels. However, it couldn't be helped that a window had to be repaired just where flour was stored and then, in an unguarded moment, we could almost always fill a pail halfway full with flour and cover it with construction debris and wood scraps. The Russians only later caught on to such tricks. We were again working twelve hours a day, with gruel and a piece of bread at noon. That was our entire wage. We got enough gruel to take some home in a liter pitcher. My pitcher was half full with flour with the gruel on top of that. That way I could pass through the very thorough inspection on the way out with at least half a pound of flour without incident. Of course, we could only pull off stealing flour now and then; we never even got near the bread.

The bakery stood in an otherwise totally destroyed district and was surrounded by a wall. There were guards at the entrance. Management used some barracks at the back of the bakery compound. The bicycles used by the soldiers and officers on the administrative staff to get to their jobs at the bakery were highly coveted. They were prepared to trade canned meat for a bicycle. Our Russians parked their bikes against the rear wall of the barracks; when I saw no one was looking, I grabbed a bike and tossed it quickly over the rear wall of the bakery where it landed in the pile of ruins. The Russians accused each other of the theft, while I went to get the bike from the ruins, fully intending to ride it home. I would have loved to barter it for food, but unfortunately I never got that far. I was overtaken by another unfortunate concomitant phenomenon of the war. Orphaned Russian and Polish children had followed in the wake of the advancing Russians. They lived in impassable fields of ruins, forming whole little gangs. They were tolerated by the Russians, who themselves didn't know how to deal with these waifs. Many of them wore colorful bits and pieces of uniforms thrown together; they also carried weapons they had found. They pestered civilians and at one point they injured Mother quite seriously. One such boy slashed Mother's hand with a razor blade as she was offering some cigarettes for sale; the gash was so long she dropped everything. Of course, that was what they intended, and they swiftly disappeared with their booty. The scar from the wound, which healed only slowly, became a permanent reminder. This was the sort of band I now encountered. Threatening me with knives and a cocked pistol, they stole my bicycle. I could just thank my lucky stars I escaped with only the loss of the bike.

One evening, there was a guard in front of our building, barring the entrance. My parents had fastened a scrap of paper to the barbed wire, telling me where they were. The Russians were gradually confiscating all the undestroyed buildings as quarters for their Russian experts, who were being sent in increasing numbers to Königsberg. My parents told me they had been given only an hour to vacate their rooms and could take only what they could carry. They lost their beloved bed frame and a whole lot more. Like most people, they moved to a cellar in a bombed-out building and gradually they made the room livable. A board served as a chair, another one served as a table. A scorched mattress frame served as a bed. They had been able to keep their blankets and bed-clothes. The feelings of bitterness festered, feeding my desire to steal back what had been confiscated. But first, my father, who we thought had typhus, had to go to a quarantine ward. At least people in quarantine were given food. My father had only a mild form of typhus and was soon discharged. The damp and cold in our cellar were pestilent, and in the long run it was unthinkable that we should stay there.

The Russian doctors (most of whom were women) were beginning to worry more and more about containing this epidemic. They needed to protect themselves against infection; they also needed slave labor and German "specialists." On occasion they took measures that almost might have been designated as humane. They even maintained a second hospital, the "Charity," which I would come to know all too well. Maybe one could say in the way of an excuse that it was impossible for the Russians in charge of organizing things to look after their own and therefore they simply weren't able to care for the Germans. But my impression is that they intentionally destroyed every resource needed for survival and thwarted every attempt people made to look after themselves. As if they wanted once again to accelerate the rate at which Königsbergers died.

Dandelions and nettles were the only edible wild plants we knew. Had I the authority to write the school curriculum, I would have every child learn which plants and fungi are edible and that a handful of grains of wheat, freshly ground and softened, produces food nutritionally superior to canned goods with who knows what in them. They would learn how to find water, how to build traps, and how to take bearings. They would learn that snails, mussels, and worms are edible. Short, simple courses in the science of nutrition, survival techniques, first aid, and medical services in desperate times, that is, how to take care of the sick without a doctor or medical supplies. At some time during the child's lifetime, this knowledge could prove vital. This alone would justify introducing such courses into the traditional curriculum. All that I had learned—from penmanship to Hebrew—was useless at this moment, although I can be thankful for my apprenticeship in the carpentry shop.

More and more Russians were arriving in Königsberg, and we observed East Prussia becoming Russian. We hadn't really expected anything else but still, every day we were flabbergasted by what we saw.

Strange clothes and uniforms, typical Russian wooden fences, the banners displaying the faces of Stalin, Lenin, Marx, Kalinin, and who knows who else. Large loudspeakers at practically every corner often emitted wonderful music as well as impressive songs of Russian soldier choruses, all of which visually and acoustically defined the character of the streets, to the extent that you could believe you were actually living in the Soviet Union.

Russians are supposed to be sentimental and good-natured, but we encountered this side of their nature only seldom. On occasion, they were kind to children—I was still almost a child—but generally the predominant emotion was hatred. And watch out for aggressive brutality once alcohol loosened their inhibitions. Let us never forget: the Germans had classified them as *Untermenschen* (subhumans) and treacherously attacked them despite a treaty—their country had been laid to waste. In their hearts, the Russians carried the pain of millions and millions of fallen comrades, starving civilians, and murdered relatives and friends. Aren't we obligated here to understand these tormented people who, with one last-ditch effort, pulled themselves together even if they abandoned all restraint in their intoxication by a victory so hard won? I only want to understand, not excuse, them. The fact that all humans are as they are is, of course, the basis of all tragedy.

The Nazis had condemned me as a Jew to passivity; the Russians condemned me to activity, which was something worse. Two opposing modes of behavior in the daily struggle to survive. Woe to anyone who gave up the daily struggle to survive now. That person very quickly belonged to the 80 percent who survived the war but not the Russian occupation.

Just as the "black market" could be found everywhere in Russia, so too such a market soon appeared in Königsberg. At first it was completely hidden in various places, then at more and more openly sanctioned spots. These black markets were the lifeblood of every provisional community and the germ cell of all economic activity. There you barter, negotiate, obtain information, and make a profit. Goods exchanged for goods, goods exchanged for money; money exchanged for goods. This primal stage of every sort of economic system quickly became for many the only means of survival. And here too the Russians were sure to harass and arrest the Germans in the most vicious way. They considered all black marketeers to be "speculators." They took the bartered foodstuffs away from them, so it took great cunning to

make a profit behind the backs of the military police. But the Königsbergers, who were acquiring the art of cunning, succeeded quite well.
The black market was the first ray of hope on the dark horizon of
the future.

Meanwhile I had been asking around about Jews who had survived
and found out that most of them had been killed in a powerful explosion in the last few hours of the war. It was one explosion that turned
the entire building of the Gamm & Son Factory, including the Alhambra House on the Steindamm, into a huge bomb crater, the largest
I had ever seen. Artillery shells stored in the basement had probably
detonated at the same time. Everyone must have been killed in this
explosion: the remaining Jews, the French prisoners of war, the Russian girls, and the German guards. The fact that our neighborhood, the
Hufen, had been taken a day earlier had saved our lives.

I learned from third-hand reports that Herr Weinberg had been shot
by the Russians. Even Concertmeister Hewers fell in the last moments
of the war. On the other hand, I met a youngster from the Jewish
school, a little bit older than I—Olaf Boenheim, who along with his
father survived the heavy barrages and the Russian assault. Olaf and I
met a few times when we were breaking into Russian quarters to steal
food. His end was particularly sad: one year later we had to worry not
only about scrounging for food but also fuel for heating and cooking.
The winter was once again bitter, bitter cold—there's plenty to say
about that—when his father came to me extremely upset, telling me
his son had been searching for wood that day and had found a little
house where there were still some wood roof beams. Olaf wanted to
hack these out with an ax when the house collapsed on top of him.
His horrified father tried to tear away the rubble, his son buried under
the debris, calling out, "Father, help me—help!" The father didn't have
enough strength to lift up the heavy rubble of the wall and ran off to
find help, which you can never find quickly at such a moment. When
they finally dug Olaf out, he was dead. The father trundled his dead
son home in a cart, watching by him as Jewish custom prescribes, until
we both could bury him as best we could. The misfortune of the desperate father and the whole story haunted me for a long time. I once
met the father Boenheim later in London, where he made a strange,
disturbed impression on me. After Olaf's death and again years later
when my mother died painfully of bone cancer, I bitterly blamed God;
I would like to repeat what I said at the end of my first chapter: of

all the injustices that most offend me about Him, or that elementary power, is that the death of each human being is uniquely painful.

The dentist Dr. Levy and a Herr Prinz were the other two Jews who had survived. I lost sight of them. Herr Prinz was caught by the military police while foraging for food and sentenced to many years of forced labor. Such sentences were basically a death sentence. After having suffered through so much, hardly anyone lasted more than a year in Russian forced labor camps. He was struck by a fate that could overtake anyone caught at anything illegal. At the time, seven years was the minimum sentence, even for stealing cigarettes. But almost everyone would have starved to death if they hadn't broken the law. For years we were caught in this double bind, and for years this predicament wracked our nerves.

Of course, it's only in retrospect that I realized the people I've just mentioned were the last members of the Königsberg Jewish community, at least of the part that didn't emigrate before 1941. This community originated with two Jews—physicians—in 1540; with the evacuation of two Jews in April 1948 an urban religious community of 408 years standing perished, in all likelihood never to rise again. The *Encyclopedia Judaica* describes the history of this community:

Significant Jewish settlements only began to appear in the second half of the seventeenth century when Jewish merchants from Lithuania and Poland attended the trade fairs in Königsberg. In 1680 they were permitted to have a place of prayer during the fair. By 1716 there were thirty-eight Jewish families, who built their first synagogue in 1756, by which time there were three hundred Jews. Emigrants also began streaming into Königsberg from Russia, increasing the population of Jews to 1,027 in 1817, to 5,082 (3.6 percent of the population) in 1880, and to 4,049 in 1925. From that point on, their number decreased until in 1933 there were 3,200 Jews in Königsberg or 1 percent of the population.

Along with Berlin, Königsberg was the center of the "Enlightenment," and educated Jewish families were acceptable in Christian "society." As early as 1712, Jews began to study at the university—mainly medicine—one of them being Markus Herz. There were even Jews among the pupils of Kant; under the influence of Moses Mendelssohn's ideas, Isaak Abraham Euchel and Mendel Breslau founded a society for the advancement of the Hebrew language in 1783. They published a Hebrew monthly *Ha-Me'assef*. Isaak Asher Francolm, an adherent of the Reform movement, was the first to hold religious school instruction. He was criticized, however, when the Orthodox majority attacked his confirmation ceremony for boys and girls, and they forbade the opening of an institute. Thereupon Francolm moved to Breslau, and Joseph Levin Saalschütz attempted to continue the work of his predecessor. He even taught Hebrew at the University of Königsberg in 1847, but as a Jew he was barred from receiving an appointment as professor. Also active at this time was the radical politician Johann Jacoby, who defended Jewish Emancipation in a pamphlet (1847). From 1830 to 1865 Jakob Mecklenburg was the rabbi. His successor Isaak Bamberger was rabbi from 1865 to 1896.

The years 1897 to 1920 were important ones for the Jewish community of Königsberg. Hermann Vogelstein took over the responsibility of spiritual leadership. He was one of the most important personalities of liberal Judaism in Germany. (No less important were the contributions of Cantor Eduard Birnbaum, 1855–1920. His research into the Jewish music of the Italian Renaissance became the basis of Königsberg Jewish liturgical music.) His contemporary Felix Perles was awarded an honorary professorship in 1924. He taught both Aramaic and modern Hebrew literature. In the twentieth century, important physicians of note are: Ludwig Lichtheim, Julius Schreiber, Max Jaffé, and Alfred Ellinger. In 1925, there were five different synagogues and several social institutions. Among the professors driven into exile in 1933 by the Nazis were Frieda Reichmann and Willy Wolflein.

What a diverse history lies behind this obituary of a religious community—it can only be left to the imagination what a rich and varied community life it was, marked by internal and external struggles as it grew. What can't be imagined is the disappointment of all those who had believed and hoped since the Emancipation that one could achieve recognition or at least tolerance from their gentile neighbors through service and patriotism (a high percentage of Jews took part in the First World War).

Now and then the beams supporting the weight of debris and rubble above the cellars gave way and suddenly collapsed. There was the time that an eleven-year-old boy came home to stand in front of his cellar home to find his mother and four siblings buried there. His fate could still move our numbed souls hardened to suffering. Now no one felt secure in the only housing available to many of us. Only on a case-by-case basis did the Russians give permission to their German servants to live in the same buildings as they did. Two years later we succeeded in being so lucky. I'll tell you a few chapters later on about our life in the Russian building on Beethoven Street.

I found my meeting with Frau B., who survived by playing the piano and singing, symbolic of our hopeless situation. Frau B., abused as were all women, gave birth to a child. No one could help or save it from malnutrition, and the baby died.

There was an obstinate rumor that ships were in the Pillau harbor to transport civilians back to the "Reich." Were these rumors figments of the imagination, scraps left over from the closing days of the war? No one knew. One day I sallied forth to reconnoiter the situation, to see what truth there might be to the rumor. I didn't get far because my hunger pains were killing me. Exhausted, I was given shelter in a village by a woman with a six-year-old child. I exchanged babysitting for some pea soup while she worked in a kitchen for Russian soldiers during the day. In the evening she barricaded the door as well as the windows with furniture and planks. Evening after evening the same circus broke loose around her house. Loud knocking, shouting, and cursing. It seemed to me that she only allowed certain Russians in and with their help was able to hold the others off. During the day I went begging with the boy in front of fences and house doors, behind which the Russians dined. This is how we learned that scraps would be dumped into the bowls that children held out. But people would also toss the dregs of their soup on the ground in front of starving children as a symbolic gesture—a course of action that horrified us.

There was no question of staying here for the long term, and there weren't any rumors here about ships. On the contrary. My "adoptive" mother spoke of Pillau as being a rubble heap and the Russians having told her that there wasn't a single ship available for transport. My exploratory foray suddenly struck me as absurd. I had deserted my family's colors. I didn't even know how my parents were doing without me, so I withdrew to Königsberg.

Before I returned, I thought I could steal a chicken from the Russians. They had some chickens in a wire mesh coop. Unobserved, I opened the coop. I should have seized one and killed it at once by wringing its neck or something. I struggled a moment with my weakness before I closed the door to the coop. Ashamed, even horrified at my failure, I slunk away. Even today I don't understand and can't really explain what happened. Possibly this hesitation prevented the chickens' squawking from betraying me—who knows?

Breaking and Entering— Episode 1

The Russians sent to East Prussia to begin rebuilding the country were permitted to bring their families with them. As a result, more and more of them were housed together in billets and apartments, which were, to some extent, the contingency housing of Königsbergers who were chased out of their quarters. We were safe from being tossed out of where we lived in the rubble or cellars only if the Russians deemed such housing unfit for habitation. My parents and I moved involuntarily six times in all. Each move—as one can well imagine—involved enormous additional effort.

The Königsbergers who hadn't found a job working for the Russians received no rations. Work, theft, and the black market were the only options if you wanted food. You must remember that a twelve-hour workday earned you four hundred grams of bread, and a meal of soup was the exception. Scavenging through rubble, piles of debris, and factory ruins had long since ceased to yield anything. So I tried to base my efforts to obtain food for my parents and me on the sound footing of the three above-named principles. I once applied for a job where there was the best chance for good wages, that is, more food. Moreover, I went on thieving expeditions to supplement what my parents and I needed. If I was able to pilfer, say, cigarettes instead of something to eat, my mother exchanged these on the black market for food. Of course, these thieving excursions posed a constant threat to my life. The Russian soldiers and officers had little enough food themselves and didn't hem and haw very long when they caught someone stealing the little bit they had. More than once I only narrowly escaped mortal danger, and the three times I was caught, I had unbelievably good luck. Due to these "jaunts" of mine I'm familiar with the life of those who break and enter, and I feel sorry for them.

It all began when I broke into a cellar of a guarded house and gradually worked up to burgling Russian apartments while the residents
were present. The tormenting pangs of hunger gave me the courage to
take such high risks—my pangs as well as those of my parents. Each
time it required overcoming deep inhibitions and each time it was a
last resort when all else failed. Looking back, I realize I displayed talent
and skill for the demanding career of burglar. On account of the mortal danger I faced on every raid, I mentally made careful preparations,
in which escape routes, measures for concealment, and ruses played a
large role. It all started with me always wearing my work overalls. For
the Russians, this was the clothing of a respected "specialist." It would
allow me to explain my presence on the pretext of some sort of repair
job in case I was discovered in the initial stages of the break-in. To that
end, I buckled on the pouch with my repair tools where I would hide
the stolen goods. In the little pocket on the trouser leg for the carpenter's ruler, I hid two skeleton keys, which I soon learned how to use
like a virtuoso. They wouldn't be discovered there even during a thorough body search. The next thing I always did was to reconnoiter the
way back before I started. The most suitable buildings had connecting
roofs. I then unlocked doors into attics and cleared my escape path.
Only then did I slip into the officers' apartments, wearing silent gym
shoes, while keeping my ears open for any sound. There was never anything much to find. A piece of bread, a pound of flour, some millet or
barley, a German clock, things like that. But this haul invariably meant
having something to eat for one or two more days.

I should also mention that the living conditions I've been describ-
ing were not getting better. They constituted our daily routine, with
small variations, for almost two years. It is beyond all comprehension
or any description. We hit low point after low point, particularly during the winter months. For years I had to make my robbery runs, often
every day, with different obstacles each time; and always there were the
enormous risks.

This one time I decide to go to a suburb. The Russians there are a bit
more carefree than their compatriots in town. At the edge of a large field
of ruins, I see some houses where some Russians are living with their
wives. Disguised as a "specialist," I scrutinize the houses to see if the
occupants are at home. If they are, I usually move on, seeking better
targets. Today, however, I notice snow-white bed sheets, even some

pillowcases, hanging on a line to dry. Since I know the black market value of pillowcases, I want to stuff some of them in my pockets. As the robbery is a cinch, I'm not careful and am immediately discovered. A woman's screams trumpet the done deed, calling to everyone in the neighborhood for help. I see at once I'm in imminent danger, and there's nothing to do but to take to my heels. As fast as I can I'm running across the field toward the next tract of rubble; I'm not a hundred yards away from the scene of the crime when the first shots whiz by. As I look over my shoulder, I see two Russians, half undressed and waving a rifle or a machine pistol about, hard on my heels. It's obvious that this chase could and probably will have a deadly finale. While I'm zigzagging across the field and making sure that there are the greatest possible number of heaps of stones between me and my pursuers, I pull my booty from my pockets and toss them high in the air. So high that my pursuers are bound to notice the white pillowcases. I'm hoping the booty will calm them down a bit, and they'll abandon the chase. This sprinting about under a hail of bullets is costing me so much strength and fear that I take cover behind a wall in the next pile of ruins, totally exhausted and gasping for breath. I know I'm lost if they keep coming after me. I just sit there barely concealed and give myself up to my fate. I wait and hope—and I've won. My pursuers overestimate my weakened condition. If only I could've run further, the labyrinth of rubble would have meant certain safety. The Russians have the same thought and give up the chase, probably only a few steps from my hiding place. I feel utterly wretched and miserable. I'm angry with myself over my carelessness and curse what I'm doing. Today I come home empty-handed. I don't have the spirit or strength left for any further attempts. Even my parents are disappointed and hungry. I had always brought something home before. My mother, however, had traded a primitive set of binoculars from a previous break-in, so at least we have something to eat. Of course I never tell my parents what I'm doing or what's happening; my parents are too old. My father always disapproves and my mother worries too much. I have to deal with what's happening on my own, but the main thing is that I'm soon game for new stunts again.

Catching Smoked Fish

Winter had now begun, making our lives considerably more complicated. Fuel had to be found and stoves had to be installed. I looked for work again where there was a chance I could also steal food. We were all laid off from the bakery after all the windows and niches had been boarded over with wood panels in the provisional manner of the day. Then I heard that the Russians wanted to set up a plant to produce smoked fish and were looking for carpenters. The phrase "plant to produce smoked fish" sounded extraordinarily enticing. I feasted in my imagination, relishing the smoked fish in advance, or at least the fish heads or other edible discarded bits. I applied and was accepted. Once again, there were the familiar tasks: here a window to be repaired, there a crate, a railing, a ladder, a bench, a table, or whatever there happened to be. Right away during the first few days we were mustered to a roll call, sort of a plant meeting. We were threatened as usual with the most dire of punishments should we be caught doing . . . In the course of our work, we didn't come into contact with any fish, smoked or otherwise. Our pay, as was customary, was four hundred grams per day of bread and meals. Not one of us abandoned the hope that something somehow could be figured out. We found only the occasional tossed fish head or tail, the leftovers of a meal, and were ecstatic. But what each of us silently hoped for we could never pull off.

The only fish we ever saw was through locked gratings. The crates full of delicious freshly smoked fish were piled there after they weighed. They had been placed in front of our noses, but at a distance from the iron gratings. The padlock was large and couldn't be unlocked without damage. We had to do something. But what? Then one day it came to me. The room where the fish were stacked behind the iron grating was really a passage way with doors. My plan was to drop wood shavings and muck in front of the grating that protected the locked-up fish. Then the fussy Russians would order us at once to really clean up the fish room. And so it came to pass. Now, I had stuck a nail through the end of my broom handle. The tip of my broom with the protruding nail had inconspicuously turned into a fish hook that reached the correct distance through the iron grating. After setting up a lookout and a warning system, I took advantage of a suitable moment to snag two smoked fish from the crates. We had to watch like the devil that the fish didn't fall off the hook before I could maneuver them through the bars. The trick worked a few times although the Russians soon got into trouble about the short weight of the crates. We could see what happened when that occurred. Then the moment came that was bound to come sooner or later: just as I caught another fish, the alarm was given, forcing me to hurry. That was not at all good for the fishing process; the damn fish fell on the ground between the grating and the crate. Hurriedly I managed to get the broom in a corner so I wouldn't be caught red-handed. As the officer—our boss—entered the room, we were all busily cleaning the floor tiles and the walls. As ill luck would have it, he immediately discovered the fish on the floor and stared at it a long time with a furrowed brow. Then he looked at each one us without saying a word. After a renewed moment of serious thought, he walked up to the broom standing in the corner, discovered the nail and sniffed it. Then he disappeared, still without having uttered a word. We feared the worst, seeing ourselves already condemned to a Siberian labor camp.

At noon there was roll call. All German workers had to line up. Our boss arrived with a translator. With a serious expression that revealed nothing, he began a speech: "Comrades! I have never seen that you can catch fish with a broom and from a locked room at that. That you can catch fish already smoked in the dead of winter is most remarkable. Nonetheless, since these incredible things happened today in my plant, I am compelled to fire some of my employees without notice or, as the case may be, assign them to a disciplinary transfer." We were so relieved that we burst out laughing and could have hugged our boss, who had a sense of humor. He really should have reported us to the military police, setting the whole process in motion to prosecute and sentence us. Since he knew the harshness of Soviet military justice, he did nothing to hand over the culprits. His genial speech was really saying, what's happened was sort of a miracle and was not theft that deserved harsh punishment. Unfortunately we were indeed, as promised, transferred to a construction site, and my activity in the smoked fish plant came to an end.

Premonitions

Mother gradually learned how to exploit the possibilities of the black market. For example, she bought or bartered packets of cigarettes and then sold the cigarettes individually for a small profit. She did the same with bread, which she bought by the loaf for over a hundred old rubles, and then sold by the slice. A laborious but ultimately profitable business. Only to her misfortune it was a business full of excitement. Once, courtesy of the military police, who were arresting Germans involved in trade as "speculators," and another time, courtesy of some brutal Russians, who simply took everything away from her. Starving Germans, too, sometimes tore the bread from her hands.

I was now working as a bricklayer's assistant for six hundred grams of bread a day. Father had finally found an undemanding job as a security guard and was now earning bread too. Mother was able to barter for some food on the black market. I was getting some additional rations from Russian apartments whenever it was absolutely necessary. For a few days everything went well. I hauled stones, mixed cement, and did what a bricklayer's helper was supposed to do. And then the most astonishing thing happened. Suddenly, I was seized with the desire to go home. The feeling was so overwhelming that I left my post during working hours and ran home. An action so unheard of that normally it meant being fired. As I was going home, I was thinking of the absurdity of what I was doing and was amazed at my impulse to go home early in the morning of all things.

Just as I'm turning into our street, I see Mother staggering oddly toward our quarters. She's as pale as a ghost and has a bad head wound. She tells me she was knocked down and robbed of everything.

She didn't know how long she had been lying unconscious in the ruins where a Russian had lured her with promises of bargains too good to pass up. Once there, he hit her in the head with a brick. After she regained consciousness, she had thrown up a few times before crawling home. She looked at me as if I were a fata morgana, so astounded was she to meet me there. I helped her the rest of the way and put her to bed. It seemed uncanny to both of us and we both were aware of the oddity of such a moment in our meeting like that. To our relief, Mother recovered quickly, but this incident was something that I'll wonder about the rest of my life. Without a doubt, her thoughts were transmitted to me. A connection between two people operating across space. If that's possible, what else might be? A connection operating across time and space? Do we forge a unity with certain people that can influence what we think and do? There is also the fact that I've been able to anticipate things, I've had the experience several times of being able to foresee—to have the premonition of—an immediate danger or an event that will occur in the future. Only in extreme situations, of course, and never deliberately. A little while later something else happened.

I've just opened the door very softly with my skeleton key, entering the quarters of some Russians. For some time I listen hard for sounds in the apartment. The lock had been easy to open as the security locks common later on were not yet in use. I had knocked, of course, and no one had answered, but today I definitely sense immediate danger. Granted, I have had this feeling several times before for no particular reason, and then later I was annoyed with myself since my fear proved to be unfounded. So I say to myself: "Don't be a coward, go ahead." I enter the kitchen as quietly as I can, and I see a large net bag of potatoes lying there, just what we so desperately want. Grabbed in a jiffy and then softly away. But then I can't. Something powerful holds me back. A premonition completely paralyzes me, and I stand there confronting the potatoes for several minutes, unable to lay hands on them. I'm dumbfounded and helpless, amazed at this phenomenon, when, still out my sight, a door is abruptly and noisily opened and the next second a Russian is rushing through the kitchen door, swinging at me with an ax. Our eyes meet, and with a look and a gesture I'm able to stop him. I immediately sense that I've influenced him, that I could develop something like hypnotic powers in extreme emergency. He stops the ax in midswing over his head and spellbound he stares at me. His terrified wife shows up behind him. I immediately start talking to him. I tell him I'm a "specialist" and have to check the electric wiring. Also that I hadn't stolen anything, he could see for himself. It took quite a while to calm him down and to convince him. My power to influence, my art of persuasion along with his good nature and credulity help me wriggle out of this escapade unharmed.

What was going on here? Luck, chance, a higher power? This unknown something that can be felt and aids our intuition, what is it? A special sensibility? Why shouldn't it have something to do with God? Especially if one understands God to be a power that is immanent in all things, as something that shapes all forms of existence—the physical and the spiritual—and thereby binds and links all things.

As usual, it took only a day before I was ripped from such meditations back into the daily humiliations of trying to stay alive. Mother brought home some mushrooms she had obtained by barter and prepared them as best she could under the circumstances. A half hour after eating them, however, we had terrible stomach cramps and were all horribly nauseous. We knew very well that mushrooms could be fatally poisonous. We didn't know that genuine danger of being poisoned—by the mushroom known as amanita—presents symptoms only many hours after eating. Our symptoms, certainly very serious, showed up immediately, weakening us still further. But we didn't—as we first expected to—face death.

The "Charity"

Professor Wilhelm Starlinger, who founded the first *Deutsches Seuchenkrankenhaus* (DSK) (German Epidemic Hospital) at the behest of the occupying power, describes the situation at that time in his terse report—I am quoting from his book *Grenzen der Sowjetmacht (Limits to Soviet Power)*:

1) The physical and mental strain hit women and children the hardest (especially as the men, to the extent they had survived the final battle, were evacuated en masse soon after victory); the vulnerability of the women was total, the disruption of the family was complete, and for a woman who had to provide for small children it was impossible. 2) The first distribution of bread, which started slowly, only in May, and then only to adults able to work, was irregular and insufficient. Very watery and limited to four hundred grams, the bread was the sole source of provisions, and irregular at that until the summer of 1946, and benefited only a small portion of the population. Most people lived on rye grain, which was gathered from the fields by those fit enough to do so or those greedy for profit. The rye seed had been planted in the winter of 1944/1945 and their stalks had remained uncut in the fields; these proceeded to sprout ever more vigorously from the summer of 1945 on. Large quantities of meat were taken from animals dug up after having long been buried. In the winter of 1945/1946 there were reliably reported cases of cannibalism recorded. Only from the summer of 1946 on were there slightly more distributions, later even payment in money to regular and necessary workers. 3) Habitable housing was in extremely tight supply, characterized by crowding into the smallest possible spaces; household goods, underwear, clothing, especially shoes were

for the most part nonexistent; there was scarcely enough wood for cooking during the severe winter and in the brutally cold winter of 1946/1947 there were many nights whole families suddenly died of cold and exhaustion. 4) At the height of the typhus epidemic, in the fall of 1945, Königsberg depended solely on the water from its wells, which, with few exceptions, were polluted, and from bomb craters when there wasn't enough well water; people washed using water from the bomb craters (the distance to the Pregel River was too far and too dangerous). They could change and wash their underwear only seldom. Sanitation was nonexistent, the existing latrines were too few and poorly maintained. People found them too far away and were too fearful to brave the distance; consequently, the filth in the courtyards and cellars was very serious. It wasn't until 1946 that a few districts saw some improvement, but only a few could take advantage of it. 5) By the summer of 1945, the infestation of flies was so severe that every container, every piece of bread, every invalid, even every fresh piece of excrement was instantly covered by a swarm of flies. The outbreak of a plague of lice began in May and flourished without a break until the winter of 1945/1946, the proliferation of rats was so out of control that people were attacked in their sleep. 6) The population had no disinfection agents, nor did they receive any; even soap was rare. Cleaning up the city was limited to clearing the main streets. Setting up latrines and using them occurred only gradually. Even burying the dead was not completed for weeks. 7) By setting up a loose network of German outpatient clinics, which were up and running by the beginning of May 1945, the first registration of those diagnosed with infectious diseases could begin, then the registration of those suspected of having an infectious disease could follow. This measure was already well under way when the first wave of typhus patients began; registration of those newly infected, however, was delayed. Those diagnosed with an infectious disease were admitted into new German Epidemic Hospitals that had just been established. Transportation was especially difficult in the first year; for the seriously ill, it was protracted, exhausting, frequently a danger in itself, and it always was in an open cart (pulled by hand!).

Professor Starlinger goes on to write about his specialty, which was combating epidemics:

5) The outbreak of a lice plague extended far and wide by the winter of 1945/1946. 6) Measures to combat the outbreak of disease were limited to placing in quarantine and isolating anyone diagnosed as being infected. Eventually, new cases were successfully registered. 7) Housing and feeding the sick in the improvised, ever expanding German Epidemic Hospitals (DSK) that were inadequately supplied ensued under the most difficult and completely deficient conditions; active medical intervention was limited to the barest essentials. The result was that epidemics in Königsberg befell a closed and homogeneous German population that (a) could not acquire immunological protection either from previous contact with the diseases or from vaccination; (b) was left unprotected by the lack of any sanitary or public hygiene measure (other than a frequently belated quarantine and isolation of a patient already exhibiting symptoms of the disease) against the unchecked spread of disease due to environmental conditions, while the utter absence of any organization in all aspects of life fostered the explosive spread of disease; and (c) suffered from such overwhelming physical and mental strain that any susceptibility whatsoever to infection in the environment or in the individual had consequences for the population, whose most basic demands for nursing or medical care were overwhelmed.—It can rightfully be said that in Königsberg the epidemics ran their course under the most primitive conditions. At that time, it often seemed to this observer as if fate and nature wanted to test what human beings could bear and how they would behave when disease had free reign.

The state of our health was desperate. Father felt terribly weak and lost weight precipitously. It seemed as if women were generally in a better position to survive on a diet completely devoid of protein. The death rate of males was strikingly higher. So it proved to be with Mother, who was the most resilient of us all. Everyone who saw her during this difficult period admired her persistent energy, willingness to help, and her courage in the face of the daily struggle to survive. She probably wouldn't have survived this awful time without me, and certainly I wouldn't have done so without her. She was most sorely tested in winter, that is, in December 1945: one morning I could no longer move. I was talking gibberish and had every symptom of high fever. The thermometer later read 41 °C (105.8 °F). That is how the end began with most people. After they had desperately tried not to starve to death, some sort of terminal illness struck. So would have been the case with me had Mother not fought doggedly without complaint. When she saw that my condition was very serious and had worsened in the next few days—I could scarcely breathe—she ran around until she found a Russian woman doctor. The physician examined me, had me say "trizet trie" (thirty-three) a few times and ordered me at once to enter the "Charity." This was a hospital that had been put back into operation, but we hadn't known about its existence at all. At the behest of the resolute doctor, who was a high-ranking officer, a Russian ambulance brought me to the hospital, which was run by German physicians. When I was brought to the admissions desk, a nurse and the admitting physician argued whether I should first be taken to the delousing station according to regulations or be put directly in a ward. I heard the physician say: "He can't go to the delousing station, he'll croak on us there." He examined my hair for lice and immediately ordered me to be admitted to one of the sick wards. I was handled with the utmost care and brought to a room with eight beds. Real beds with white bed linen. Four beds stood along the right wall and four along the left, each jutting out into the room. The passageway in the middle was a little bit wider than the space between the beds. Here I felt safe and for the first time encountered an official institution concerned with my physical well-being. Inevitably, it was very quickly apparent how limited its resources were. But for once I was lying in a clean bed and didn't have to do a thing, didn't have to think about a thing. My worries even diminished when Mother, after a difficult week, announced her idea of bartering for some food for her and Father. Luckily, I had stolen a rather large amount of *Muckefuck* (Mocha faux, a coffee substitute) in a break-in. Father was to prepare this while Mother, outfitted with a hot coffee pot and a few cups, sold this on the black market by the cup for a ruble to freezing Russians. The profit was enough for them to survive and brought me that peace of mind crucial for my slow recovery; a very slow one.

Dr. Frank took X-rays and diagnosed infection in both lungs and dry pleurisy as well as malnourishment. The two doctors who oversaw my ward were Professor Böttner and Dr. Schaum. If they could hardly do more in my case other than wait—there simply were no medicines—their care and personal interest were absolutely decisive for my gradual recovery from a very grave illness. Now is the moment to give these two men my heartfelt thanks. Dr. Schaum could not possibly imagine what it meant when he talked with me on occasion. The state of being taken seriously, the feeling of being able to let go gave me a sense of well-being I hadn't felt in a long time. I lay quiet in my bed, all happy and filled with hope. Once a day there was something to eat—mostly a gruel, but sometimes bean or pea soup, which were exquisite delicacies for us. Sometimes there were even some snacks in the afternoon. It wasn't enough to keep my roommates suffering edema from starving to death. They died one after another, and their beds were immediately filled with cases just as hopeless. Everyone had edema or wounds that wouldn't heal or they were terribly bloated. Dr. Schaum untiringly aspirated pleura and pericardia. It was really the only thing he could do. When a thirteen year-old boy who had been put next to me died—his pericardium too had been aspirated several times—I was very upset. No one came to visit him; he expired in the next bed almost without a sound and was put into a mass grave together with countless other nameless victims. That certainly would have been my fate if Mother hadn't come almost every day and begun to bring black market purchases. A slice of bread, some horse fat, some canned food, and some more bread. She quickly realized that without her efforts I would never get well again. When she could no longer hold the coffee pot because her tendovaginitis was acting up, she made a vendor's tray herself for the coffee pot, which she could hang around her neck. Now she looked like a real market woman. On her feet from morning to evening, with only one goal: to obtain bread or food. She managed to do so only by pushing herself to the limit. Father's job in all this was to fetch wood, keep the fire going, and make the coffee, while Mother tirelessly hawked and sold her hot refreshment in the market.

She tucked whatever she brought me in the hospital under my covers. I ate it at once and as inconspicuously as possible. It would have been inconceivable to save the food for later since someone only would've stolen it as soon as I fell asleep. Nor did I share the food with anyone else besides the young boy in the next bed. You can't share the slender reed to which you yourself are clinging. It was a terrible dilemma. Anyone who wasn't completely apathetic talked about food, about nothing else but food. Nonetheless, I was happy in this state of resting in bed. It was not at all a secret to me that within the walls of this hospital, a number of people, like parasites, were trying to ensure their survival. Everyone was living on rations distributed by the military government that were all too meager for the hospital personnel and patients. Rumors about the corrupt distribution of food and theft in the kitchen made their way to the wards.

I began to read again. In the hospital library there were many books on philosophy, and I read everything that I was given as if truly possessed. The seemingly logical view of the world of the Pre-Socratics— Anaximander, Heraclitus, Thales of Miletus, and others—entranced me beyond measure. Here a hypothesis is proposed and an entire world is thereby explained; scarcely has one said everything is like this, then another one comes along saying it is like that. I found it fascinating and exciting, and read and read.

Outside, winter was making life decidedly more difficult, and there were rumors of cannibalism. Doctors had identified meat for sale in the market as human flesh. Likewise, meatballs turned out to have been made of human flesh. And then the Russians discovered a regular human butcher shop in the city's ruins. Victims were lured to the site, where they were killed and their flesh, lungs, and heart were processed.

Mother was trying now to increase her profit through petty trade— buying and selling. She told me how the military police kept a sharp eye out and how difficult it was to carry out a deal behind their backs. When the military police realized it was impossible to stop the Königsbergers' struggle to stay alive by engaging in their barter and trade, they spread the rumor of poisoned food Germans were selling to the Russians. If they had their way, we certainly wouldn't manage to stay alive.

I had been in the hospital for five months and was just beginning to get well when suddenly I came down with a high fever again. The next day it was gone, then it returned and so on. I had come down with malaria, a disease that was beginning to sweep through the city; it was thought to be caused by the polluted ponds used for fire fighting. These ponds were artificial lakes installed by the Nazis to double as reserves in case water capacity should be knocked out. Now they were filled with decaying cadavers and garbage people had tossed there. Flies and mosquitoes could breed undisturbed and had turned into a plague the same way that lice, rats, and other insects had been for a long time. As a result, diseases suddenly appeared that had never appeared in Königsberg before. But how do you treat malaria without quinine, which of course was unavailable. This illness was a serious relapse for me. The fever eventually cured itself, and bit by bit I recovered from the malaria, which left me with a damaged spleen as a souvenir.

The month of May precipitated a severe crisis when there was nothing more to eat. At first the soup became thinner and thinner, then

there was no soup at all. What was happening? The military government that had run things until now was to be replaced by a new civilian government, which wouldn't take over until the first of June. And
since the military didn't care about anything anymore in May, there
was a deadly interregnum. (By decrees dated April 7 and June 4, 1946,
by the Presidium of the Supreme Soviet of the USSR, Königsberg was
formally annexed into the RSFSR [Russian Soviet Federated Socialist
Republic] and thereby into the Soviet Union.) There were simply no
more deliveries to the hospital and everyone was left to their fate.
People were desperate and the misery surpassed all description. Anyone who didn't get any additional food from the outside was lost.
About a week after the Red Army stopped deliveries, the death rate of
the patients rose so dramatically there were up to forty dead a day.
People were always dying around me, and the business of covering the
faces of the deceased with bed sheets became a formalized, repetitive
gesture. The burly hospital orderlies then came to fetch the dead and
hauled them away like dead batteries. Just as before, human life was not
only worthless, it was unwanted. The lovely chorales the nurses sang
in the corridors couldn't conceal this fact. The more quickly someone
died, the better. In the end, I would estimate that over 100,000 of the
120,000 to 130,000 civilians who once existed here did the Russians this
favor. Hitler wanted to make Europe *judenrein* (Jew-free), Stalin wanted
to make East Prussia *deutschrein* (German-free). Even so, the one can
never be compared to the other. But that I was allowed to survive both
is incomprehensible to me.

In an act of desperation, the doctors ordered all hospital patients
and nurses to go out to the fields and ruins to collect edible mushrooms. Everyone who could go to the toilet without assistance had to
help. Once again, it was a question of life or death. That is how I came
to go on my first excursions on very wobbly legs. The only positive
thing was that I finally learned to recognize edible plants—especially
stinging nettles, goutweed, common orache, and dandelion. Soup was
then made from what was gathered each day. I cannot say if this
reduced the death rate. Mother made heroic efforts and was more in
need than ever of my help. Everything was far too much for her. To
procure food for three people was a monstrous impossibility. That she
had been successful up until now for two, funneling a bit to me was
already a miracle. Long before I was well I left the hospital to throw
myself once again into the wild fray.

Breaking and Entering—
Episode 2

When I came home from the hospital, my parents had moved again. They were now living on the ground floor of a burnt-out building. They had a room with a roof, protected against the rain, whose windows were boarded up. The previous tenants, now deceased, had constructed a very solid entryway. Since these were very good quarters, my parents had taken in an old acquaintance, a music teacher Gerda S., whom Father knew from old times. "The Gerda," as my parents called her, had shared the hard fate of women, but as the spirited daughter of an estate owner she still had her sparkle. With the help of anthroposophy and music, she amazingly knew how to keep body and soul together. She migrated from one Russian family to the next, from one soldiers' club to the next, giving piano lessons and performances to earn a meal or a piece of bread. At the time, her good spirits and her lively mind, which served to protect her from permanent damage, lifted our spirits as well. Conversations about her "religion" were stimulating. My parents of course understood as little as I did when she tried every so often to explain anthroposophy to us. Her eyes glistened and her hands waved about. She spoke of ethereal or astral bodies, ghosts and spiritual beings, conjuring up mental images whose colorful splendor brought joy to the believer, whose belief is based more on emotion than reflection. For all that, I would prefer to feel in colors, tones, and music. From words I hoped for more clarity. I once said to her something to the effect that because the sublime lies in the inexplicable, an inexplicable philosophy is not necessarily the sublime. But she may have possessed too little self-confidence about her own ability to think logically, believing what is within our comprehension could not be spiritually sublime enough—I don't know. We were all crowded together in our room only on our days off and at night. Gerda survived these years, but was very ill when I saw her not so long ago. Her spirit, still unbroken, hadn't been able to let go of what she had gone through. She was no longer her confident self and she bore these years as a burden— physically as well as mentally—throughout the rest of her life.

My parents had aged considerably. They looked as if they were in their seventies. They were both full of lice. Father was constantly squashing the creatures between his nails. There was no other way to get rid of them. Urine was the only available disinfectant, which proved here to be totally ineffective. I had tried early on using it to get rid of my scabies, but to no avail. Looking back, I see now that the healing power of nature helped those of us who had survived to defeat disease—diseases for which one would normally use medicine by the pound. The general state of affairs, however, was bad and our situation was as desperate as ever. Something had to be done once again to obtain food. Unfortunately, I was too weak to think of starting again right away as a cabinetmaker or as a mason's helper. I was happy if I could go a hundred yards without having to rest. I was beating my brains out again to come up with something. Small thieving excursions resulted in little success. I couldn't concentrate and I couldn't always muster the nerve necessary.

In the summer of 1946, the Russians were beginning to restore and expand the electric grid, and they were desperately looking for electricians. The work of an electrician wasn't very physically demanding, and so I claimed to be an electrician. But the powers that be, of course, checked this out. A German master electrician handed me a piece of paper and a pencil and told me to draw a changeover switch. He discovered at once I was no electrician. Nonetheless, he gave his approval and recommended that the Russians give me a job. This was another huge stroke of luck and played a key role in our constant struggle to survive. Every Russian had great respect for specialists, especially for electricians. They were impatiently waiting to be hooked up to electricity and the electricians were going to help them. This not only opened the Russians' doors for us, but allowed us to help ourselves to many a contribution in the form of bread or potatoes. Furthermore, I scouted out opportunities that were suitable for my renewed enterprise of breaking and entering. That was, as it had been before, a last resort on account of life-threatening risks; we really did make the supreme effort to keep from starving by trading on the black market and through work.

Once the first Russian apartment blocks had been furnished with electricity, the demand for lamps and ceiling lights was enormous. Consequently, I searched for lamps that didn't work or for anything that would hold a light bulb. I refurbished everything with house wiring and somehow made it look presentable. As a result, I came into possession of articles easily sold on the black market. I wasn't as handy as others who could conjure "gold wedding rings" from a piece of brass piping. In my new field of endeavor, many-tiered chandeliers were the most lucrative objects. The Russians were really eager for these old-fashioned, cruciform iron monstrosities. Now and then you could find such things in the trash in burnt-out attics. For the most part, they didn't work at all, but could usually be repaired. This led me to undertake expeditions to inspect the attics in buildings where Russians lived. There weren't many "colleagues" who dared to go directly into the lion's den, and I was occasionally able to find usable things lying around on the floor.

When I enter the four-story apartment building, a feeling of trepidation comes over me that is stronger than usual. I can't say definitely it's a premonition that's warning me. But the uneasy feeling is particularly strong. As usual, dressed in my overalls and gym shoes, I quietly mount the stairs all the way to the attic, which is astonishingly still intact in this building. I hear no sounds, no one is opening a door; and unseen, or so I think, I reach a door that's locked. The heavy locks on this iron door are not so easy to open with my skeleton key. They often stick. I patiently work it open and enter a storage room that's still quite full. Before I look at anything, I hide the skeleton key in the ruler pocket in the leg of my overalls. I never forget to do that. On closer inspection, I see that there is scarcely anything of use here. Only a few sockets, no lamps. I take nothing but two sockets. Slowly I go down the stairs. I don't feel up to breaking into one of the apartments today. As I'm coming down from the third story to the second, a door is torn open and a young, Jewish-looking lieutenant rushes out. He hurls himself at me, beating me with such venom that I am knocked bleeding to the floor. I get a few more kicks and then am seized by my hair and throat, and shoved down the steps to the street. We must be a curious sight, for more and more Russians are watching us curiously and smiling at us complacently. Everyone feels satisfied when "evil" is punished. In this fashion, we go straight to the military police post. I'm always in front, my lieutenant who is foaming with rage behind. Perhaps he considered the possibility of just shooting me. For a moment there on the stairs, I had a feeling he would. He probably didn't because I had no stolen goods on me. I later found out someone had broken into this building a few days before. My colleagues apparently had been more successful than I, and my officer may have been one of the victims. Stealing from Russians was seen by everyone—except by my father—as a heroic deed, a justifiable act. There had long been scores of people, mostly very young, at work who were trying like me to ensure their survival. Only no one said where he had broken in. Therefore, no one knew what places to avoid for a while. This time I'm out of luck, and as had already happened with a number of Königsbergers, I'll be sentenced in summary proceedings and ordered to a work camp in Russia. That's how they dealt with thieves they caught. But once again it doesn't happen that way: at the station, my lieutenant is still yelling. He stands me in front of him and clearly distraught, yammers away without pausing for breath to the station officer, who's somewhat older and doesn't seem at all disturbed. I note, however, he even eggs on my officer with a question now and then. My officer ascends into a more furious rage, and he starts hitting me again. At the same time, he's patting me down, once more looking for stolen goods and thoroughly going through my tool pockets. He doesn't find the skeleton key. That would've been the end of me. He continues to address me more and more angrily, shoving me backwards against the wall. There he starts to strip me. Intentionally, I pull down my pants so that the sign of our commonality might soothe his hostility. But it has the opposite effect. He grabs my hair and bangs my head against the wall until my knees, no longer able to support me, give way and I crumple to the floor. Then he turns on his heel and goes over to the table where the police officer is sitting.

Still a bit dazed, I notice the police officer is disgusted as he takes a seat at the typewriter. He begins to write up the diatribe as it's being dramatically dictated. It takes quite a while before they finish and my tormenter affixes his name below the typed report with a flourish. Then he disappears after making another threat, probably directed at the policeman. It's obvious the military policeman doesn't care for this officer. Maybe he's anti-Semitic, maybe he doesn't care for all the theatrics, and maybe the fact that not one item of stolen goods is presented or found is the deciding factor in his attitude.

I am sitting in my corner, waiting to see what would happen. Every so often I try to explain to the military policeman that I hadn't stolen anything. Not one word does he say, so I spend the rest of the afternoon at the station. After a few hours, probably just before the change in shifts, the officer approaches me; holding the paper with the written charges in his hand, he addresses me. I understand only fragments of what he's saying: "I'll let you go this time, but make sure you never cross the path of this officer again or I'm in trouble too." Then he tears up both copies with the signature of my accuser, opens the door, and lets me go.

Human kindness in a military police officer. Hatred in a Jewish officer—to comprehend such things wasn't easy for me.

Water and Electricity

I thought of yet another new trick. I would loosen the phase changer in the distribution panel where the live lines came into the buildings—generally, the distribution panel was near the entrance. Then I would wait until a few Russians had been helplessly fumbling around in the fuse box. At that moment, I would appear as if by chance. The "specialist" would be hailed with gratitude, and I would in all apparent innocence offer to help. After fiddling importantly with my inspection probe, I would correct what was wrong and demand bread as pay. That worked a few times until I tried it at the wrong house where a Russian electrician was living. He saw through the maneuver and with blows threw me out of the building. After that, I wasn't so pleased with the trick anymore, and I specialized in building antennae. These were simply wires strung from one porcelain reel to the next, nothing more. This earned me a half loaf of bread as pay. But no matter how hard I worked, it wasn't enough to fill the mouths of all three of us. At least not enough for several days running.

My relationship with my father was extremely tense. It isn't easy to reconstruct the arguments with him that surely took their toll on us both. Each of us was always trying to justify our philosophy of life. His questionable inactivity and my questionable activities could be defended by even more dubious philosophical structures of thought, as good or bad, or as right or wrong ways of acting. There was talk of the curse of the evil deed—what I understood as a reference to my thievery—and of the effect of someone's wisdom making the world better, continually increasing peace and love. His examples were those who submitted such as Gandhi and Buddha; my men of action were Moses and Wilhelm Tell. He was definitely Gandhi only insofar as he did little, and I was Moses because I stole from the Russian "Egyptians." But who could live up to his examples? It always came back again to the question: Are noble ways of acting applicable in every circumstance? Didn't we need other principles in our extreme situation? Was it noble and right to die doing nothing instead of surviving by stealing?

Thank heavens my father wasn't ready to die. He always became furious if he thought I got a larger piece of bread than he did. Mother divided the little we had, taking into account that I needed more calories for my work and other things I did, not to mention that she perhaps favored the younger man for other reasons. Father hated me for this "unfairness," and I hated him for this hatred. His claim, which was seldom expressed—and which I basically accepted—hung in the room, namely, that he had been the reason we had survived the Nazis, therefore we were responsible for his surviving the Russians. That his presence had prevented us from being transported to the gas chambers didn't balance out with our efforts now. And in addition to such thoughts, there is definitely a moral duty to care for the members of your family. This was as true for him under Hitler as it was later for me under Stalin. My only problem was to induce Father to take a more active role in the struggle to survive. But to talk with him about these things was difficult, especially as his ability to formulate his thoughts was superior to mine. What remained was always a great and deep feeling of unease, which made everything all the more difficult.

Then Father gradually became more and more apathetic and couldn't be moved to do anything anymore. He lost so much weight he looked pitiful and no longer wanted to get out of bed. At the same time, however, our lives had noticeably improved. We had been allowed to move to a ground floor room in a Russian building. This building was on Beethoven Street and stood alone among the ruins. We three were given permission to move into the room if we took over the janitorial duties. We were very happy about this. Surviving the next winter in our unheated quarters would've been impossible. We had no idea what we would use to heat the room, but to have an actual, closed room was one of the most important prerequisites.

We didn't need to haul water in buckets from the Luisenwahl anymore. For some time now, hydrants had been set up in various places that could be tapped, making the problem of water supply easier. For bodily needs, the ruins, in which impressive vegetation was beginning to grow, had to serve as before. However, the residents of our building practiced another method. In one of the kitchens on the ground floor—of course virtually destroyed and unused—they had hacked a hole in the floor and through this hole they crapped. The swelling mound in the cellar was growing in the shape of a cone up to the hole in the kitchen. They were about to knock out another hole in the floor in another location when something happened to put an end to this practice. Just as they had been hooking up electricity, the authorities were gradually connecting up single buildings and streets to water mains. One day when I came home, I found the residents standing helplessly out in front while water was splashing cheerfully everywhere. Our building had been connected to the water main by some invisible plumbing genies and now every defective or open water faucet—and the pipes themselves—were spewing forth jets of water. The residents were all totally helpless and greeted me as their savior in their hour of need. I sensed their hope and felt a duty to fix the problem. After all, I was their "specialist." I asked the Russian major who lived on the second floor if they had even turned off the main supply valve, which of course had to be somewhere in the cellar. He confirmed it hadn't been and said somewhat embarrassed that you couldn't go in. I ran downstairs at once, already suspecting what he meant. The entire cellar was already knee-deep in water, and floating on top was all the shit. There was a break in the pipe or an unsecured water faucet in the cellar directly under the kitchen, from which gushed heavy streams of water. That had set the ceiling-high pile in motion. Of course there was nothing to do but remove my socks and shoes—my pants, too—to wade into the brown soup, searching for the main supply valve. It took some time before I finally found the dammed valve and could turn off the water. To repeated cheers of *"Otchen kharasho!"* (Very good!) I emerged from the stinking glop, happy that I had lived up to their expectations. However, I took this opportunity to make it clear to my fellow residents that it wasn't a good idea if they continued to use the kitchen, that they should perhaps . . . They nodded their heads and from then on I ran into the major more often over in the ruins.

This building was not fixed or put into working order for years; too much was beyond repair. But right at hand, in one of the other ruins, water burbled now without pause, and that was closer and more convenient than one of the hydrants in the other nearby streets. Electricity and water were now available in the building, making our lives considerably easier.

Break and Entering— Episode 3

One of the last nerve-wracking robberies I pulled was perhaps my riskiest venture. Hunger was gnawing at us again to such an extent that we had to find something. Obviously, I never stole from the Russians living in our building. Not only on moral grounds, but also not to jeopardize the enormous advantage of living where we were secure against the winter.

So off I go and come to three multifamily dwellings in a row that are inhabited exclusively by officers. In my overalls, with my tools and skeleton key in my pocket, I try to discover which apartment is empty at the moment. On the third floor of the middle building I boldly open a door and hear a loud conversation in the living room. Hoping that no one will leave the room during such an animated exchange, I enter the kitchen and see a whole hundred-weight sack of potatoes, sitting there like manna from heaven. But I can't lift all hundred pounds at once anymore, not to mention carry it a rather long way, although I could possibly drag it along on the ground. But if I'm caught now, the game is up. This time it's beginning to frighteningly resemble Russian roulette. Even to think of dragging away a sack of potatoes under the eyes of the Russians who are continually coming and going would be impudently challenging fate.

I vaguely remember seeing a wheelbarrow in the courtyard at a nearby construction site. So I leave the apartment again, setting the door ajar— in order to save fumbling around with the skeleton key when I return— and go to the construction site. I have to go around the block, and there is indeed a wheelbarrow sitting there. I place it on the curb in the street in front of the main entrance and look around for bits and pieces of roofing felt to cover the potatoes. While I'm doing this, I encounter two highly decorated Russians. When I return to the apartment door on the third floor, it's been closed and locked, evidence that someone has come or gone in the meantime. I open it a second time—which goes more quickly this time—and again I hear loud voices. I sneak into the kitchen. I have to summon all my courage to seize the sack of potatoes. I begin to haul it along. Whoever stumbles across me now would immediately see what I was up to and would take the usual immediate action. I don't even bother to think up an excuse in case I'm caught. What would be the point? I must be demented; how can I even think of escaping unnoticed down the stairs and out the building. Moreover, the sack has to be heaved into the wheelbarrow.

I'm already outside the apartment and the sack has made quite a bit of noise going over every threshold, leaving in its wake a sandy tow path. Anyone could see what was going on. With a thwump, thwump, thwump, I drag the sack down the stairs. I manage somehow to get to the wheelbarrow unobserved, where I heave the sack into the wheelbarrow with my last ounce of strength. I pack the potatoes with the roofing felt and take off. Any Russian who crosses my path now sees only the worker and not the potato thief. Then just as I'm crossing the next intersection—it happens. A loud hue and cry comes from behind. Fear paralyzes my limbs for a second. I look around and see two uniformed Russians hurtling towards me as fast as they can. The jig is up. Nothing can or will save me this time. That's obvious. At that point, a strange passivity and submissive resignation to my fate comes over me—I recognize this from before—as if my life has no reason for being and in the inner reaches of my soul I'm prepared for the possibility that the "great Owner," from whom I've borrowed my life, has the right to reclaim it at any time or merely to do something terrible with it. I move on at a slow pace and wait for the cursing Russians to reach me and interrogate me, shoot me down, or at the least beat me to a pulp. But no such thing happens—and as I look back again, I see an empty street without a soul, with no one running in my direction. It can't be that once more a miracle has happened! Either they followed a different trail at the intersection, or the cursing, running Russians didn't have anything at all to do with my break-in. I have no idea. This time I'm more frightened than ever, and a peculiar numb feeling won't leave my limbs. It is as if the "great Owner" wanted to say, "That's your last warning!"

For the umpteenth time I swore to myself not to gamble my life so foolishly again, my life that's been spared until now. But when hunger became, as it did, unbearable, I was at it again. There was no other choice. When I came home, I immediately cooked a few of the potatoes, which, alas, turned out to be frozen. That diminished our enjoyment, and we were quite disappointed. But we did live on frozen potatoes for days, happy to have the certainty of a next meal.

On one of the following evenings, a young Königsberger—a bit younger than I—is running quickly along the Luisenallee. Following him is a Russian soldier with a drawn pistol. Moments later—out of my sight— I hear a shot. They got him in the head.

Electric Heat

We electricians were supposed to get a former movie theatre up and running again. Our main task was actually to smuggle the last scraps of a valuable parquet floor home to use for heating. The oak slats still had traces of tar and burned well. But the winter of 1946/1947 was so bitterly cold that all our efforts to find enough fuel fell short. Along with starvation, freezing loomed as a mortal threat. The scraps of wood from the parquet flooring warmed us for only a few hours. This winter, however, seemed especially long and cold. Soon there were nights with temperatures dropping to −25 °C (−13 °F). We had to do something. My boss, a fully qualified electrician, found a way. In the movie theatre where we worked, there were quite a few electrical resistors, coils wrapped with high resistance wire. They allowed you to turn the theatre lights smoothly up or down. If you short-circuited the resistors, they began—as with a normal electric oven—to glow and give off heat. There was already current available, and all the fuses were bypassed with wire that was way too thick. They weren't really fuses anymore. Real fuses would have blown had you connected such primitive heating devices and used several thousand watts of current. There weren't any electric meters yet. Our "resistance" saved us from freezing. We could raise the temperature in this way. This was a huge blessing, especially at night. We lay in warm clothing on pieces of mattresses that had been scavenged together. Once a horse hair mattress section began to glow in the dark. It had inched over too near our hot "resistance." Mother was the first to smell it, discovering it just in the nick of time before it caught fire. Then in the very last second, she seized the mattress section and managed to hurl it quickly through the open door of the balcony into the courtyard. At that moment it burst into flames and as we fought the blaze we calmed down the alarmed

Russians. A fire in the room would've been catastrophic. Our water supply was too limited to extinguish the blaze.

This dreadful winter is indelibly linked in my mind with all sorts of impressions and experiences. The Russians had set up huge loudspeakers on every corner. Most of the time they broadcast propaganda speeches or news. But in between they played the most wonderful music. There I would be, hurrying home in the dark beneath the clear starry sky and the icy, sparkling landscape covered in snow like a Christmas card would be flooded with the sounds of the sublimely played double concerto for violins by Bach. A dreamscape and the sound of David Oistrakh playing the violin both exhilarated and bewitched me. How can I describe it? I would dash from corner to corner to hear better. In such moments I believed in the existence of a better world, in a realm of the soul where there had to be the most splendid things. This music brought tidings I couldn't dismiss. And at the same time, my eyes saw the figures of people huddled together, frozen to death. Stiff, as if turned to stone, they sat or lay there. Sometimes they were under a blanket of freshly fallen snow. These were the people who couldn't find a stove for warmth or had given up the vain search for food. Most of the time it was older people lying there, but once there was a child too. How was an empathetic person to react to this? Too great were the contrasts between the world of music and the reality of Königsberg. How many were struggling with no help at all and just froze to death? These people became bitter warnings. Often they just lay there in the cold for several days before they were hauled away.

Baiser Bakers

The temperature continued to fall, and the business of fetching water and going to the bathroom turned into a complicated affair. You didn't dare expose any body part to the freezing cold for any length of time. Now that I've become older myself, I wonder how my parents survived all this. I can't even remember anymore if we caught colds. That would've had unfortunate consequences. Our electric heat was the source of our salvation and the reason all our acquaintances came by from time to time.

One day even Frau Stock, who baked *baisers* on occasion to sell on the street, dropped in. Even she wanted to get warm. While there she took in our critical situation at a glance. Father was lying in bed too weak to do anything else. Mother could scarcely find anything on the black market, and I was working from morning to evening without a prayer of bringing home enough bread for three. It was only a matter of time before we too would lose the overwhelming struggle to survive. The Stocks, who worked in the households of Russian officers and who formed a quasi cooperative living arrangement with them, had it much easier than we did. They bought extra food from the sale of *baisers*. They discovered the Russians loved buying this confection— which was unfamiliar to them. To bake *baisers*, you needed egg whites and sugar, expensive products seldom available on the black market. Frau Stock would teach us the trick of baking *baisers*. The prerequisite was, however, an oven whose temperature could be independently controlled both at the top and the bottom.

Since her suggestion seemed to be our only chance to survive, I wracked my brains for ways to get such an oven. We had built our wood-burning stove ourselves. I could easily find bricks, and even cement was available. Only, how do you set up an oven whose temperature could be independently controlled at both the top and the bottom? It was a technical problem that wasn't easy to solve, but the oven seemed our only real chance at survival. So I simply started to build: in the living room in the wall with the chimney, I constructed a brick form around an iron baking box I had scavenged from the rubble—the innards of a burnt-out stove—and made sure there were two independently regulated sources of heat. I figured that a wood-burning source would be the source of heat below and an electrical resistor would simultaneously be the source of heat above, sort of a combination wood-burning and electric oven. Once I had the idea, construction wasn't very difficult. And behold! The thing actually worked. Frau Stock could begin with her lessons. We had to beat the egg whites stiff, sweeten them, and then drop the meringue in small mounds onto the baking sheet, which we had to bake, carefully adjusting the heat above and below. With luck, we got a whole batch of small, snow-white, sweet *baiser* portions from one egg. With no luck, we ended up scraping a brown candied mass from the baking sheet. With dogged determination we hurled ourselves into this task, our last hope, for it was high time that something happened. Without scruple I stole all the remaining electrical resistors, which were probably still needed in the movie theatre, and exchanged them, or the money I got for them, for eggs and sugar and we began to bake. The first sheet was a flop, but we consoled ourselves by happily consuming the remains of our mistakes. The second attempt came out quite well. After a few mishaps and successes, I slowly got a feel for the proper dose of heat, a sort of sixth sense, and this was the turning point that, undoubtedly, saved our lives. Now we could produce something the Russians weren't familiar with and liked to buy. This way we not only made something of a financial profit, but we also kept the egg yolks for ourselves. They kept us from that dangerous condition known as "exhaustion apathy," the preliminary stage of starvation.

Soon we three were a team again. I baked, Mother bought and sold, Father—who had regained strength from the egg yolks—helped split wood and beat the meringue. Now we had the feeling that we could master our fate. After two years of the most awful misery, after the coldest months of winter, and possibly just short of our demise, we chanced upon baking *baisers*. It was our salvation. My thieving excursions, which only by the greatest good fortune hadn't ended in disaster and had never been worth the effort and risk, became a thing of the past. The arguments with my father also became a thing of the past even though the tension and estrangement lasted a long time. None-theless, it would be wrong to think that our new life had become in one fell swoop a piece of cake. *Baisers* often burnt or didn't turn out. The containers we used to display them for sale were often knocked from my mother's hands, her money stolen. The military police arrested any street vendor they caught. You had to keep a sharp eye out. If they caught you, then everything was seized and imprisonment was threat-ened, but thank goodness, not always imposed. More than once Mother didn't come home because she was spending the night in the basement of a military police station. There weren't always eggs to buy in the market, and then, of course, we couldn't bake anything. It was becom-ing more difficult by the day to find wood. The profit was minimal. We sold a tiny *baiser* for two rubles and—if I recall correctly—had to pay eight to ten rubles for an egg. Our *baisers* were a lot smaller than those you get today at the baker's. In spite of all the losses and setbacks, we now had a way, a ray of hope, and a tangible possibility to escape the consequences of malnourishment and slowly but surely regain our powers of resistance.

We owe Frau Stock a debt of gratitude. Her reward is only slightly diminished by the caution that was typical and understandable for all behavior in those days: only when she had definitely been told by her Russian officer that her application for an exit visa would be con-sidered did she disclose her baking secret. She told us that herself, so I have to assume that if the permission to leave had not calmed her understandable fear of competition, we would've remained without help. That was completely a matter of course in the extraordinarily difficult struggle to survive. It doesn't change the fact that the decisive turning point in our lives was that she gave us her *baiser* recipe. She exhorted us to keep this knowledge secret as long as it was our only means of existence. Eventually we could help a few people with the egg yolks and, later, we made cookies from the yolks to give them something extra nice. The inevitable result was that we were besieged with requests for help, which we could only respond to in a small way.

I heard that a German prisoner of war wanted to exchange a violin for bread and rubles. I was very excited, for I yearned to have a violin. The exchange took place and now I had a cheap, badly stringed violin with a bow of equally poor quality. But now I could practice when I had a chance and do something that required conscious thinking, something that wasn't just important for the next few moments, but for my whole life. My heart responded to this violin and even today I become attached to my instrument—it's an Italian violin now—it's exactly the same love. When I could take the time, I practiced scales and chords as well as the Beethoven romances from a score I had found somewhere.

On one occasion we all had reason to be particularly thankful that the Russians, probably more than any other people, love and admire artists. A young man practicing violin was enough to suggest art, just the sight of which made them forget their all too well-founded suspicions.

In our room, which smells slightly musty, I'm all alone and I'm devotedly practicing Beethoven again. Suddenly Mother, a military policeman, and a plump Russian woman noisily burst in, everyone speaking at once. The Russian is wearing a quilted jacket and the obligatory head scarf of Russian peasant women. An impressive number of medals for bravery jingle on the uniform of the policeman, who glares at us menacingly. Mother anxiously keeps repeating, "*Nischevo, nischevo!*" (It's nothing! It's nothing!) Without any greeting or explanation the woman immediately begins searching through our residence. No further explanation is necessary; I know what's happened. Mother had been to the black market to exchange a small tablecloth from one of my earlier break-ins and some other things for sugar. It's obvious that the robbed owner recognized it and, not incorrectly, suspected she could reach the thief through the fence. Our situation is, once more, precarious. Was brutal Russian justice going to seize us after all? Now, when everything was taking a turn for the better and the days of my desperate thieving expeditions were finally a thing of the past? Somehow I sense that my quite passable violin playing is distracting the two. They must be thinking whoever can produce such beautiful sounds can't possibly be a thief too. I see my chance and immediately feign indifference by continuing to practice while taking no notice of them. Meanwhile, I'm striving to play with great feeling and prudently repeat the few passages I've mastered. It makes an impression. Already the military policeman is looking friendlier, and more and more his attention is focused on my violin playing.

The whole time my mother is trying in the most irritatingly awkward manner to divert their attention from the makeshift shelf where a pair of gloves from the tainted source still lies. She looks so pale and worried that this alone should raise suspicion. I try, as inconspicuously as possible to indicate with glances and head shaking she is to remain calm, but the more the policeman admiringly watches me the less opportunity I have signal to Mother. Gradually things become uncomfortable for the Russian woman, who is basically easy-going. With increasing carelessness, she rummages through our wretched, disordered room. She gives up too soon to find anything and indicates to her escort she was probably mistaken. For a few seconds, the two stand there helplessly. Embarrassed, she begins to apologize, which we, greatly relieved, graciously accept. Almost like ghosts, both disappear as quickly as they came and the whole thing is over.

Even now, I still think how these easy-going Russians, certainly as poor as we were, assumed I couldn't have done anything wrong only because I was playing the violin.

Gleanings

When you write about what happened you have to make choices. Apart from the events in well-defined order, there are dozens of images inhabiting my memory that refuse to line up in a correctly dated sequence. They are like pieces of a puzzle that belong to my three-year-long "Russian puzzle." Whether they reflect events that happened somewhat sooner or later isn't really that important to me.

Today I am going to the Office of Cultural Affairs with my violin. A Jewish captain receives me. I tell him in Russian that I would like play something in order to be employed as a violinist. I tell him that a group of musicians has been formed to entertain the troops and prisoners. He wants to hear the Beethoven Romances, which I perform as well as I can. Then he fetches a few sheets of music from the cupboard. They have lots of accidentals and unusual rhythms; I'm supposed to play this at sight, which I do less well. Nonetheless, he says something about wanting to try me and I could play for a while without pay. I'm happy with this success and think I've taken an important first step.

As I stepped out on the balcony, I discovered all my clothes had been stolen. Mother had hung them there to thoroughly air out one fresh sunny day. I don't remember anymore exactly what I did. In any case, everything was gone. I somehow had to come up with some new clothes. In the market, we ask the Russians what they want for their shirts and their coats and they name a price. We've just had a good period with *baiser* sales, so I come into the possession of two faded Russian military shirts and a navy coat. This was heavy and uncomfortable, but warm. To complete the outfit, I wore an old pair of military trousers found on some junk pile, which I cleaned up, and a pair of gym shoes I had kept. This was both a droll and at the same time fashionable ensemble.

Williott Schwab gave me violin lessons. He took great pains and his lessons were given with a great deal of warmth. I owe him much. We worked very hard.

The currency reform devalued the ruble from ten to one. The money was new. They set up so-called "magazines" where little by little food was available for sale. You had to stand in line for hours and ruthlessly drive out the line-jumpers.

In the "German Club," there was dancing. Mostly it was Russian soldiers. The band needed a *Stehgeiger* (stand-up violinist). I tried out, and lo and behold! I got it! Herr Simonsohn, a former band leader, played the piano and arranged all sorts of pieces for piano, violin, saxophone, and drums—mostly Russian dance tunes that I especially liked, but also Viennese waltzes, German hit tunes, for example by Peter Kreuder.

I no longer have any idea when this German Club started or what its purpose was. My connection to it was limited to playing at dances twice a week, for which I received a few rubles from time to time. I was, as was almost every German at this time, anti-Communist. I associated Communism with what I had experienced and certainly was also influenced by the incessant Nazi propaganda. There was no possibility of an intellectual debate where there was only one point of view. Later, books and conversations helped me to a more nuanced judgment, which however never did away with my emotional antipathy. Those familiar with Soviet affairs claimed that the number of victims of Stalinism exceeded ten million. Unimaginable!

Stalin was another Hitler for me in those days—someone who abused his unlimited powers as dictator to enslave and to terrify his people. In addition to that, Stalin in no way came to the aid of those of us who were victims of the Nazis, at least not in East Prussia. Yes, he had been victorious over Hitler, but in Königsberg we didn't have associations such as the VVN (*Vereinigung der Verfolgten des Naziregimes* [Union of the Victims of the Nazi Regime]) or *Privilegien für Opfer des Naziterrors* (Privileges for the Victims of Nazi Terror). I detested, of course, with heart and soul every form of dictatorship; democracy, which I had never experienced, seemed to me heaven on earth. In spite of my rejection of Communism, I gradually found the Russian character likable:

their exuberance of feeling, their folk music and dances. As their way of life became more familiar, I began to get used to them. And there was now more and more contact and conversations with them.

One day a Russian heard me playing the violin. He knocked, entered and said that he was connected with the conservatory in Riga. He could make me an offer to study music on a Soviet scholarship. However, I would have to agree to sign up for several years and would have to become a Soviet citizen, otherwise there was no way. Despite the appealing prospect of being relieved of all worries while studying music, this proposal was out of the question. First of all, there were my parents, who still depended on me. Then there was the political and military education that was also part of the curriculum. This was totally out of the question. As a result, the music education I longed for remained only a daydream.

The "German Troupe" was supposed to go on tour to entertain soldiers. I was taken along as the "obligatory violinist." An old opera hand, Herr Mühlhoff, took me under his wing. This was necessary because the arias they all sang were not at all easy for me to accompany. There was the leader of the group who could sing splendidly, Herr Imkamp, and Herr Augustin, and a soprano (whose name I've unfortunately forgotten). She had a tendency to break out in tears, for example, the *Bajazzo* prologue with its accidentals and changes in tempo or the "5,000 Taler" aria. Williott Schwab played, in addition to other tunes, the gypsy songs of Sarasate, accompanied by Frau Fietkau at the piano. Gerda danced, Herr Schulz did the comedy, and the Lilliputians did stunts. We were quite a colorful troupe!

One time we were loaded onto the back of an open truck and driven to Rauschen when it was −30 °C (−22 °F). There the idea was to make the New Year's Eve a bit special for Soviet soldiers who were taking a break. We were so completely frozen that it took hours before we thawed out. By then the Russians were so drunk we only had to play half the program. It was even so cold on the podium of the meeting hall that the walls glimmered with a layer of frost and ice. Schwab tried to play his violin, wearing woolen gloves, a feat he actually pulled off. While we were in the middle of a number, a fierce fistfight erupted for some reason or other. Fists whirled and objects flew through the air. Those knocked to the floor were kicked and beaten to a pulp. A wink to us indicated we should keep on playing. We were quite worried

about how all this would turn out. But soon there were tears, recon-
ciliations, and embraces. Later, I often witnessed similar scenes, and it
amazed me every time to see love follow hatred so quickly.

Finally, finally the first emigration transports begin for German civilians.
This gives hope to anyone still alive. You have to file an application, and
just as with the lottery, someone sometimes receives the emigration
propusk, a Russian visa. There is absolutely no way to figure out what
criteria are used to grant permission to leave.

Mother earns some money by helping applicants fill out the Russian
questionnaires. Father is, at last, needed as a violinist. A pop orchestra
had been formed in the "Club of the Red Army"; a cheap, factory-made
violin is found for him and he is asked to play the second violin part.
The real pay is a full meal. But the most important thing here is that
Father is active again. The club is in the former girls' trade school on
Beethoven Street, right near where we live.

It was 1948 and the previous three years of Russian occupation lay
heavily on us like a terrible eternity. We hadn't received a response to
our application to emigrate. Once again, we were becoming nervous
and discouraged. More and more Germans were emigrating, but we
heard nothing. To watch Germans for more than half a year being
allowed to leave for freedom and not to be among them was, again, a
bitter test of our patience. I had ceased to haggle with fate. To stay alive
was the most important thing.

Just within the previous few months, a young German—his name
was, I think, Siebenhaar—was sentenced by a court to seven years of
forced labor. The charge was a minor theft that would normally be
called theft of comestibles for personal consumption. Whenever I
heard such news, I was always seized with terror, and I had to marvel
that so far I'd gotten away with things so lightly. Such a long sentence
meant the end of every hope.

Mother was advised to help the process of getting our *propusks*
along a bit with a bribe. So off she went to the application office where
it was said that they processed the emigration applications. She took
all the money we could scrape together and gave it to the official,
saying that he would receive a similar payment if he could get us the
emigration *propusks.* We had to wait, straining to earn such a sum
again. As usual, I was playing for dances while Mother "speculated" on

the black market and Father puttered around the house while also playing in the pop orchestra four times a week. But we basically earned our extra rubles by selling *baisers*. This continued to be the basis of our existence. One evening when I came home from playing for dances, my mother greeted me in tears. She told me that the official she had bribed had come up with two emigration *propusks*, but didn't have one for me. I asked Mother at once if she had given or shown him the three hundred rubles that had been the deal. But the shock of no exit visa for me had made her forget the most essential thing. I was almost certain that the missing *propusk* was intended first and foremost as a demand for payment of the remaining bribe. And that turned out to be the case. When Mother rushed off the next day with our rubles for the official, he pulled my completed documents from a drawer. Grinning, he tucked the rubles away without counting them. Mother happily quipped that we very well could've handed him a smaller bribe.

On a certain day, we were supposed to show up near the train station with hand luggage and enough food for seven days. I was drunk with excitement and couldn't believe there was finally going to be an end to the fifteen years of living under an ever more stifling lack of freedom, persecution, discrimination, wretchedness, and threats of death hanging over our heads. I was now nineteen years old and all my ardent hopes for an education had only been dreams. Was I really going to have the chance now to make up for what I had missed? How glorious that would be. Even Father and Mother were walking on clouds, and we found it difficult to keep on baking and selling *baisers* when our thoughts were already in Germany. In a Germany we hadn't the foggiest notion of, a Germany we endowed with a multitude of grand expectations, and which we assumed, after its terrible fall, had become tolerant and wise, a Germany that had forsworn for all eternity its delusions about race and its craving for status.

The days passed slowly, agonizingly slowly, until the day of the transport arrived at last and we found ourselves at the collection point. These collection points, so reminiscent of events of the recent past, had been until now symbols for the beginning or end of something that was always painful: people gathered for party indoctrination, deportation of Jews, evacuation after air raids, escape for refugees, transport before imprisonment or forced labor; but now it was for transport to freedom. This time, it couldn't possibly be the beginning again of something awful, for I considered freedom to be the highest human good. An indescribable feeling of happiness had taken hold of all of us. We had to be careful our joy didn't get out of hand. We joked and laughed and told ourselves all would be well.

We repressed any thought about the final farewell from what had been our homeland for hundreds of years, from the graves of our fore-bears and what had been their domain. We wanted to shake off every-thing as a bad dream as swiftly as possible and to forget as much as possible. To begin a new life, without danger, in new surroundings with completely different people; to see my sister again, who had been living now in Scotland for ten years, separated from her entire family; to study; to eat our fill: this is what was whizzing about in my head. Theatre, concerts, movies, travel, friends, chocolate and oranges—if possible, all of these at once.

We knew about the freight cars from prisoner transports. You could only stand up in the middle of the car as both sides were divided in half along the length of the car so that twice as many people had a place to lie down. In the middle, there was a coal stove and next to it was a pile of briquettes, coal, and some wood. Again there was a barrel, a tin bucket the height of a chair, just as it was in my worst memories of Rothenstein; a makeshift toilet for both men and women alike—right where everyone could see.

It was a large transport with well over a thousand people. After we had been thoroughly checked, the freight cars were filled, one by one, with men and women in no particular order at all. The older people lay down below and we younger ones scrambled above. I was lying next to women and girls, who soon found it very merry to have me in their midst. They sensed my lack of experience—one could call it chastity—and in the very first night caused me deep embarrassment with hands that groped as if by chance. It was an embarrassment that in no way checked my happy giddiness. Even during the day it was rather dark: the heavy doors of the freight cars were bolted from the outside. The air vent flap installed high in the side of the car didn't let much light in and afforded only a few the possibility of looking out. They told the rest of us what they saw, calling out the place names if they could see the signs at the train stations.

The train stood still more than it moved forward. Sometimes the train moved for a few minutes, then stood still again for hours. The trip through Poland took several days, but on occasion the freight cars were opened up and we could get out for a stroll about in nature and to take the first steps on German soil—soil that was still German. Liberated, deep breaths filled our lungs with lovely spring air. Then once again the journey continued its accustomed leisurely pace, meandering back and forth, or so it seemed to us. Somewhere, there was something hot to drink, and then for the first time we were together with people from Germany, who were noticeably unwilling to tell us anything—we were in the Soviet Occupied Zone.

Even we had heard rumors that there were more things to buy in West Germany and that each Occupying Power had introduced its own social order into its German sphere of influence. On that basis alone, the Eastern Zone was less congenial to us than the Western Zones, in which we hoped to make a democratic, in our sense of the word, new start. This all sounds as if we were more knowledgeable than we actually were at the time. Most of us knew what a democracy was only second-hand; and in general, the tales of better supplies available in the Western Zones was the deciding factor. But only those who could prove they had relatives in the West were permitted to go there. We found this out in the quarantine camp of Kirchmöser, which became our destination after five or six days of traveling around, when we were finally permitted to leave the train.

Before any contact, measure, or procedure confronted us, the first thing that greeted us was a thorough delousing and an even more thorough dousing with DDT powder of our clothes in the delousing ovens. The camp officials, irritated by my scraps of Russian uniform, dumped on me and my clothes half a box of a poison later banned, visibly disgusted by the fact that a German could find favor in such clothing—as if the choice had been mine.

I used every free moment to practice violin as if possessed. I got to the point where I could play the violin concerto by Max Bruch and Sarasate's gypsy melodies quite well, taking such joy in the music that nothing in the world mattered more to me.

My parents sent letters to acquaintances living in Berlin as well as to distant relatives; the word quickly spread among them that the "Wiecks" had arrived.

It is certainly easy to imagine my thoughts and those of other young Aussiedler (German resettlers to Germany) in the quarantine camp when a meeting was called to talk about the future and jobs. Every male inmate was ordered, almost under duress, into a room, whose exit was blocked by several officials. We heard a propaganda speech about life in the Russian Occupation Zone, and we quickly caught on this was a recruiting campaign for work in uranium mines. After someone had glowingly described life in the uranium mines as heaven on earth for over an hour, in which the only important criteria seemed to be good pay, housing, and plentiful food—the work itself was not mentioned once—they pulled out prepared lists with our names already printed on them, passed out indelible pens, and told us to sign. When no one wanted to sign, they were going to force us to listen to yet another lecture. At the same time, they blocked the exits to anyone who made a move to leave the room. Immediately, we all realized what was happening, and in a few moments we young men from Königsberg became an enraged mob, capable of anything. We threatened the officials blocking the exits with such an awful beating they feared for their lives if they didn't let us leave at once. We wouldn't hesitate to lay hands on them. With our flashing eyes and a defiance borne of everything we had survived, we compelled them to capitulate without resistance. Our path no longer blocked, we left the room. It was our first shock in the land of our dreams; there would be others.

After this episode, I wanted to escape the camp, and soon found the opportunity. Igna was the daughter of my mother's cousin Lotte Beth, who had committed suicide. Like my sister, Igna had been sent in time to England, and had returned to Berlin after the war. She worked there as a reporter for DEFA, the only state film company in the GDR. They also made newsreels. When Igna heard that we were in Kirchmöser, she persuaded her superiors to make a newsreel feature about our camp, with particular emphasis on the resettlement of the "known musician couple Wieck." And so it happened that one day a truck came rolling into the camp with spotlights, ladders, and cameras, as well as a motor car with several imposing gentlemen to film the story. Of course, cousin Igna was there. After greeting us heartily, and after I had checked out the truck a little bit, our plan was set: I would break out of the camp using the truck to reach Berlin. In Berlin everything would somehow sort itself out. The cameramen were willing to go along.

I didn't need to worry about my parents at this point. They had no obstacles to fear on account of their age, and they could come to Berlin after a three-week period of quarantine with no difficulty. But things were different for us able-bodied men. We could no longer be sure that somehow with subtle coercion we would not find ourselves under some sort of obligation. We would be forbidden to leave the Soviet Zone or they would apply cunning means of persuasion.

After they finished filming, I climbed on the truck when no one was looking. Without being questioned I passed through the fence in the direction of Berlin. There weren't any conspicuous farewells because I thought I would soon see my parents again. But Father soon left us for good right after the quarantine period. His former pupil Gerti took him to Elmshorn, and with that my father disappeared from my life. Two or three visits in Elmshorn and his attendance at a couple of concerts in Hamburg when I was playing there didn't change the fact that we didn't care about each other any more. He divorced my mother and married for a third time. His new beginning brought him twenty happy years, which he considered his reward for courageous endurance. At the age of eighty-eight he died an easy death, while a most painful death by cancer awaited my mother. An incomprehensible trial after a truly difficult life.

By the way, I did see the newsreel feature in a Berlin movie house. I saw with amazement they had used my parents to claim that even old people had been evacuated from East Prussia. But my parents were the only ones over sixty in the camp, and I maintain today that in 1948 there were scarcely any young children or older people of their age among the 15 to 20 percent who had survived. Father and Mother were the exception.

My arrival in Berlin was the great long-awaited moment in my life, a second birth. Now I finally had the chance to decide my own life, to make decisions and carry them out. For the first time, I was free to do as I pleased, to study, to learn, even possibly to travel to a foreign country, or to become what the Berliners call a *jelernten Berliner,* a native-adopted Berliner.

Berlin

The frustration, confusion, and overwhelming challenges a South Sea islander suddenly faces when transplanted to Sydney or an Eskimo encounters in New York couldn't have been greater than what I went through. Igna lived on a side street off the Kurfürstendamm, right near a traffic circle in the center of West Berlin. Just days after I arrived, she took me to see the operetta composer Eduard Künneke, whose wife was a distant relative of my mother. The Künnekes lived on Sybelstrasse in a large Berlin apartment with high ceilings, a main entrance as well as a service entrance, and an enormous music room that could be partitioned with a curtain. Frau Künneke, once a sought-after operetta celebrity, still behaved like a star: unbelievably temperamental and original. She inspected her intimidated relative and immediately determined, not without reason, that this half wild boy first needed to be civilized. She found me not lacking all appeal. So she arranged for me to accompany her and her husband—whom I didn't meet that afternoon—to the movies that very evening. She would take care of getting the additional tickets right away. With that, I was dismissed until the appointed time.

Igna also sought help from the Jewish congregation and got useful suggestions for helping me over a series of bureaucratic hurdles. I went through all of this as if in a trance. My first day of freedom in the great city of Berlin, without fear of Hitler or Stalin—how could I absorb anything like this so quickly? What I really wanted was to retreat to some quiet place and in gratitude contemplate and reflect on my fate. A religious concert would've been more in keeping with my mood than the proposed movie. I looked forward to it well enough, although I really wanted to decline. Nonetheless, I showed up at the promised time at the Künnekes and for the first time met the famous composer with wavy white hair—a conspicuous phenomenon who stood out from everyone else as did the Berlin radio tower from other buildings. We set out together to see the movie *The Twelve Chairs* at the British Information Center. The Berliners twisted around to peek at us, for they recognized the Künnekes as easily as they did Berlin's Mayor Reuter.

I didn't understand a word of the film. I couldn't follow the pace of the story or catch the allusions. I found the spirit and the jokes of the trivial plot intended only as amusement to be totally alien. Frau Künneke also provided running commentary so loud it could be heard all over the theatre. There were moments when people were paying more attention to her than to the film. Since I was sitting right next to her, they were ogling me too. I was very uncomfortable. Anyway, I was close to losing my identity; I was straining to reorient my sense of reality. In such a state, what a person wants to do most of all is hide.

I lay down now at night on the air mattress with a new and unaccustomed sense of inferiority. I was trying to make sense of my emotions and sensations and the impressions of the big city assaulting me. I was struggling to bring them into harmony with the self that had been formed up until now under entirely different circumstances. My points of reference had been set during my life in Königsberg and weren't so easily changed from one day to the next. Once again, it was with my violin where I found refuge. In the tumult that was my soul it gave me something to hold on to. Only here I knew what was really important to me and only through the violin did I have a way to express myself. I practiced as much as I could and could only enjoy the feeling of finally being free when I was practicing. How I had longed for this very feeling.

I was told to join various organizations, for example the VVN (*Vereinigung der Verfolgten des Naziregimes* [Union of Victims of the Nazi Regime]), as only then could I receive a Care package on occasion (these were packages of donations from Americans in the form of canned goods and clothing). I did everything I was told to do, and for the first time, three years after the end of the war, I discovered there were advantages to having been persecuted.

A visit to the synagogue in the Fasanenstrasse left me ambivalent. This no longer had anything to do with God, whom I had felt so close to in Rothenstein. It no longer required the beautiful chanting of the cantor or other mediating rituals for me to turn to God; nonetheless, the melodies always triggered painfully melancholy memories.

An American clothes depot provided me with dark green army underwear that was much too large, gaudy shirts, and a wonderful wool jacket. One of the depot employees asked me where I was from and what I was planning to do. I bitterly recounted a little bit about my Russian experience, whereupon he gave me an address where I could go, saying he had recommended me. They would help me there without delay. He had sent me to an office of the CIC (Counter Intelligence Corps) and probably thought I was qualified to work for this organization on the basis of my experiences. He was very much mistaken. When I saw what was going on, I became quite angry, which I emphatically expressed, since I felt solidarity with the Russians as a people who had been persecuted and horribly mistreated by Hitler. No one was to take me back to a world full of hatred with the intention of harming others.

Not long after I found out that the VVN also was being used to bring about political confrontation. Namely, this organization had been controlled since 1945 by the Communists. I sat down at once to write a blazing letter to the directorate of the VVN, and included my resignation. That was in the fall of 1948. After having barely arrived in Berlin, I personally experienced the ever increasing enmity between the Russians and Americans. After only two months, the Berlin crisis led to the infamous blockade of all roads to the city. This Berlin Blockade has become a part of history. In an unparalleled effort the Allies set out to counter the Russian ploy. The *Luftbrücke* (airlift) saved West Berlin, and me too of course, from falling once more under Russian sovereignty.

But before the American and English planes were flying food into Berlin without a break and before we held a protest in front of the Schöneberg Rathaus against Russian aggression, I enrolled in the Berlin Conservatory to study music. Unfortunately, the semester (or trimester) at the university for music was well under way. Since Professor Heinz Thiessen, the director of the Stern Conservatory, which in those days was independent of the *Hochschule für Musik* (Academy for Music), was originally from Königsberg and remembered my parents quite well, the normal entrance procedures were waived and I was accepted. With that, I finally received the long-awaited official permission to move to West Berlin, where I had been living illegally. My entrance examination was accompanied by Professor Thiessen on piano—I played the first and second movement of Bruch's violin concerto. I got into the class of Professor Lessmann, whose playing, although very good, lacked spirit. Nonetheless, I applied for a place at the acclaimed Music School for the summer semester. After successfully passing the entrance exam, I studied with Rudi Schulz, a violinist whom I knew and venerated from listening to radio with earphones in Königsberg. I had a strange feeling that the powers of fate were at work here too.

Meanwhile, my mother had arrived in Berlin and established contact with a number of people who came from Königsberg. She could stay with the Künnekes, who gave her a room. It was heated with a small stove—a so-called "cannon stove"—that was put up where there had once been central heating. The stovepipe was simply rammed through the wall to the outside. All Berlin was full of stovepipes protruding from the walls. If Mother wanted some heat, she heated with briquettes and coal, which were still rationed at the time.

I moved in with other acquaintances: the family Weise, who lived at Breitenbachplatz No. 12, welcomed me like a son. Frau Weise was the former Eva Stern, whose father was a well-known Königsberg physician who had taken his life when he was about to be deported. The head of the household was Little Paul Weise, who so resembled the conductor Wilhelm Furtwängler that he was often taken for him. Their lovely daughter Andrea was seventeen years old and already had a serious boyfriend. This made it possible for our relationship to be an uncomplicated brother-sister one. While living there, I enjoyed a wonderful period of youth and studies. I had a chance to develop. Wonderful is certainly not the definitive word for the condition in which I found myself: not only did I have something new to digest every day, but I also had to make up for lost time. My lack of general knowledge, current information, understanding of politics and its ideological ramifications forced me to read, to question, and to discuss everything possible. There was at the time a very good newspaper in the American Sector of Berlin, the *Neue Zeitung,* which had highly qualified people writing for it. The *Monat,* too, was a magazine with very high standards. In these forums, there were discussions about the past and attempts to understand the present. My thinking was very much influenced by both journals. Unfortunately, both these publications later folded.

For most people, the only thing of any importance was to rebuild.

Everybody pitched in, worked hard, very hard, and with work as an excuse they repressed a lot. With undiminished intensity, I kept thinking about the phenomena of National Socialism and anti-Semitism. There were too many open questions. At the same time I was fascinated by Spinoza's *Ethics,* and ever since I have called myself a Spinozist. My views of God and man were definitively formed by him. Spinoza defines God in Propositions 14 and 15 of his *Ethics* (Part I): "Besides God no substance can be granted or conceived.... Whatsoever is, is in God, and without God nothing can be, or be conceived." And in Proposition 43 (Part III) it says: "Hatred is increased by being reciprocated, and can on the other hand be destroyed by love." How very true! Such theorems answered many questions, and when he also says that every human can, through his own cognition, grant reason that dwells within the strength and power to choose (Part V), that was also just as important.

I had quite a lot to do to catch up with other students on the violin and was practicing up to ten hours a day. I now know the countless hours spent practicing were fairly pointless, but I hoped to prove myself worthy of the privileged fate of "someone who had gotten out" with energy, hard work, and determination. That, by the way, was the case with a lot of people.

My brother-in-law's family invited my mother and me to Edinburgh. The reunion, so long dreamed of, with Miriam, her husband, and my niece, Barbara, was an encounter of brother and sister who had become strangers. Many years later, after we had come to understand each other better, Miriam said how strange she had found my letters and admitted that before our reunion she had been worried and anxious. In my letters, unreal assumptions about her life and English liberty must have been sprinkled with references to my Russian experiences that were equally incomprehensible to her. The reality, however, was that the brother and sister who were meeting now had each been formed for exactly ten years by very different worlds of experiences; even their laughter, gestures, and appearance, once so similar, could not overcome the abyss that now separated them.

Miriam's husband, Hans, a mathematician and son of Viennese emigrants, belonged to a circle of respected Jews living in Scotland, whose views and beliefs originated in a different world. That I felt horribly ill at ease despite their generous hospitality was rooted in this difference. All the pleasurable little things, such as going to the pubs, walking around the city, visits to the castle, conversations, light jokes, gave me a stomachache. It was as if I were squandering costly time in wanton idleness. Several times I fled to a garage, where I could practice my violin to my heart's content. For me, that was the most important thing in the world.

Our emotional lives were filled with such different pictures, sensations, sorrows, and habits that we assumed it was too difficult to comprehend each other and gave up before we made an attempt in this direction. How lonely my thirteen-year-old sister must have felt in a strange land—first in college, then in Edinburgh—how her love for Hans enabled her, like Cinderella, to become part of a successful Jewish emigrant circle. Here, however, she was obliged to fit in with different ways of living and thinking. With no means of her own and dependent on charity, her self-esteem suffered. And when she was finally able to study and was successful—the conductor Sir John Barbirolli wanted her in his famous Hallé Orchestra—she discovered she was pregnant. The dream of independence, music, and liberty she had struggled so hard for was shattered and her life began as a wife and mother at the side of a scientist who advanced only slowly at first. At that time we didn't understand that music and our violins always offered salvation in our hour of need—just as much for me as for her—and that very thing could have been the bridge that connected us at once.

I returned to Berlin earlier than planned, probably insulting Miriam's in-laws, who had paid for the trip and my stay. Today, I'm ashamed that I needed years before I could understand my sister's life. My lack of understanding lasted the same length of time as it took to consider my own life in some perspective.

The Allies broke the Russian blockade. We made a special trip to the Tempelhof Airport to watch the transport planes landing and taking off in a continuous stream, bringing all the foodstuffs and other goods that Berlin needed. Some deliveries were already spoiled foodstuffs that had probably been pulled from warehouses with ancient inventory. None of this prevented us from enjoying life. Only I was increasingly hindered by my growing shyness in dealing with other people. Anywhere I was invited I found it impossible to be relaxed and spontaneous. This in turn affected everyone there, so I turned down invitations, choosing instead to practice my violin and to cultivate eccentricity. I was tormented more than anything else by the curse of reflection. I constantly worried about how others were reacting to me.

But as had so often happened in my life, the right thing happened for me at the right moment. A school friend named Hildegard came to visit Andrea. I fell in love and found in Hildegard a sympathetic person who gently began to take me, a somewhat eccentric stranger, in hand and slowly, with clever psychology, she turned me little by little into a "useful person." We were married in 1950.

Birth Pangs

What I loved doing became my profession: playing the violin. My children were born. Friends came along. Everything that had been a nightmare slowly faded away. Nonetheless, there were reminders that proved past events still cast a shadow.

Why did I so completely lose my temper if I was late for a subway train and encountered an official in the ticket booth armed with his ticket punch—they still punched tickets in those days. I was convinced that the fellow took his time with my ticket, just long enough until he was sure that I couldn't catch the train waiting on the platform. I cursed him out as a KZ guard and damned Nazi, no longer able to check my outbursts. The same thing happened in a government office after a bureaucrat doubted me when I gave the wrong date that the Star of David had become mandatory.

There was an acquaintance who, with the arrogance of youth, seemed to enjoy picking at my wounds. It went something like this: "Herr X, who's a Jew himself, thinks that Jews are themselves responsible for the hatred in the world around them. What do you think?" Or: "Herr Y, who's a Social Democrat, said that the Treaty of Versailles, unemployment, and Jewish influence forced Hitler to act." Or: "The Russian atrocities and the inhumanity of the Russian and English air raids on the civil population were just as bad." After surprise attacks like these, he took delight in the awkwardness I then suffered when I couldn't refute his assertions in a few sentences.

Of course, one can't abolish evil with evil, just as one can't eradicate black with black. Hitler could only be defeated by force. It wasn't enemies but his delusions of grandeur that made him act as he did. Certainly no one will contest that Jews, too, are human beings. But for me, "the Jews" were people who watched over my childhood; "the Jews"

were relatives, school friends, and teachers. All of them dear, honorable, industrious people who were cruelly "exterminated." I couldn't
bring them back to life to introduce them to those who never had met
a Jew. I found unbearable that such talk assumed the fate of these poor
souls was partly self-inflicted. I blanched and began to stutter. Instead
of being able to gradually unload the burdens of the past, I was forced
first of all to prove with facts and arguments what the horrible events
had been. In addition, everyone wanted me to absolve them specifi-
cally of any responsibility. In this way, I came to learn that the capacity of the self-righteous and the conceited to blind themselves to the
truth knows no limit.

Remorse and mourning generally existed only in reference to oneself. Most had suffered terrible losses themselves and had been forced
to make sacrifices. Which of the victims were the cause and which were
the consequences was no longer the issue. Suffering was suffering.
There had been killing on both sides and in the end the suffering on
both sides was an even score. Over, done with. And that wasn't even
the mildest form of unwillingness to comprehend. I preferred to hide
my Jewishness in order to avoid repeated stabs to the heart. But concealing it just stirred up the feelings of guilt again. I can't describe the
galling feeling that lasted for weeks if I remained silent when I should
have spoken out, where an immediate word of protest should have
been spoken and the lack of opportunity, courage, strength, or time
had stopped me.

The desire to emigrate occurred more and more often. In 1956, I
finally went to Israel—on my own. I wanted to look around and see if
it could become home for me and my family. That, however, turned
out to be impossible. The intolerance of the Orthodox Jews would have
made life for my gentile wife and my children like that of Jews in so
many countries. The young state wanted to exist solely for its own
people. The Arab population gave them problems enough. For us,
Israel as a new homeland was out of the question.

Our little house was cozy and in winter it was warm. In the autumn,
we even had grapevines spreading across the canopy to the terrace we
had built ourselves. My work was satisfying; I played the violin from
my soul and often was overcome with emotion. We lacked for nothing, why was I seeking something else? The urge to emigrate finally
surfaced again and couldn't be suppressed. Dreams were so frightful
that when staying in hotels on concerts tours I was always worried

about frightening my colleagues by calling out in my sleep or yelling or talking and betraying my problems.

What was that in Rothenstein when I swore eternal gratitude to God and promised that I would always be satisfied with fresh sea air and smoked fish as the greatest happiness? To what extent did my life now relate to my thoughts then? Did my new beginning mean that the oath of those days no longer counted for anything, that the claim of my classmates to some sort of justice and vindication no longer needed to be considered just because they were dead? Was the exhortation to remain a Jew only routine habit of the rabbi, and was the congregation weeping at the sight of the empty seats an outlandish scene from a tragedy—and nothing more? No, I shall never forget anything of what happened. But these are solely my personal wounds, others have theirs—and who knows, perhaps even worse ones. Let's not go on blaming each other. Only I draw the line—I and I alone—when I must answer in order to remain true to myself and to those who have perished. Do I draw the line at Lorenz and Globke? Or preferably much further back, at Eichmann and Himmler or Hitler? Or not at all? Reconciliation, forgiveness, and a new beginning for murderers and their supporters too?

A Conversation

There probably will never again be a time in my life that my heart doesn't begin to pound or I don't become agitated when there's talk somewhere of "the Jews." Is it fear of encountering hatred and contempt even now or is it, each time, a deep hope of finally meeting an understanding and unprejudiced person? One often talked of "the Jews." "The Jews" were this or that, did this or that, wanted this or that; therefore for everyone who spoke like this there must have been something fundamentally different about "the Jews." Something that made them different not only on account of their different faith (which was of little matter anyway to assimilated Jews), but of their nature. If Jews were basically considered as something different, what then was the difference? If I criticized such notions, they looked at me with pity as if to say, "Ah yes, but you too are indeed one of 'them.'"

There were also friends and many young people who made an effort by their convictions alone to make the world a more tolerant and peaceful place. The hours I spent with them have remained important moments in my life. When we got together back in those days—after the war—we sat on crates. We didn't have any money for furniture and we washed our children's diapers by hand. Economic recovery and reconstruction were just beginning. The manufacturers of consumer goods produced whatever was in demand in spasmodic waves. The surge in the production of radios, washing machines, and refrigerators came only later, and later still, television. In its place we enjoyed visiting each other often and held animated discussions on all sorts of topics, sometimes with considerable knowledge. I'd like to relate one such conversation, freely reconstructed—even though I'm well aware that short discussions about anti-Semitism can't ever do justice to such a complicated subject.

V.: There's always a reason for the hostility!

M.: You mean anti-Semitism, perhaps?

V.: Yes, that too.

S.: I'm sure you can only overcome this hostility if you know what causes it.

K.: But there are sometimes so many complicated reasons, many of which are buried in the subconscious, and they can't be examined rationally simply because you don't even know that they're there.

M.: I believe a person is able to analyze his biases and their causes if only he makes an honest enough effort.

V.: Let M. just try to explain anti-Semitism.

G.: But please leave out the primitive reasons such as the Jews are the ones who killed the son of God, they are guilty of everything, they can cast spells, and so on.

K.: What do you mean by primitive reasons? Are religious reasons primitive ones? Religious people are aware of nothing if not their religion.

M.: Religious reasons are certainly the main cause. Historically, the Christian persecution of the Jews reached its first high point at the Third and Fourth Lateran Councils during the reign of Pope Innocent III (1198–1216). They accused the Jews of being allied to heretics and passed terrible laws that discriminated against the Jews. That happened when the papacy was historically at the height of its worldly power, against which even the Staufer empire shattered. Intolerance became a state doctrine and simultaneously the essence of Christianity—Christian compassion—was sacrificed to greed for worldly power. Christians were forbidden to employ Jews to work for them, to live among them, and Jews were excluded from all public offices. So that everyone would know who was a Jew, they were forced to publicly wear a badge or a tall Jew hat to mark them so that they were visible to everyone. From that moment on, Jews became outsiders stripped of their rights by the virtue of state doctrine, and so they remained with slight variations into our own time. Each of us knows, of course, that outsiders easily become scapegoats.

K.: That the Christian religion and Christian culture had a Jewish origin disturbed the Nazis the most. Hitler fought the Church in an unsuccessful attempt to shake off the Jewish inheritance they hated; that and Auschwitz and a revived Germanic cult strengthened Christianity in the long run. At the same time, this fortified the Jews' determination to found their own state.

V.: What was going on in the time before Jesus?

M.: The pagans were tolerant of other religions as long as their cult practices weren't disturbed. In antiquity, it was the Jews who, unfortunately, must be called intolerant. They had a "jealous" God—Yahweh. Jews were not allowed to show religious reverence for other gods or kings. It's explicitly stated in Deuteronomy (17:2–7).

V.: Reason enough for anti-Judaism among non-Jews at the time.

S.: You could explain the past with all these historical tales. But today there's no longer the influence of the Church, and in most countries Jews are citizens with equal rights. Nonetheless, you can make the case for an anti-Semitism motivated by more than religion.

M.: Anti-Semitism motivated by something other than religion usually comes from feelings of fear and envy; from the fear of new ideas and the changes they bring (Marx, Freud, Schoenberg, Einstein), as well as envy of a group that seems to be more independent and more successful.

G.: There aren't just Russian, American, German, Yemeni Jews but, besides the whole spectrum of human types, there are also Orthodox, free-thinking, rich, poor, smart, and simple-minded Jews. You can't overlook the fact that Jews have argued and fought violently among themselves: Orthodox, liberal, free-thinking, and agnostic Jews. Also, Polish Jews looked down on Lithuanian Jews, Russian Jews on Polish Jews, and German Jews on Russian Jews. You would have to first find characteristics that differentiated all Jews from non-Jews and not just the peculiarities of a few before you can advance a rational reason for an anti-Semitism that's not based on religion.

V.: I believe there is a Jewish sense of community that connects all the members of a club or a sect. The solidarity of people who are threatened by the same thing, who know about their past sufferings and worry about future ones. They are used to thinking rationally; that in turn enables them to meet a challenge better than other groups. America, the land of equal opportunity for all immigrants, proves this quite convincingly. Moreover, Jews are often afflicted with neuroses that form in all minority groups and that's quite a catalogue: from craving admiration to over-sensitivity.

S.: Any way to refute that?

K.: If at all, that's true only for minorities—not for those people, then, living in Palestine (Israelis).

M.: ... and is only to be seen as a sweeping statement.

K.: Why should Jews of all people be used to thinking rationally?

G.: Because a group that has been threatened with extinction over the centuries can't afford to assess the facts incorrectly without paying for it—frequently with their lives. They have to try to protect themselves, and the only trump cards they could hold and play were knowledge and, if need be, money. There were scarcely any illiterate Jews since a requirement of the bar mitzvah is that a thirteen-year-old read from the Torah.

S.: Isn't knowledge and money often compensation, a means of acquiring greater security and social prestige?

K.: Oh yes. But here you shouldn't forget the myriad of professional restrictions Jews had to contend with.

M.: In this way, people are formed by the world in which they live—be it socially, ethnically, religiously, even racially, et cetera—but at the same time they have an effect on the world that shapes them. So the links between cause and effect are infinite.

V.: Couldn't minorities too be made responsible for their fate as well?

M.: Among the countless links between cause and effect, the decisive, determining fact in human relations is power and powerlessness, which I generally hold to be the most important in its effect on human behavior. Minorities are, as a rule, always in the position of being weaker and therefore more threatened (except for some typically colonial situations such as in South Africa). And as in politics or in every workplace the stronger person, the more powerful one always has responsibility for the welfare of those who are dependent on him. Among all the formative causes, power and powerlessness have a very special significance and as such these concepts are a topic for discussion in themselves.

K.: Are you trying to say that guilt always belongs to the powerful?

M.: Yes, inasmuch as the terrible, enormous guilt is mostly a result of abuse of power and the more powerful person has a greater latitude to act. As, for example, Pope Innocent III or Hitler with respect to the Jews.

V.: But you could always say that the characteristics of Jews we've already mentioned provoked anti-Semitic reactions.

M.: Even if they seem occasionally more talented, richer, more sensitive, held different beliefs, and stuck to themselves, that wouldn't really be characteristics that could be called negative. Those who hate Jews have invented something bad or generalized from individual cases. Apparently, they assume, if they feel hatred there must, of course, be reasons for it. Studies and statistics prove, however, that all the accusations of the Nazis were untrue. The criminality of Jews had been at times a percentage—depending on the type of crime—nearly five times less than their percentage of the population. Only, such examples of numbers have little effect on anything, and Theodor Herzl—the author of *Der Judenstaat* (*The Jewish State*) and thus the founder of Zionism—said of a similar statistic: "Such studies, like many other 'defenses,' are based on the mistaken notion that one can refute anti-Semitism with logic. They truly hate us supposedly just as much for our merits as for our flaws."

S.: With the Nazis it was also a question of ideology according to which the Aryan race was of higher value and all other races—the Jews in particular, which can't really be called a uniform race by the way—were inferior. So inferior that they either had to be "exterminated" or were just good enough for slavery, like the Slavs for example. National Socialism with its ideology of race was one of the most momentous monstrosities of the human intellect.

M.: . . . and the proof that humans can be turned into heartless monsters once they succumb to delusion.

V.: I would like to know whether the arguments offered here are sufficient to explain a hatred that made possible the incomprehensible events under the Nazis?

K.: No, absolutely not!

V.: So then, our attempt to do so is a failure.

M.: We wanted to find the reasons for the hatred and prejudice. If hostility is inflamed by demagoguery—be it religious or political—to feelings of hatred, the line of irrationality and madness is crossed. Irrationality and madness are immune to logical explanations.

S.: . . . and that seems to me to sum up our conversation.

Such conversations surely didn't bring exhaustive analysis to bear, but nonetheless they helped us gain greater insight into certain questions and revealed how deeply rooted the causes of a given phenomenon can be.

Birth Pangs 2

This eternal on-the-one-hand-and-then-on-the-other!

> We become friends with a very nice man. A reference to his time in the
> military in the Lichterfeld Barracks pops up in a subordinate clause. I'm
> thinking: Weren't the Lichterfeld Barracks SS-barracks, where they shot
> Hitler's opponents by the hundreds?

When I visited my cousin Dorothea Wieck, she told me—at my
request—about her meeting with Hitler. These were pretentious receptions where the party bosses invited famous artists, and Dorothea was
one of the best-known UFA stars. Hitler requested or ordered her to
be his dinner companion. Dorothea thought that her simple tempera-
ment made Hitler feel relaxed and that was the reason why she was the
recipient of this dubious honor. The conversations, however, were banal,
and mostly they talked about the disadvantages and problems of being
famous personalities who could no longer move about unselfcon-
sciously, freely, or anonymously. He was really very charming, she said!

My father-in-law remarked several times that Jewish scientists had
managed to emigrate early enough to save themselves. But wasn't the
company for which he was working at the time also responsible for
Hitler's successes and his ability to operate freely? He also told of his
time in the Buchenwald concentration camp. Not the one guarded by
the SS where most of the inmates did not survive, but the Buchenwald
concentration camp that the Russians continued after the surrender.
They too had it bad, and my father-in-law organized lectures and worship services.

The catalogue of this sort of on-the-one-hand-but-on-the-other-
hand stories went on without end, and I kept it to myself that these

stories made me ill. Stories of officers who refused (only after the period of initial victories was over, of course) to be the "devil's generals," stories of resistance fighters who had previously voted for Hitler, then failed when they tried to save what still could be saved, or stories of erstwhile deceived Hitler Youths and girls who were executed during the war for failing to carry out orders.

Just where were those who said, "Because I did this or that at the time, because I believed, said, wrote this or that at the time, I am also responsible for a development I most deeply regret. Based on this experience, I shall be especially on guard that something like this will never happen again. I shall always point out to people the fatal danger of certain tendencies, which although they are now in a completely different context, can lead to similar events involving the same principles." Surely there were many such people, only I practically never encountered them. I would have liked to have flung my arms around their necks—in my imagination, at least. Instead, people persistently glossed over things, kept silent, downplayed things, made excuses, blamed others, and justified themselves, for so long until most people believed themselves that everything had been completely very different from what it had really been.

I decided to emigrate for a number of reasons. The Wall built in 1961 closing off West Berlin was one of them. Another came from New Zealand, a country I discovered on my tour of Asia with the Berlin Chamber Orchestra. An enchanting country. So much pristine nature, where else could such untouched nature still be found? In addition, there was the offer from the University of Auckland of a teaching position, which meant new tasks and responsibilities for educating young people. Auckland is the largest city in New Zealand, surrounded by infinite ocean and lovely beaches. Volcanic hills and subtropical vegetation account for a diverse and beautiful landscape. The clear air, stirred gently by breezes, is always delightful.

Together with my family I left what had been my home until now, certain of finding a better one. I define "home" here as the human and cultural shell, for my East Prussian home was lost never to be restored. We directed our eyes and thoughts from the steamer toward the distant horizon as it came into focus, where a speck of land would appear that we would call home. But soon I came to compare home with parents; you can't change them according to whim. After seven years we finally realized that our roots couldn't be torn from German soil. Only at the other end of the world what those roots meant to us became clear. Wishing and wanting had little effect. What nourished these roots suddenly became more vital to us than the sun on the lemon tree and the beach behind the house. It was as if it had to be rammed into my head that certain values cannot be misused as commodities and easily exchanged. Home, without a doubt, is one of them.

Oddly enough, it just happened to be my New Zealand colleague who turned out to be a wily anti-Semite. We played chamber music together very well. I could also not rule out a similar attitude on the part of my immediate supervisor, the head of the department. I had emigrated to the other end of the world precisely not to have to put up with this. (The anti-Semitism of two Englishmen who had immigrated after the war was not at all typical of New Zealanders. There weren't more helpful people on the face of the earth. It was just striking that I of all people ended up exposed to these exceptions to the rule.)

What had been a belief of mine for a long time became after my far-flung flight a certainty: all people, be they musicians or politicians, Germans or New Zealanders, Jews or Christians, the persecutors or the persecuted, are frighteningly the same irrespective of different temperaments, ideals, and conventions. In all of us resides the potential for every possible action, even those actions born out of hatred. There are, moreover, powerful compulsions that are triggered when people find themselves in certain kinds of situations, whether of unlimited power or impotent dependency. Particularly critical here is that timid obsequiousness of the latter feeds the appetite of the former to dominate the other and vice versa. People only become likeable when they have an aptitude for reason and the possibility, based on insight and recognition, to counter their disastrous compulsions—consciously deciding in favor of love. All my hopes are based on human nature being endowed with this ability.

During my stay in New Zealand, the reasons that had once prompted us to leave Germany dwindled. Not that the horror pushed far away seemed any less horrible. But wasn't it true that Hitler had branded me a Jew and then Stalin, a German? Didn't the years of suffering shared with East Prussians mark me too? Yes, after everything that had happened, it depressed me to belong both to the nation of perpetrators as well as to the nation of victims. If you have experienced, however, as I have, how quickly even completely normal people can become perpetrators or victims, then it is with great trepidation that you always see both possibilities in every person—no matter what group that person happens to belong to.

The difficult decision to return was made. In the music profession there is always the particular risk of wanting to begin again at forty. Our children had to be uprooted a second time. By now, Thomas had reached the age of seventeen; Miriam, sixteen; David, thirteen; and Emmanuel, nine.

Mirror Images

Enjoying life, music, and all lovely things marked my life after my return, for which I thank God—whom else?—with all my heart. But there were developments that darkened the heavens: developments that recall the story of the frogs that hop out at once if put into hot water, but die miserably if the water is heated slowly because they fail to recognize the danger.

To what extent will we poison our world with chemicals and radioactive materials? There isn't any doubt at all that a lot of this harm is irreversible.

Why are so many young people attracted to those who, with clenched fists, demand more "security," "fair borders," and "Germany for the Germans"—and what do they actually mean? Border corrections through strength? Laws against minorities? Have they already forgotten how the former perpetrators also hid behind euphemisms for ideas that were taboo? Back then, they shouted about the "Fatherland" and invaded neighboring countries; they demanded "Germanness" and destroyed culture; they glorified the "Aryan" and murdered millions.

The steps on the way to disaster are very much the same even if Nature in her inexhaustible wealth of invention varies the circumstances. Somewhere one group always marginalizes another, latent hostility that's never vanished grows into enmity and hatred. And the next catastrophe doesn't occur because only the available weapons are so destructive—who can be certain even of that? Hope? Yes! There's the thing called human reason. As long as our final destiny still lies open, each one of us must and should hope.

When yesterday's wartime enemies, now that they've become friends, dramatically shake hands against the backdrop of military cemeteries, the last war is neither rendered undone nor can it stop the next one.

To stop that one, the enemies of tomorrow absolutely must shake hands today and not just for the television cameras or for the sake of propaganda. The hand that is held out in reconciliation, the deeds that offer it and the renunciation of abuse of power must be a matter of daily practice; this is the only way to secure a peaceful coexistence.

> At the funeral for the father of his best friend, Emmanuel asks me to play with him the slow movement of the Mozart duo for violin and viola. In the cemetery chapel after the ceremony, a group of older men, about ten or so, glowering darkly, suddenly drape their *Ritterkreuze* (Knight's Crosses) around their necks and march in front of the coffin.

The medals they're still so proud of today—how many lives did the members of the deceased's club kill to earn them?

In working with Conductor C., we could study at close quarters the behavior of an impulsive, egocentric genius as well as that of the people he dominated. C. uses the power he has by virtue of exercising his talent and strength of will without much scruple; he arouses both fear and admiration in the hearts of others. But this fear has the effect of turning many people each time in a new and frightening way into compliant underlings, silent sufferers, and only one or two heroes. But it is the compliant underlings who feed the desire for power that grows into dizzying self-delusion.

> Once again I'm on a concert tour and after a stop in Moscow and several more hours of flight we suddenly recognize the coastline and the broad sea. If you look closely, you can see the exact outlines of the Courland Spit—just like those on a map—and I'm already feverish and trembling. Now we are flying right over Königsberg, and my thoughts are pulled back to the time when I was very young and back to the cursed war and postwar years. Thirty thousand feet above Königsberg I feel as if I'm my own ghost and want to understand what life and my personal fate are supposed to mean. There below, I lived for years in the most dire need, and now I'm flying over it all while I sit in the lap of luxury. I'm searching my memory for anything that would've allowed me to foresee my future back then. I can't recall anything of the sort, although I did have, without a doubt, premonitions of imminent danger or immediate peril to people close to my heart.

According to the teaching of the Zen master, individual awareness cannot be fixed. The memory must safeguard instantaneous certainties. For me awareness is also sensation. A definite feeling of something "lying behind it all" that always resists being put into words. Very early on, I was fascinated by the fact that behind everything we know there is always something lurking, like a constant provocation.

To communicate something of whatever is lying behind it all, in notes, colors, or poetry, seems to me what all serious artists are really concerned with. But too often their works have only the characteristic of mirrors. After all, the mirror has been the symbol for thousands of years of only the reflection of what is already there. It cannot make visible what is invisible or add anything itself.

I experienced just how strong the sensations in me can be when these sensations revealed whatever was "lying behind it all" on my second concert tour in Israel. This was with the Radio Symphony Orchestra of Stuttgart, of which I was now a member. The sun shone, as usual in Israel, bright and warm. We had a morning free, and I went to the Wailing Wall in the Jewish section of Old Jerusalem. This impressive wall with its huge rectangular blocks of stone that centuries and human destructiveness have barely touched bears witness to the distant past about which we surely know less than the bible lets us believe. On the fenced-off stone surface directly in front of the bare Wall, there were men in black milling about. Some were praying, continually bowing according to ritual. Others came or went, while small groups were holding celebrations at several tables set up in front. It was Sabbath, and several boys were being bar mitzvahed. It was obvious that the thirteen-year-olds felt their Jewish promise to God to be a momentous event. Right near me was a boy who very much resembled me at that age; he was chanting his Torah portion directly in front of me. The Torah was lying on a beautiful blue velvet cloth. The rabbi, a cantor, and relatives and friends, so I assume, were standing close by. All were wrapped in white talliths. Then it happened: against my will, the gap between me and this bar mitzvah disappeared. Awestruck by the boy's solemnity, the reality of Jerusalem turned into my own Königsberg past. Now it was I who was standing before the Torah, and it was as if all my joys, sorrows, doubts, and memories washed over me all at once; they burst forth from the depths of my soul with such force that I lost control. Bitter tears were proof of wounds not yet healed—either they were an agonizing warning not to forget—or they were a thunderous voice, saying, "Hark, Michael, 'the Eternal' is Thy God, 'the Eternal' is one!" I do not know.

In Israel, Ruth Auerbach, formerly Ulla Pik, and Tamar Peled, formerly Hannelore Winterfeld, have organized a reunion of former pupils of the Jewish school of Königsberg. Many of them had emigrated to Israel in the mid-thirties. The cozy little living room in the Maagan-Michael Kibbutz is filled with people. They want me to tell them what the end of the war had been like. When the nine of us former Königsberg pupils— in the company of our spouses—begin to speak, we discover a coincidence. It is April 9, six o'clock. On this day at this very hour, the Königsberg Festungskommandant Lasch signed the surrender that came too late. This hour was therefore the hour of death for Prussian Königsberg, which we and our parents had so loved and which had been our homeland.

I am greatly moved by the reunion, but it seems unreal to me and is way too brief for me to learn everything I want to know and to tell what everyone wants to hear. Nonetheless, we speak of the circumstances that enabled each of us to survive and we remember those whom we can only mention by name. A meeting after forty-five or fifty years is already a gathering that is a memorial service to remember those left behind, the relatives, friends, teachers, and schoolmates who were murdered.

Surely, the most important thing, more important than anything else, is the constant worry about the future of our children and grandchildren and the constant reminder that we—and we alone—bear responsibility for the circumstances we create for our children's future. But a prerequisite for doing justice to this responsibility is knowing what happened and hearkening to the voices of the dead. This book is dedicated to them.

Afterword
To the Seventh German Edition

It mustn't happen again! It is imperative to know that we must make the outbreak of war between nations impossible in an age of terrible weapons of inconceivable mass destruction.

The Königsberg philosopher Immanuel Kant expressed the idea over two hundred years ago that the key to perpetual peace (the title of his essay) is a state consisting of nations. In Kant's state, the individual nations must conduct themselves in the manner of responsible citizens in a federal republic. I believe that to establish such a state of nations, before it is too late, is the most pressing task of every person alive today.

The time when war is the continuation of politics by other means must be relegated to the past. Every new war carries innumerable risks for everyone in the world. Before we even begin this effort, we must overcome many a false premise and outmoded tradition—traditions that have only served until now to mold a country's subjects for war. We must overcome the glorification of territorial expansion achieved by aggressive war; we must reject the commemoration of deeds considered manly and heroic that are no more than men killing fellow men. Every advantage secured by force to the disadvantage of another plants the seed for new hatred and new violence.

Global cooperation among human beings is the path to peace, national conflict is the path to war.

Reader Response

I have received over four hundred letters and they all touched me deeply. They describe unbelievable fates. Even now I recall the cruelty I experienced without comprehending it; I consider the hatred, the obsessed dictators, and the orgy of violence that was the war to be the most terrible of evil. Some responses supplemented my own account with important details. Two of my classmates, whom I assumed were dead, contacted me. I was sent the *Deutsche Reichsbahn* (German Reich Railway) report confirming the deportation from Königsberg (which I described at the beginning of the book) and a copy of the original execution report, the *Geheime Reichssache* (Top Secret of the Reich), written by SS Colonel Jäger. I also received reports by telephone from eyewitnesses who had been present and watched what the murderers did. In every case, words fail to convey and the mind cannot grasp what cannot be imagined. It worries me to see how the memory of evil deeds is misused as a sort of drug to titillate, a drug which the media peddle to entertain the consumer. By doing this, we waive a critical chance to learn from the past.

In looking back on my life, I can see that even without war we are in the process of destroying the basis of our existence—nature. I believe a fundamental misconception is our notion of God, which is too childish, resulting in an arrogant and egoistic view of ourselves. More and more, we pay a terrible price for the notion of a personal God (Our Father, who art in Heaven), which secularizes nature. There is a price to be paid for the idea that man is made in God's image, which prevents us from seeing fully our own potentially dangerous and destructive natures. Of course, our human nature also has constructive and loving elements. We are no more, no less than a tiny little particle (perhaps in substance even immortal) of the wondrous whole that is still beyond what we can imagine—before which I bow down in awe. "Besides God no substance can be granted or conceived" (Benedictus de Spinoza).

February 2001

Appendices

Glossary

Works Cited

Appendix 1

A Letter

September 1, 1987

Dear Menachem and Shoshana,

I was delighted to receive your prompt and spontaneous response to my book manuscript, and I can't thank you enough. Shoshana's compliments were good for me and the corrections and commentary very useful. Most pleasing was your characterization of my book as "A Requiem for an Admittedly Small But Beautiful Community." And that's exactly what it's supposed to be.—

Menachem is asking questions about my "identity," and I admit that it isn't an easy question for me to answer. To do so, I have to take a position I've long since abandoned. Today I find that a given identity is always a mental uniform. Often these uniforms serve only to tell friend from foe. My enemies are not specific groups of people, but destructive tendencies in all people. (I'll try to explain this later.)

Your question is "Is the Michael who escaped Stalin in 1948 now an uprooted East Prussian of Jewish faith, shaped by everything that happened during the Nazi period, or is he a Jew who has finally found his true and final identity?" In Berlin, perhaps, I was an uprooted East Prussian. I yearned for the beautiful East Prussian landscapes and the sea. The city of Königsberg, however, had been destroyed. A pile of rubble buried tragedies and catastrophes, which I can think of only with a shudder. The rubble pile also buried my lovely memories of childhood. I felt my student years that followed in Berlin to be a gift from heaven itself—a rebirth. We were so thankful then to be among those who had survived. I posted these thanks to the same address that I used in times of my greatest need and that recipient had long since ceased to be only a God of the Jews. I do admit that experiencing the bar mitzvah at the Wailing Wall in Jerusalem revealed to me that Judaism was deeply rooted in my heart, but my musings have taken me far beyond the prescribed beliefs, laws, and customs.

The fact that I am Jewish will occupy my thoughts as long as I can think. Today, however, this is less pressing than in times past. As I've indicated earlier, I find other questions more important. For example, whether all people (no matter what

243

race, nationality, or religion) aren't subject to fatal psychological mechanisms that are genetically programmed—how can it be otherwise? Such mechanisms surely govern all our reactions and not just those in extreme situations, such as in positions of great power or in the deepest moments of fear for our existence. They fatally govern what we feel, think, and do. (Mechanisms that will, ultimately I fear, endanger our continued existence.) I have too often seen how quickly people succumb to self-delusion, how relentlessly and egoistically they abuse power, and how it's not just those paralyzed by fear when their existence is threatened who lose their ability to resist. Both groups—the abusers and the paralyzed—just like all people everywhere, are related to each other by these inclinations. In more or less different degrees, of course. The quick change in attitudes when Königsberg fell frightened me.

As if there is a "reactive instinct"; instincts that are triggered by certain situations. The Russians had only just won the war and power had barely shifted when persecutors who had gone around as *Herrenmenschen* (members of the master race), turned into fear-ridden creatures, and the persecuted, once quaking with fear, turned into ruthless persecutors. I saw with my own eyes how the Nazis became whining, groveling beggars after their arrest and the liberated Poles became vicious despots who bullied every German, Nazi or not. I might have said this was due to the suffering inflicted on them were I not absolutely convinced everyone is ruled by his instincts. In a given situation, everyone is also ruled by those psychological mechanisms I mentioned earlier—unless people consciously struggle against them. It's sadly true our genetically programmed readiness to hatred and aggression lies in wait for us just as much as self-delusion awaits the powerful or inhibitions await the fearful. Why then does the same thing happen in every group of people, no matter what group it is?

Intermezzo: I've just finished reading a biography of the Jewish philosopher Theodor Lessing, who was murdered by the Nazis in 1933. All the perfidy and ruthless coldness of the anti-Semitism of the 1920s came to life. What particularly upset me was that at this time there was still freedom of expression and, for the most part, the rule of law. My mind rebelled against such infamy in a presumably peaceful time. I had believed that this sort of single-minded and unfair provocation had only occurred later under the Nazis. You have to ask: Is Germany really a country where people are worse than those in other countries? A country where people, like certain breeds of dogs, are meaner and tend to bite? But that's just what I refuse to believe because that would be biological poppycock. First of all, Germans aren't a race. They're Europeans, they are people just like everyone else. Aren't there atrocities anywhere people abuse power? Without a doubt, the cruelty of the Nazis surpassed anything known before. But that mustn't distort the view of those of us who survived. The Chinese too were unbelievably cruel during their Cultural Revolution. It's said that ten million were tortured to death. In Russia twelve million accused are supposed to have been killed in the Stalin era. When the Americans dropped the atomic bomb on civilians, when they dropped napalm in Vietnam, they were cruel. When the Spanish exiled the Jews in the fifteenth century, the officials of the Church were the servants of the Inquisition, when the Africans were locked in feuds—people were always unbelievably cruel.

I have to admit, so soon after the events of the 1930s we all vividly remember, after Auschwitz and after two World Wars, the virulent anti-Semitism, militarism, and the violence we have today directed at foreigners seem to me to express ineradicable human stupidity. What can be done about this besides making people aware of it and working to increase the ability to think critically? What can be done without demonizing or idealizing anyone, what can be done besides being willing to understand and to reconcile at all times, and acting responsibly toward future generations and the environment? Whatever group of people we belong to, whatever identity we may have, all of us are sitting in the same boat. We are living in a fragile world we mustn't destroy, which we can preserve only if we cooperate.

Dear Menachem and Shoshana, my Jewish heart cringes when we pray at the Seder (and not only then): "Pour out Thy wrath upon the nations that know Thee not" just as much as when I hear, "Kick out asylum seekers!" Woe to all of us today if God "pours out" his wrath—especially if He uses poison gas or the atomic bomb—anywhere in the world. And woe to us if we aren't willing to help those who need it. We would very soon become the ones who need help ourselves.

What many people can't understand is that acts of war and revenge lead only to escalation or chaos, that they neither resolve a problem nor bring about reconciliation. (I don't mean you shouldn't defend yourself.) But what I demand of others I must first be willing to demand of myself. I'm thinking here of acceding, sharing, seeking out the point of view of the other person, forgiving if there's genuine understanding, and remorse. For I'm totally certain that I'm no better a person than the next fellow—and if I want to do some good, I have to work hard on my own motives.

I think all these detours are necessary to answer your question about my identity. Besides enjoying an Orthodox Jewish education, I also was brought up culturally—as you were too—a German. Only with the slight difference that in those days because my father was a gentile, I was perhaps more aware of my German side than of my Jewish side, which was rejected by the Nazis. But that's not really right, for my mother felt herself to be at least as German as my father. In Menachem's opinion, the definitive line was crossed when the Star of David disappeared from our clothing and a struggle to survive began in Russian-occupied Königsberg, in which everyone became an animal of prey fighting for food. You grasp things perfectly when you write "I have the impression that at this point when everything changes the author is increasingly beginning to identify with his world; indeed, more so than circumstances require, which are those forcing him to scrabble for his very existence and his fate that the Russians do not acknowledge him as persecuted Jew." Such a circumstance is hard to conceive unless you imagine a sinking ship. Here no one would expect even one passenger who is swimming away to save his life to be concerned with *Vergangenheitsbewältigung* (coming to terms with the past) or national or religious differences. That's what it was for me at that time when I took off the Star of David. "But after you reached the shore safe and sound, then what?" I hear you ask. I had long harbored doubts whether Judaism was the satisfactory religion for me, and the many gentiles who hated Jews made their own religion almost an abomination to me. I have to admit though at that time—and at any time—the seldom practiced postulate "love" was the only key to peace, and remains the only key in my eyes. It is the most precious thing we have. If love is lost, then so are we. Even the commandment "to love thy enemies" is profoundly true. How else do we break out of the devil's circle of hatred and counter-hatred? Aggression and acts of revenge?

Yes, Menachem, back in those days when I found myself once more part of a community, one that had to endure terrible things and was destined for "eradication," I identified with the victims of abuse and starvation. It was Germans who selflessly helped me when I lay at death's door (in KZ Rothenstein, for example). We were all poor creatures struggling to survive and in that struggle we no longer differed from any other poor creature in this world. It could very well be that the person who helped me had been a Nazi—I didn't ask. For I saw only the "victim" in all people. The misguided, the obedient, the suffering and dying victim.—Do you see here a betrayal of our dead? That's my question to you, to you both.

Even if I'm not a genuine Jew or Christian or whatever (perhaps calling myself a Spinozist comes the closest), I am most certainly a sentient and thinking man and thus related to billions of similar people. Related—as already noted—by virtue of the same fateful susceptibilities, passions, feelings. Related, not least of all, by virtue of the joy that life can offer, despite everything. But to this day I always feel the most closely related to those who are, as I once was, oppressed and persecuted, who are in pain, who have suffered or are suffering, who find themselves in dire straits. These include persecuted Jews and in those days included German civilians under Russian occupation, even if you say this was the inevitable consequence for all their delusions of greatness and terrible deeds.

Perhaps you both now understand why I don't feel any need of an "identity," why I don't feel I have to belong unambiguously either to Judaism or to Christianity or to any other group. My identity is to be a human among other humans—in a broader sense of the word, a living thing among living things, and in a still broader sense of the word, a tiny part of an infinite, ungraspable whole.—

I reached these conclusions only after I had emigrated from Germany and had spent seven years in New Zealand looking in vain for a new homeland. It was of course important that we were now a family where each individual member took into consideration the welfare and the needs of the other members. (That mustn't sound like an excuse—even if it were one.)

Your impression is correct—dear Menachem—I tried then and am trying today in spite of everything that's happened to begin something new through music with many people of good will, and people who want somehow to make reparations, together with youth (who learned only later what happened) shocked about the past. And what we began then looked so promising because, after all, no other country experienced as we did what hatred, dictatorship, and racial delusions can bring. Back then, I thought Germany would be immune for centuries against any repetition of such a calamitous course of history. We were fully aware that the mortgage for the thoughts and deeds of the perpetrators could only be paid off over a long time.—Was that also a betrayal of our relatives and the friends who were so ruthlessly murdered? Please give me your honest answer—no "on the one hand and then on the other"!—It is certainly true that I have found no

real sense of security in the bosom of any community (nor did I have that feeling before) on account of my mixed religious heritage. Today, I don't seek it
anymore and precisely for that reason I feel intellectually more independent. And
besides, I wonder if we aren't given a true blessing of security, genuine peace, only
after death, which comes to us all?—

Hope everything is going well for you. With gratitude, sympathy, and heartfelt
greetings,
Michael

Appendix 2

Travel Report

October 1, 1992

Dear Friends,

We're back from our trip to Kaliningrad (Königsberg), somewhat dazed by everything we saw and did. I knew that the city where we spent our childhood, honorable old Königsberg, no longer exists. After all, when the *Vertriebene* (expellees) left Königsberg after 1945, they left behind a pile of ruins that didn't look as if anyone would ever build a house there again. But now, forty-seven years later, a new and different city stands there, one whose buildings and streets are definitely very much in need of repair but seems to give four hundred thousand people a place to live and work—Kaliningrad. A city consisting of many plain "socialist" buildings, quickly slapped together, like those we know from the former Soviet Union and its satellite countries. A city with soulless squares around a monument to Lenin or Marx, with dreary streets and almost everyone wearing dark clothing engaged on their daily search for something to buy. Cars and buses are so battered that you doubt they can survive bouncing over streets pock-marked with potholes. In this city desperately in need of repair, it's as difficult to say who has the authority over these things as it is to figure out what common purpose they serve.

The restoration, initiated by Marion Gräfin von Dönhoff, of the impressive, newly recast monument to Kant on one side of the University Square is as significant as the General Lasch bunker on the other side. (This is the place where on April 9, 1945, Lasch capitulated; today it is a museum.) These two memorials facing each other symbolize the extraordinary zenith as well as the absolute nadir of a city's history. Even when the Russians occupied Königsberg from 1758 to 1762, Russian officers attended the lectures of Immanuel Kant and were deeply impressed by the knowledge of this Königsberg inhabitant, who wrote about his city: "Such a city as Königsberg on the Pregel River can be assumed to be a seemly place for deepening what we know of man as well as what we know of the universe, the acquisition of such knowledge is possible without the need to undertake a journey." Königsberg was the most important city after Berlin for the Enlightenment and liberalism, and it wasn't only the Russians who participated in those days in the cultural and intellectual life.

When Commandant Lasch surrendered, Königsberg had been destroyed and conquered with heavy losses (the Russian frontline soldiers had fought their way to the door of his bunker); this was the declaration of bankruptcy of the political system in Germany that had sustained for years hatred and arrogance against others, that had armed for war and started it to achieve imperialistic ends. But the flowers the Russians lay at the foot of the Kant monument and on Kant's grave are for the citizen who envisioned wise, pragmatic concepts, all too infrequently put into practice, for a peaceful community of all nations free of prejudice (just look at Kant's little essay "Zum ewigen Frieden" ["Perpetual Peace"], prescient and still very timely).

Anyone who goes to Kaliningrad today shouldn't expect to find Königsberg. Alas, Königsberg, as someone once said, didn't survive the last war. This fact makes me think bitterly about generals, government officials, and an entire nation that couldn't manage to rid themselves of a dictatorial clique that had, in the eyes of all, already lost a criminal war. If the July 20th Plot had led to the end of the war, Königsberg would have been spared destruction, the East Prussians would not have become refugees, and there wouldn't have been any reason for the Russians in the final battle to have obliterated Königsberg.—

There is a building here or a place there that recalls the past, but these leftovers from Königsberg's existence are like finding bones in a cemetery. The most astonishing "bone" for me is the Jewish Orphanage, completely undamaged, sitting in the middle of a completely destroyed city. That's where I went to school after the vicious desecration (November 1938) destroyed the large, beautiful synagogue of the Reform Jews, where I studied Lessing, Goethe, Schiller, Shakespeare, and others while Hitler Youth stood outside throwing stones and painted "*Juda verrecke*" (Death to Jewry) on the walls. At the time, we didn't understand why adults were always whipping up this frenzy of hatred against us children, against neighboring countries, against anyone who was considered different; but we did understand that every expression of hatred results in enmity, heartlessness, and destruction and that anyone who stirs up hatred—of whatever sort—is responsible for the deeds that follow. The bleak ruins of the bombed-out cathedral stand there now as a depressing, almost resigned witness for what hatred produces.

It should be quite easy to learn from the past. But you wouldn't believe the sort of things that were said by some East Prussians my age who were on the trip with me armed with their D-marks. They were unchanged in their disastrous arrogance and a comment meant for us exposed their old anti-Semitic prejudices. Many behaved like lords of the manor on vacation coming to check whether the steward put in charge of their property was administrating their holdings well. And of course, the steward can't possibly do it as well as the heir who manages his own property. But the steward is still supposed to do a better job. It was, however, the deep sigh from one East Prussian woman that let the cat out of the bag. She opined as how only a Hitler could help in the present chaos. (Frau F., who had traveled from Israel just for this trip with her husband, who was a native of Königsberg, heard this and told me. As a child, Frau F. had crawled one night out of a pit where she and her younger brother had been thrown when her parents and other Jews of a Russian city had been lined up on the pit's edge and the shooting began.) So, a new Hitler would help! Quite. Wasn't it then Hitler whom we can thank for the loss and destruction of Königsberg? I ask myself, more and more discouraged, in fact, more and more desperately, did more than fifty million people perish in the last war in vain if only a short time later—meaning today—so many can no longer recall the cause of that vast catastrophe?

I don't want to be unfair. There are definitely many tourists who seek contact with people there and selflessly give help. Frau Professor S., for example who went out to the countryside with a backpack full of things to give to the very poor and needy, of whom there are so many. Most of them had been cast up here by some horrific fate (if they aren't of the generation born here). I won't forget the especially cordial embrace of the woman who now lives in the apartment we had, now fully rebuilt, and who told us her story—father and brothers had been killed in the war! She gave us some apples and generously invited us to stay with her.

The Kaliningrad writers, who wanted to meet me in the offices of their association, seemed to be unsure whether it is better to receive pay and suffer censorship or to work for no pay but without censorship. They told of meeting with young Germans who had told them that as far as they were concerned East Prussia didn't belong to Russia. Such comments left those who live there now feeling unsettled and threatened. On television, a retired officer who can't live on his pension commented bitterly and as a warning that he wouldn't forget how to handle a gun. "It takes time," said our Russian translator Maxim, but he couldn't say what should be happening in the time it would take.

In a Russian television interview, the question comes up what I would recommend for Königsberg to become a cosmopolitan city once more, perhaps similar to what it once was. How can anyone answer that? As long as intellectual energy has to be expended on obtaining the necessities of life, energy and time for music, literature, and painting are limited. It's always been like that. And, still, the philharmonic was well attended when we played Mozart, Schuman, Beethoven, and Sarasate; and, finally, children study at the *Städtische Musikschule* (City School of Music), their talents shining through despite the poor quality of their instruments.

I don't really like luxurious surroundings, so I wasn't too upset when the rain came in at Hotel Kaliningrad, when the elevator was out of order, or when the water, which was only seldom warm, was turned off from time to time. But if these things still happen decades after trying to make improvements, one does have to ask what's wrong. For gardeners and for people who take care of animals, the answer is nothing new. If the environment doesn't correspond to what plants, animals, or people need, nothing thrives. The ideology of Communism was specious and therefore the social structures based on it were spurious too. They shipwrecked on the impossibility of ever fulfilling their stated ideals.

Our visit to the places where Königsberg once stood seemed to me like being in a Fellini film, where scenes changed for no rational reason. In the hotel restaurant, we are dining on one course after another for three D-marks or less while outside the hotel children are begging, street hawkers are doing business, prostitutes are trying to ensnare customers, and taxicab drivers are waiting. In the mornings, I practice sonatas by Schuman, Mozart, and Beethoven with a Russian pianist; in the afternoons we visit what had been the KZ Rothenstein, where German civilians had been brutally tortured. In the evenings an adorable Jewish children's choir sings songs for us that bring tears to our eyes while my sister reminds me what one did with similar children fifty years ago. Ivanov, the mayor for cultural affairs, tells us that he can still remember me well playing dance music as the *Stehgeiger* (stand-up violinist) in 1947 and how he loved dancing to the music. I can't easily deal with all these abrupt changes in moods.

It's only when we visited the Courland Spit that a sense of calm returns, thanks mostly to the landscape that so entranced us as children. The white beaches along the Baltic, the tall sand dunes on the shore of the lagoon, and the friendly forests were practically unchanged even though the former fishing villages have given way to vacation homes. A row boat ride on the quiet lagoon beneath the clouds scuttling across the sky, with the sand dunes gleaming brightly when the sun breaks through puts us in a conciliatory mood and brings back happy feelings. We saw an elk running across the path one evening. She let us film her as she stood about twenty paces from the road. This seemed almost like a deliberately staged event with special effects—or was it a plea from an animal threatened with extinction not to destroy her too in our merciless race for affluence?

Dear friends, our city of Königsberg would have been 690 years old in 1945. Hubris, hatred, and the compulsion to lay waste to everything caused its destruction. Thus, the Königsberg that has perished should become a fiery warning against the horror that stems from hatred—for the serious danger conjured up by those who incite to hatred (often without being aware of doing so). A warning to future generations, which calls for the spirit of human cooperation and makes vivid what can happen when nation is set upon by nation, what disastrous consequences can come from anyone who thinks, speaks, or writes aggressive slogans such as "Giving up is treason!" or "Kick the foreigner out!"

When we returned to Stuttgart, we felt liberated for the first time. Seeing desperate need everywhere without being able to help, or being reminded of the past without having hope for the immediate future is almost unbearable for any length of time. You become very aware of how much was accomplished after the war when Germany was rebuilt, but I cannot shake the fear that we are beginning to repeat our mistakes and that internal and external excesses make precarious what we have achieved.

With cordial greetings,
Michael Wieck

Glossary

Shown in parentheses next to the defined term is the name of the chapter in which the term first appears.—Trans.

"*Wehrmacht* marched into Vienna" or *Anschluss* (The War Begins)

"Union." The Treaty of Versailles explicitly prohibited the union of Austria and Germany. Throughout the 1920s there had been support for at least a customs union. Hitler regarded union between Germany and Austria to be indispensable. Austrian Nazis murdered Chancellor Dollfuss on July 25, 1934, hoping to stage a coup. Hitler supported the illegal Austrian Nazis. In 1936 Hitler recognized Austria's independence by treaty. In 1938 he invited Chancellor Kurt von Schuschnigg to Berchtesgaden to demand concessions for the Austrian Nazis. The chancellor, realizing that neither Britain nor France would step in, was forced to yield. To forestall the success of the Nazis, the Austrian chancellor promised a plebiscite on the question of Austrian independence. After sending troops to the border, Hitler demanded on March 11, 1938, Schuschnigg's resignation in favor of the Austrian Nazi party leader Artur Seyss-Inquart. Despite Schuschnigg's resignation and cancellation of the plebiscite, Göring ordered Seyss-Inquart to request German aid "to restore order." On March 12, 1938, German troops crossed the border and Hitler declared *Anschluss* had been achieved.

Ernest Ansermet (Prologue)

1883 (Vevey)–1969 (Geneva). Conductor principally associated with the Orchestre de la Suisse Romande (Lucerne). As the new director of the Kursaal Orchestra of Montreux, Ansermet met Igor Stravinsky, who advised Diaghilev to engage him to conduct the Ballet Russes.

Babi Yar (Bar Mitzvah)

September 29–30, 1941. Massacre of over 34,000 Jews in the ravine of Babi Yar on the outskirts of Kiev. When the Nazis captured the city of Kiev in mid-September 1941, the Jewish population was 175,000. Jews—men, women, and children—were herded into barbed-wire areas at the top of the ravine, guarded by Ukrainian collaborators. After they were forced to strip, the Jews were led down the sides of the ravine, where the Germans machine-gunned them to death. Layer by layer, the Jews were killed. In their haste to dispatch so many in two days, the Germans did not make sure that all were dead; a few managed to crawl away and survive. Yevgeni Yevtushenko (b. 1933) wrote a somber memorial to Babi Yar (1961), in which the narrator bears witness; Dimitri Shostakovich (1906–75) set Yevtushenko's poem to music in the Babi Yar Symphony No. 13 in 1965.

Bajazzo Prologue (Gleanings)

The opera *I Pagliacci*, by Ruggiero Leoncavallo (1858–1919). The opera is known in German as *Der Bajazzo*. Bajazzo was the name of an Italian actor with a band of strolling players who murdered his wife in a jealous rage behind the stage in the small Calabrian town of Montalto on August 13, 1865. The jealous husband then murdered the wife's lover, who was the servant of the Leoncavallo family accompanying the seven-year-old Ruggiero to the performance. The opera, based on this incident, consists of a prologue and two acts and was first performed in Milan in 1892.

Sir John Barbirolli (Berlin)

1899 (London)–1970 (London). Conductor. Barbirolli studied at Trinity and the Royal Academy of Music. In the interwar period, he was the conductor of the British National Opera Company and Covent Garden. In 1936 he succeeded Toscanini as the conductor of the New York Philharmonic. In 1943 Barbirolli was asked to restore the Hallé Orchestra in Manchester; he remained its director for twenty-seven years. From 1961 to 1967 he was also appointed conductor of the Houston Symphony Orchestra. He died of a heart attack during a rehearsal in London with the New Philharmonia Orchestra.

Marshal François Achille Bazaine (Prologue)

1811 (Versailles)–1888 (Madrid). French army officer. Bazaine served in Algeria, Crimea, and Mexico. Emperor Napoleon III gave him supreme command of the army in the Franco-Prussian War. On October 27, 1870, Bazaine capitulated at Metz with his army of 180,000 men. He was captured, court-martialed, and condemned to death, but he managed to escape to Madrid, where he wrote his memoirs justifying his conduct.

Berlin Blockade / Airlift (Berlin)

Early on the morning of June 24, 1948, the Soviet Military Administration closed off all surface traffic from the western zones to the three western sectors of Berlin, cutting off a civilian population of about 2.5 million people. The Blockade was the response to the Western Allies' moves to consolidate their occupation zones in West Germany into a single independent state. As one step of this consolidation, the Allies had introduced into the western sectors of West Germany as well as into the western controlled sectors of Berlin a new currency over which the Soviets would have no control. The Chief of U.S. Forces in Europe and American military governor of the American Occupation Zone, Lucius D. Clay (1897–1978), approved the order to begin resupplying West Berlin by air on June 27, earning himself the name "father of the Berlin Airlift." General Curtis LeMay was in charge of the Airlift, which had C-54s taking off and landing at Berlin's Tempelhof Airport every two minutes. "LeMay's feed and coal company" brought in 5,000 tons of supplies a day or over two million tons in all by the time the Soviets lifted the Blockade on May 12, 1949. This first serious crisis of the Cold War established the commitment of President Truman, who was advised against such measures, to anti-Soviet policies.

Otto Besch (Nidden)

1885 (Neuhasen bei Königsberg)–1966 (Kassel). East Prussian musicologist and composer. Besch first studied theology before he turned to music. From 1918 to 1945 he taught composition at the Königsberg Conservatory and was a well-known contemporary music critic. After the war he was an editor in the music section of the North German Radio station in Hamburg. He composed chamber works for piano, violin, and cello. He wrote: "The spirit of my music comes only from one source—the landscape of East Prussia."

Cantor Eduard Birnbaum (Conflicts and Personal Fates)

1855 (Cracow)–1920 (Königsberg). Composer, cantor, and musicologist. Birnbaum studied *hazzanut* (Jewish liturgical music) in Vienna. He served as cantor in several German cities before he became chief cantor in Königsberg in 1879. His reputation as a Jewish musical scholar and as a collector of musical manuscripts and materials attracted young cantors to study with him. He published many works on liturgical music. His papers, now at the Hebrew Union College in Cincinnati, constitute the most important collection of eighteenth and nineteenth century European Jewish music and archival materials.

Pastor Friedrich (Fritz) von Bodelschwingh (*Kristallnacht* and After)

1877 (Bethel bei Bielefeld)–1946 (Bethel bei Bielefeld). Pastor. Taking over from his father, Bodelschwingh operated Bethel, homes for the disabled. He became a Reichsbischof (bishop) in 1933, but resigned in protest over Nazi control of church. In 1940 and 1941 he protested the Nazi euthanasia program in vain.

Philipp Bouhler (*Kristallnacht* and After)

1899 (Munich)–1945 (Berlin). Early member of the Nazi party. He worked on the newspaper *Völkischer Beobachter* (*Racial Observer*). From 1925 to 1934 he served as business manager of the party. In 1933 he became the *Reichsleiter* (Party Leader) of the NSDAP and was elected to the Reichstag from Westphalia. In 1934 he was appointed the police president of Munich and chief of the Führer's personal chancellory, which handled Hitler's personal affairs. He wrote a school text on the history of the Nazi Party, first published in 1939, *Ein Lesebuch für die deutsche Jugend* (*Reader for German Youth*). In 1939 Hitler appointed him and Dr. Karl Brandt to head the euthanasia program. In 1940 Bouhler was designated to be the head of the Madagascar Plan. The plan, which proposed to resettle European Jews in Madagascar, was never implemented however. At the end of the war, he and his wife committed suicide to avoid arrest by the Americans.

Dr. Karl Brandt (*Kristallnacht* and After)

c. 1904–48 (hanged at Landsberg Prison). Personal physician to Hitler and his staff. He was one of the main defendants in the Doctors Trial that commenced on December 9, 1946, against twenty-three SS physicians and scientists. At his trial, he defended medical experiments on humans: "[A]ny personal code of ethics must give way to the total character of war." His last words, stopped mid-sentence by the executioner, were "This is nothing but political revenge. I have served my Fatherland as others before me . . ."

Otto Braun (The Chemical Factory of Gamm & Son)

1897 (Berlin)–1918 (Marcelcave, France). Poet. Privately educated, Braun volunteered for the army in 1914. He was wounded in November 1916; after he recovered, he returned to the front, where he was killed by a hand grenade. His poems were published in 1921 under the title *Nachgelassene Schriften eines Frühvollendeten (Posthumous Writings of a Genius Who Died Young)*. His poems are typical of the elliptical, telegraphic style found among Expressionists.

Max Bruch (Gleanings)

1838 (Cologne)–1920 (Friedenau). Conductor and composer of violin concertos, chamber music, and symphonies. Bruch received his early music education from his mother. He conducted in various cities, including Liverpool and Breslau. In 1891 Bruch was appointed professor at the *Hochschule für Musik* (Academy of Music) in Berlin, where he taught until he retired in 1910. Well known are his Concerto for Violin in G Minor, op. 26 and Kol Nidre for cello and orchestra, known in English as "Hebrew Melody." It is based on the liturgical melody for the central prayer in the service for Yom Kippur or Day of Atonement.

Marshal François Certain Canrobert (Prologue)

1809 (Saint Céré)–1895 (Paris). Marshal of France, aide of Louis Napoleon. A Crimean war hero, Canrobert distinguished himself in the Franco-Prussian War and later as a senator of the Third Republic.

Sergiu Celibidache (Prologue)

1912 (Roman near Iasi)–1996 (Paris). Romanian conductor. In 1945 Celibidache worked with the Berlin Philharmonic Orchestra until Furtwängler returned, then with the RIAS Berlin Radio Orchestra. He held a series of guest conductor positions. From 1972 to 1977 he was the Artistic Director of the Radiosinfonie Orchester Stuttgart. In 1979 he was appointed director of the Munich Philharmonic Orchestra.

Certified Jew or *Geltungsjude* (book title)

Classification of racial status under the Nazi race laws. What was known as the *Judensternverordnung* (Star of David Decree) was officially titled the *Polizeiverordnung über die Kennzeichnung der Juden* (Police Decree Regarding Identification

Badges for Jews) and was issued on September 1, 1941, and effective fourteen days later. The order mandated that all Jews over the age of six could not appear in public without the *Judenstern* (Star of David); section 3 described the size and color, how it must be worn, who was exempt, and what the penalties were for noncompliance (up to 153 Reichsmarks or six weeks of imprisonment). Exempt were Jewish spouses living in mixed marriages to the extent that there were children from the marriage and these children did not qualify as Jews *(diese nicht als Juden gelten)*. Thus, a *"Geltungsjude"* was someone who qualified as Jewish under the bizarre and elaborate Nazi classification system of purity of race.

Chelmno (Aunt Fanny)

Village about fifty miles from Lodz in Poland. Death camp operations began under Herbert Lange on December 7, 1941, although they were suspended on March 19, 1943. They resumed on June 23, 1943, and continued until January 17, 1945. Here, the first mass killings of Jews by gas took place, using gas vans. The estimated number of deaths is between 150,000 and 300,000, mostly Jews. It was from Chelmno that on January 20, 1942, Jacob Grojanowski escaped from a work detail burying the bodies of those who had been gassed. He told a rabbi in the nearby village, "Don't think I'm crazed and have lost my reason. I am a Jew from the nether world. They are killing the whole nation of Israel. I myself have buried a whole town of Jews, my parents, brothers, and the entire family." He reached Warsaw and the Ghetto leaders, to whom Grojanowski told what he had witnessed. The information was passed to the Polish Underground, which transmitted it to London by June 1942.

Lovis Corinth (Nidden)

1858 (Tapiau, East Prussia)–1925 (Amsterdam). Painter and graphic artist. Corinth is known for his psychological themes in his painting. In 1911 he took over the office of president of the Berliner Secession from Max Liebermann. In 1914 he greeted the outbreak of First World War as a radical new beginning.

Courland Spit (Nidden)

The narrow spit of land, the Kurische Nehrung, between Memel and Königsberg, between the Courland Lagoon and the Baltic Sea, about 58 miles long and from ⅓ to 2½ miles wide.

DEFA (Gleanings)

Deutsche Film Anstalt (German Film Studio). Licensed by the Russians in May 1946, DEFA was established in Babelsberg, which had been a studio city since before World War I. The studio was famous for avant garde films but became a propaganda factory under Goebbels. The Soviets took control in 1945, handing the studio over to DEFA in 1946. The first postwar film, *Die Mörder sind unter uns* (Murderers Are among Us) (1946) by Wolfgang Staudte (1906–84), was typical of the period's *Trümmerfilme* (rubble films), dealing with fascist/anti-fascist themes; later, conflicts between the state and filmmakers and social themes were typical of DEFA films.

Deutsche Reichsbahn (German Reich Railway) **report** (Afterword)

The schedule dated June 24–25, 1942, for the *Sonderzug* (special train) to take 465 resettlers from Königsberg to Wilkowiski (Lithuania). Its journey began at 10:34 P.M. from the North Train Station and arrived the following afternoon at 4:30 P.M. The final item in the instructions forbade disclosure of details of the schedule to bystanders as well as to those being transported.

Deutschland, erwache! (The Star of David)

"Germany, awake!" Anti-Semitic slogan and song. The slogan and song was a rallying cry to arouse the mob against the Jews and glorified the martyrdom of those who died in the cause of Germany. "Storm, storm, storm, storm! / From tower to tower peal bells of alarm! / Peal out! Sparks fly as hammers strike, / Come Judas forth to win the Reich. Peal out! The bloody ropes hang red / Around our martyred hero dead. / Peal out! That thundering earth may know / Salvation's rage for honor's sake. / To people dreaming still comes woe. Germany, awake! Awake!" The song was written by a friend of Hitler, Dietrich Eckert (1868–1923).

Marion Gräfin von Dönhoff (Appendix 2)

1909 (Castle Friedrichstein, East Prussia)–2002 (Crottorf bei Friesenhagen). Journalist. Influenced by the economic crises of the 1920s, the countess began the study of economics at the university in Frankfurt am Main. When Hitler came to power, she became an activist against the Nazis, ripping the swastika from the university roof, tearing down posters warning against Jewish teachers, and distributing anti-Nazi flyers. The "red countess" fled to Basel. In 1937 she returned to East Prussia and took up the administration of her family's estates. She was a key contact to foreign diplomats for the Stauffenberg group in the July 20th Plot, but she escaped with a Gestapo interrogation when the assassination attempt failed. As the Russians entered East Prussia, Dönhoff fled to the west, leaving her estates behind. She attended the Nuremberg Trials and was critical of the Allies' one-sided view of Germany, which did not acknowledge the existence of a German resistance movement. In 1946 she became a stringer for *Die Zeit*, one of the great liberal newspapers in postwar Germany. In 1955 she became the editor for political affairs at *Die Zeit*. She was a sharp critic of Adenauer's policies and an ardent advocate for a conciliatory policy toward Eastern Europe and Russia. In 1968 she became the editor-in-chief of *Die Zeit* and, in 1972, the publisher. Her conciliatory positions on relations between the Germans and the Poles and between the Jews and the Arabs were controversial. In 1992 the Kant monument she donated was unveiled in Kaliningrad. Both conservatives and liberals honored Dönhoff as a journalist and admired her intellectual and personal integrity.

Grand Admiral Karl Dönitz (The Reunion)

1891 (Grünau bei Berlin)–1980 (Aumühle bei Hamburg). Supreme commander of the German navy and Hitler's appointed successor. During World War II he created the "wolf pack system," which devastated Allied shipping in the Atlantic at the beginning of the war. In 1942 he was promoted to the rank of admiral; less than a year later on January 30, 1943, he succeeded Erich Raeder as supreme commander of the German fleet. Convinced that Hitler had been sent to the German people by heaven, he was rewarded with Hitler's designation on April 29, 1945, as President of the Reich and Supreme Commander of the Armed Forces. On May 1, 1945, Dönitz announced his appointment in a radio address after stating the Führer had fallen fighting Bolshevism. When the Americans rejected his offer of a partial surrender, Dönitz capitulated. The first instruments of surrender were signed in Rheims on May 7, then again in Berlin on May 8 to include the Russians. On May 23, 1945, the British captured Dönitz after he had held office a little more than twenty days as Führer. At Nuremberg he was sentenced to ten years imprisonment, which he served in Spandau, and he was released October 1, 1956.

Dr. Oetker's Pudding Powder (The Königsberg "Cemetery")

Dr. Oetker is perhaps best explained as the "Betty Crocker" of Germany. Dr. August Oetker was a real person, a pharmacist in Bielefeld who in 1891 developed a formula for packaging the right amount of baking powder for one pound of flour. The family enterprise went on to package powder in envelopes to make perfect puddings and a host of other products (including instant Bavarian dumplings and potato pancakes).

East Prussia (Nidden)

A former German province, in the interwar period bounded by the Baltic Sea, Lithuania, Poland, and the Free City of Danzig. The first Christian settlements by the Knights of Teutonic Order date back to the thirteenth century. Its capital city was Königsberg, renamed Kaliningrad after World War II. In 1945 the province was divided between Poland and the USSR; German inhabitants were expelled, were killed, or escaped, and the area was resettled by Russians or Poles.

Adolf Eichmann (Birth Pangs)

1906 (Solingen)–1962 (Ramle, Israel). Chief of Office IVb4 in the *Reischssicherheitshauptamt* (Reich Security Main Office) charged with the deportation of the Jews. In 1932 Eichmann joined the Austrian Nazi Party. In late 1937 he visited Palestine on orders to explore the possibility of deporting Europe's Jews there and in March 1938 Eichmann was appointed *Referent* (Special Officer) for Zionist Affairs. In July 1939 Eichmann was transferred to Berlin to head the Gestapo's Jewish office. By the end of the year, Heydrich appointed Eichmann to head Department IV of the RSHA, responsible for "handling" the Jews from the eastern territories. Eichmann's Department was also in charge of organizing the transport of Jews from other parts of the Reich. It was Eichmann's recommendation in 1941 that the camp commanders use Zyklon-B to gas the Jews and it was his efforts that ensured the chemical was supplied to the camps. Eichmann attended the Wannsee Conference on January 20, 1942, and prepared the minutes. In October 1943 Eichmann was put in charge over all matters concerning confiscation of property of persons hostile to the *Volk*, and such persons were, by definition, Jews. In October 1944 Eichmann reported to Himmler that, although the camps kept no statistics, four million Jews had died and that two million

more had been shot or killed by mobile units. After the war, Eichmann was captured, under the name of Adolf Karl Barth, by the Americans near Ulm, and a
second time under the name of Otto Eckmann. Identified as the man in charge
of the extermination program against the Jews at Nuremberg, Eichmann escaped
again. In July 1950, he slipped into Italy, with the help of the *Organisation der SS
Angehörigen* (Association of SS Members) and eventually, under the name of
Ricardo Klement, arrived in Buenos Aires. In 1960, the Israeli secret service kid-
napped him and brought him back to Israel, where he was tried from April 11 to
August 14, 1961. Eichmann's diaries, written as he awaited execution, were released
in spring 2000 by the Israeli government. Eichmann's entry for September 6,
1961, reads:

> I will recount the genocide against Jewry, as it occurred, and describe my think-
> ing both yesterday and today about this. For not only the fields of death did I
> have to see with my own eyes, the battlefields where life itself died, I saw much
> worse. I saw how, by a few words, through a single, abrupt order of one indi-
> vidual, whom the regime empowered, fields of annihilation were created. I saw
> the eeriness of the death machinery; wheel turning on wheel, like the mecha-
> nisms of a watch. And I saw those who maintained the machinery, who kept it
> going. I saw them, as they rewound the mechanism; and I watched the second
> hand, as it rushed through the seconds; rushing like lives towards death. The
> greatest and most monumental dance of death of all time.
>   This I saw.

Isaac Abraham Euchel (Conflicts and Personal Fates)

1756 (Copenhagen)–1804 (Berlin). German author who wrote in Hebrew and
leader of the *Haskala* (Jewish Emancipation). He was a pupil of Kant and influenced by Moses Mendelssohn. In Königsberg he was, despite his scholarly reputation, rejected as a lecturer at the university because he was Jewish. His writings
called for education, training, and civil rights for Jews. In 1788 he published a
biography of Moses Mendelssohn. Euchel advocated Hebrew as a modern language, founding, along with Menahem Mendel Breslau (d. 1839), the Jewish
monthly *Ha-Me'assef.* His desire to bring Jews out of the ghetto into modern life,
however, was not assimilationist: he prepared a free translation of the prayer book
in German and he published a commentary on the Book of Proverbs in German,
using Hebrew letters.

Der Freikorps (My School Days Are Over)

German private paramilitary groups after World War I. A number of Freikorps
first appeared in December 1918, made up of ex-soldiers and others who were less
than enthusiastic about the new German republic. Mostly very conservative and
nationalistic, they were unofficially employed to put down left-wing uprisings. At
first, they were supported by Defense Minister Gustav Noske and General Paul
von Hindenburg, but by 1921 they were seen as a threat and eventually replaced
by a regular army and police force. Many became units of the Nazis.

Der Freischütz (School Days 2)

"The Free Shooter," best known opera by Carl Maria von Weber. The first German Romantic opera, it premiered on June 18, 1821, in Berlin. The opera uses music to express German, instead of universal ideals, spoken dialogue, natural setting, supernatural elements, and folk songs.

Roland Freisler (Air Raids over Königsberg)

1893 (Celle)–1945 (Berlin). Lawyer and judge. A brilliant man, Freisler learned Russian in captivity during World War I. After 1933 he participated in reshaping the law to reflect Nazi principles. In 1942 Hitler appointed him president of the *Volksgerichtshof* (National Socialist People's Court), which convicted thousands for "treasonous" utterances and thoughts. He so bullied defendants that on occasion even the Nazis were embarrassed. He was a participant at the Wannsee Conference in January 1942. He went to Munich to preside over the trial of the White Rose resistance members Hans and Sophie Scholl and Christoph Probst in February 1943. Freisler sentenced them to death by guillotine. In his judicial capacity, he was a vindictive scourge toward the leaders of the July 20th Plot. When his court was cleared by an air raid alarm on February 3, 1945, Freisler was killed by a bomb as he returned to fetch some files he had left behind. He was denied a state funeral by Hitler himself and was buried anonymously in his wife's family plot.

Ferenc Fricsay (Prologue)

1914 (Budapest)–1963 (Basel). Conductor. Fricsay was a pupil of Béla Bartók and Zoltan Kodály. He became the musical director of Budapest Opera in 1945. From 1948 to 1954 he served as the musical director of the RIAS Symphony Orchestra in Berlin and from 1949 to 1957 as general music director of the Deutsche Oper in Berlin. In 1954 he was the director of the Houston Symphony Orchestra. From 1956 to 1958 he served as the chief music director of the Munich Opera. In 1959 he returned to the RIAS Symphony Orchestra in Berlin as musical director.

King Friedrich Wilhelm IV (Winter Storms)

1795 (Berlin)–1861 (Sanssouci). King of Prussia 1841–61. After the period of reaction following the Wars of Liberation, there was great hope for reforms and progressive policies when Friedrich Wilhelm IV was crowned King of Prussia. Although he ended the Karlsbad Decrees of 1819 against the fraternities and gymnastic societies that advocated a national, unified Germany, the King failed to undertake substantial reforms. He declared solidarity with the revolutionaries in the streets of Berlin, but he used his troops to put a bloody end to the fighting. He curtly refused the emperor's crown offered to him by the National Assembly and rejected the proposed constitution; after the National Assembly was dissolved, he imposed a reactionary constitution on Prussia by decree. If Germany was to be united, it was not to be from the *Dreck* (dirt) of the people, but through royal fiat. He saw himself as the instrument of divine will.

Frisian (Nidden)

Refers to Friesland, a region along the North Sea. West Friesland is part of the Netherlands; East and North Friesland, where dialect (Platt) is still spoken, lie in Germany.

General Charles Auguste Frossard (Prologue)

1807 (Versailles)–1875 (Chateauvillain, Haute-Marne). French general. The young Frossard took part in the campaigns of Belgium and Algeria in the 1830s. He fought in the Crimean War and was wounded at Sebastopol. He fought at the side of Napoleon III in the Italian campaign in 1859. His defeat at the hands of General Karl von Steinmetz in the Franco-Prussian War in the battle of Forbach (Spicheren) on August 6–8, 1870, left the Lorraine open to the Germans. He returned to France in 1871 and published his *Rapport sur les operations du 2e corps pendant la campagne de 1870* to explain his defeat.

Wilhelm Furtwängler (Berlin)

1886 (Berlin)–1954 (Baden-Baden). Symphony conductor known for his interpretations of Beethoven, Brahms, Bruckner, and Wagner. When the Nazis banned Hindemith's *Mathis, der Maler,* Furtwängler resigned all his posts but decided to remain in Germany, thereby becoming a controversial figure after the war.

Cardinal-Archbishop Clemens August Graf von Galen (*Kristallnacht* and After)

1878 (Dinklage)–1946 (Munich). Cardinal-Archbishop after 1933. In 1933 Galen issued a pastoral letter against the National Socialist racial doctrine and continued to criticize Nazi practices he deemed incompatible with Christianity. In 1941 he publicly denounced the Nazi euthanasia program for the mentally ill.

GDR (Gleanings)

The German Democratic Republic *(Deutsche Demokratische Republik).* The Soviet Occupation Zone responded to the formation of a West German government by establishing the GDR in October 1949 with the Soviet sector of Berlin as its capital. The government instituted a planned and collectivized economy that struggled to rebuild after the war. In 1952 the GDR sealed its borders against the Federal Republic of Germany (FRG), but Berlin, under the Four Powers that enforced freedom of movement, continued to provide an escape valve. Mounting dissatisfaction with the regime led East German workers to strike on June 17, 1953, and the uprising spread quickly throughout East Germany. By 1961 the flow of refugees through Berlin was rising rapidly, and on August 13, 1961, the East German government sealed off East Berlin and began building the Berlin Wall. On the night of November 9, 1989, pressures from activists and dissidents as well as the liberalizing policies of the Soviet Union under Gorbachev led to a dramatic reopening of the Wall; both East and West Berliners joyfully took to the streets. Shortly thereafter, on October 3, 1990, the Federal Republic of Germany absorbed the GDR.

Dr. Hans Josef Maria Globke (Birth Pangs)

1898 (Aachen)–1973 (Bad Godesberg). Lawyer notorious for his commentary on the Nazi race laws. He never joined the Nazi Party, but he held the position of *Ministerialrat* (administrative advisor) in the Reich's Interior Ministry. He helped to draft the emergency legislation that gave Hitler dictatorial powers in 1933. He created the legal instruments by which the exclusion and elimination of Jews could "lawfully" proceed. He helped to draft the Nuremberg laws on race, including the *Gesetz zum Schutz der Erbgesundheit des deutschen Volkes* (Law for the Protection of Hereditary Health: The Attempt to Improve the German Aryan Breed), which mandated compulsory sterilization and killing the mentally ill and the handicapped, and the *Gesetz zum Schutz des deutschen Blutes und der deutschen Ehre* (Law for the Protection of German Blood and German Honor), which prohibited marriage and sexual relations between Jews and non-Jews. He participated in drafting the regulation by which all Jews had to add a middle name (Israel or Sarah) to their identity papers and decree under which the belongings of Jews killed in concentration camps were transferred to the ownership of the state. After the war, Globke was arrested but did not come to trial. He became a member of the Christian Democratic Party (CDU) and a member of parliament. In 1953 he became the state secretary of the chancellory under Adenauer, who rejected Globke's offers to resign five times. He retired in 1963.

Paul Joseph Goebbels (*Kristallnacht* and After)

1897 (Rheydt)–1945 (Berlin). Reich Minister of Propaganda. Born to a factory worker, Goebbels was exempted from military service in World War I because he had a clubfoot. He studied philosophy at the University of Heidelberg, where he received his Ph.D. in 1921. Not until 1924 did Goebbels become involved with National Socialism, and soon rose in the ranks of the party. By siding with Hitler against Gregor Strasser, Goebbels was named the party leader in Berlin in 1926. As propaganda minister, Goebbels created the Führer myth around Hitler. As head of the Cultural Ministry he was in control of movies, plays, books, and the content of education. As Germany was collapsing, Hitler named Goebbels chancellor and, having held the position for one day, Goebbels took the life of his wife and six children and then his own on May 1, 1945.

Johann Wolfgang von Goethe (*Kristallnacht* and After)

1749 (Frankfurt am Main)–1832 (Weimar). Dramatist, novelist, poet, essayist, scientist, theater director, government minister. Goethe was the first modern German author of worldwide fame.

Hermann Göring (*Kristallnacht* and After)

1893 (Rosenheim, Bavaria)–1946 (Nuremberg). Son of the German consul general in Haiti, Göring was brought up in the castle of Veldenstein, whose owner Ritter von Epenstein, a Jew, was the lover of Göring's mother. He held one of the twelve Reichstag seats the Nazis won in the election of 1928 and after the Nazis won 230 seats in July 1932, he was elected president of the Reichstag. During the Third Reich Göring accrued an impressive number of titles: Master of the German Hunt, Minister for Economic Affairs, Plenipotentiary for the Four-Year Plan, Chairman of the Ministerial Council for the Defense of the Reich, Reich Minister without Portfolio, Reich Commissioner for Air, Prussian President, Prussian Minister of the Interior. He was Head of Security for a while until he ceded the office to Heinrich Himmler. He held a special rank created by Hitler as *Reichsmarschall des Grossdeutschen Reiches*. Göring surrendered himself to the Allies in 1945, expecting to be treated as the head of Germany. At Nuremberg he denied any complicity in the extermination of the Jews, which he said was the secret work of Himmler. Found guilty, Göring requested that he be shot, not hanged; when this was denied, he committed suicide with a capsule of cyanide he had hidden in a jar of pomade.

Göring's commission to Heydrich (Bar Mitzvah)

Written order dated July 31, 1941, initiating the Final Solution. This written order from Reich Marshal of the Greater German Reich, Plenipotentiary for the Four-Year Plan and Chairman of the Ministerial Council for the Defense of the Reich Hermann Göring to the Chief of the Security Police and the *Sicherheitsdienst* (Security Police) SS Major General Reinhard Heydrich commissioned him to carry out all necessary preparations, organizational and financial, for a total solution of the Jewish question in all territories under German control in Europe. Göring charged Heydrich promptly to submit a plan showing the measures to be taken. The order began, "As a supplement to the task which was entrusted to you in the decree dated January 24, 1939, to solve the Jewish question by emigration and evacuation."

Rudolf von Gottschall (Winter Storms)

1823 (Breslau)–1909 (Leipzig). Author of historical novels who wrote under the pen name of Carl Rudolf. Having studied law and philosophy at the universities of Königsberg, Breslau, and Berlin, Gottschall began his literary career as a dramaturge in Königsberg in 1847. He edited *Blätter für literarische Unterhaltung* (Magazine of Literary Diversions) until 1888 and thereby exercised considerable literary influence. Among his earliest literary works were revolutionary poems *"Barrikadenlieder"* (Songs for the Barricades), which appeared in Königsberg in 1848. Later, his novels and plays expressed a conservative and nationalistic attitude. In addition to his literary activities, he also founded of the German Chess Federation.

Grand Elector (Winter Storms)

1620 (Berlin)–1688 (Potsdam). Friedrich Wilhelm I, known as the Grand Elector. He succeeded to the title in 1640 toward the end of the Thirty Years' War (1618–48). When France revoked the Edict of Nantes in 1685, which protected the Huguenots (French Protestants), the Grand Elector issued the Edict of Potsdam, under which over 20,000 refugees were welcomed to Brandenburg. Through treaties and warfare, Friedrich Wilhelm enlarged his holdings and laid the foundations for Brandenburg-Preussen to become a sovereign European power.

Ferdinand Adolf Gregorovius (Winter Storms)

1821 (Neidenburg, East Prussia)–1891 (Munich). Author of historical novels who wrote under the pen name of Ferdinand Fuchsmund. His early writings were satires, dramas, novels, and poems; however, with historical novels that were often set in medieval times, he became a popular author. His eight-volume opus *Geschichte der Stadt Rom im Mittelalter* (History of Rome in the Middle Ages) is now considered historically accurate, but contemporary historians considered the work too novelistic to be good history.

Battle of Gumbinnen (Winter Storms)

August 19–20, 1914. Disastrous defeat for Germany in World War I. Germany's Eastern Front was defended only by the Eighth Army when, contrary to all expectation of the German High Command, the Russians attacked with its First Army or Vilna Army under P. K. Rennenkampf and its Second Army or Warsaw Army under A. V. Samsonov. The Germans under the command of General Max von Prittwitz suffered heavy losses and defeat at the Battle of Gumbinnen, a town in East Prussia (now Gussew, Russia). To escape the Russians, who were about to converge on the Germans, Prittwitz ordered retreat to beyond the Vistula River, leaving East Prussia open to the enemy. The German High Command immediately replaced Prittwitz with Paul von Hindenburg, who was called from retirement, and appointed Erich Ludendorff as Hindenburg's chief of staff. As heroes of the Battle of Gumbinnen, both generals played a key role in the failure of the Weimar Republic and the rise of Hitler.

Ha-Me'assef (Conflicts and Personal Fates)

"The Gatherer." *Ha-Me'assef* was the first important Jewish journal in Europe and marked the beginning of a modern Jewish press; its first issue was published in Königsberg in 1784 and its last issue appeared in 1812. It adopted the form of the "moral weeklies," then popular in Germany. Founded by the disciples of Moses Mendelssohn, who even contributed a few Hebrew poems anonymously, the monthly was intended to develop a Jewish press closely connected with the *Haskala* (Jewish Emancipation). The publishers considered Yiddish to be an unsuitable language for the paper that was to advance the ideas of the German Enlightenment even though Yiddish would reach the largest audience; they rejected German, although eventually some supplements were entirely in German, as that would reach too few readers; they chose to publish in Hebrew, and thus *Ha-Me'assef* marked the beginning of the revival of Hebrew as a modern language. The intent was to replace the rabbinic Hebrew of traditional Talmudic studies in the yeshiva curriculum of the day with a pure, scriptural Hebrew.

Annexation of Hanover (Prologue)

As a result of Prussia's defeat of Austria in 1866, the Kingdom of Prussia was enlarged by the territories of Hanover, Electoral Hesse, the Duchy of Nassau, and the city of Frankfurt am Main.

Hasidim (Cabinetmaking)

"The pious." The term has been used at different times to describe various movements in Judaism. The most current Hasidic movement was founded by the mystical rabbi Baal-Shem-Tov in eighteenth-century Poland. It stressed joyous religious expression in music and dancing. The movement was a reaction to the influence of the Enlightenment, and emphasized moral teachings through the use of legends and stories rather than the interpretation of Talmudic law. By the 1830s the majority of Jews in the Ukraine, Galicia, and central Poland was Hasidic, with the tradition handed down through great rabbis. In the present-day Hasidic movement, now centered in the United States and Israel, the emphasis is on traditionalism to defend against secular influences.

Markus Herz (Conflicts and Personal Fates)

1747 (Berlin)–1803 (Berlin). Physician and philosopher. Son of a Torah scribe, Herz rose to prominence as a philosopher who disseminated the ideas of Kant, and as a physician who brought the principles of the Enlightenment to the practice of medicine. Although showered with honors, including an appointment by King Friedrich Wilhelm II to a chair of philosophy, Herz's religion barred his election to the Royal Prussian Academy of Sciences. Today his fame is eclipsed by that of his wife, Henriette Herz, whose literary salon was the center of Berlin intellectual life in the late eighteenth century. He lies buried next to his good friend Moses Mendelssohn.

Theodor Herzl (A Conversation)

1860 (Budapest)–1904 (Edlach, Austria). Founder of national Zionism and the World Zionist Organization. The Dreyfus affair convinced Herzl that assimilation was not the answer to anti-Semitism, that the Jews needed a Jewish national state as their homeland, and that they needed to return from the diaspora to Zion. Herzl discussed these concepts in *Der Judenstaat* (*The Jewish State*, 1896). He convened the First Zionist Congress in Basel, which established the World Zionist Organization and formulated the Basel Plan. By 1902, after six Zionist Congresses, Zionist activists had established the Jewish National Fund, a newspaper *Die Welt*, and other organizational tools for advocacy of a Zionist state in the land of Israel. At the Sixth Congress Herzl suggested a homeland in Uganda, but was met with opposition. His efforts ultimately culminated in the declaration of the state of Israel on May 14, 1948.

Theodor Heuss (The Königsberg "Cemetery")

1884 (Brackenheim)–1963 (Stuttgart). Politician. Heuss was a political journalist in Berlin after World War I. He served in the *Reichstag* (parliament) as a member of the *Deutsche Demokratische Partei* (German Democratic Party), and later as a representative of the *Deutsche Staatspartei* (German State Party). He voted for the Enabling Act, which gave Hitler total power in 1933. Active in politics, Heuss entered the Bundestag (parliament) of the new Federal Republic of Germany and became its first president (1949–59). Heuss gave a speech in December 1949 to the

Gesellschaft für christlich-jüdische Zusammenarbeit (Society for Christian-Jewish Cooperation), in which he said, having first rejected the notion of collective guilt as an invention of the occupying forces, "But there is something like a collective shame that grows and remains from that time [the Nazi era]. The most terrible thing Hitler did to us—and he did a lot—is this: that he forced us to be ashamed of bearing with him and his henchmen that we are called 'Germans.'"

Heinrich Himmler (Birth Pangs)

1900 (Munich)–1945 (Lüneburg). Head of the SS. Turned down in World War I by the Navy because he wore glasses, Himmler volunteered as a *Fahnenjunker* (officer cadet) in a Bavarian infantry regiment but never saw action. After the war, he marched on Munich with the *Lauterbach Freikorps* to overthrow Kurt Eisner's Räterepublik (soviet republic). In the 1920s he joined the Nazi Party and participated in the failed Hitler Putsch on November 9, 1923. In 1927 he was appointed the head of the SS *(Schützstaffel)*, which he built into an organization independent of its original place within the SA *(Sturmabteilung)*. By 1932, just before Hitler came to power, the SS had over 50,000 members. At the beginning of the war, the Gestapo, the criminal police, and the SD (*Sicherheitsdienst* [Security Service]) were consolidated into the RSHA (Reichssicherheitsamt [Reich Security Main Office]) directly under the control of Himmler. His full title after June 1936 was Reichsführer-SS und Chef der deutschen Polizei (Reich SS Leader and Chief of the German Police). Himmler organized the persecution and murder of Poles and Jews in Poland with the help of the *Einsatzgruppen* (Task Forces). In 1941 Hitler charged Himmler with the security of the occupied territories in the East and thereby Himmler was Heydrich's superior in carrying out the "Final Solution of the Jewish question." The failed assassination attempt on July 20, 1944, gave Himmler even more power, and by March 1945 he tried to contact the Allies to make a separate peace. Furious, Hitler stripped him of all his offices and issued an arrest order on April 28, 1945. He fled in the uniform of a Gestapo agent, having disguised himself by shaving his moustache and wearing a black patch over one eye. The British quickly arrested him on account of the uniform. When his real identity was discovered, Himmler committed suicide by swallowing a vial of potassium cyanide.

Paul Hindemith (Aunt Fanny)

1895 (Hanau)–1963 (Frankfurt am Main). Composer, conductor, violinist. Along with Schoenberg, Stravinsky, Bartók, the composer Hindemith was one of the four founders of modernism. In 1938 he left for Switzerland, then moved to America. From 1940 to 1953 he taught at Yale. In 1953 he returned to Switzerland.

Freiherr Leopold von Hoverbeck (Winter Storms)

1822 (Nikelsdorf, Kreis Allenstein, East Prussia)–1875 (Gersau, Switzerland). Founding member of the *Fortschrittspartei* (Progressive Party). In June 1861, a group of left liberals founded the Progressive Party under the leadership of Max von Forckenbeck, Freiherr von Hoverbeck, Theodor Mommsen, and others. It was the strongest party in the Reichstag during the constitutional struggle with

Bismarck and reconstituted itself as the Democratic Party of Germany after World War I. The Progressives espoused the democratic principles of the French Revolution of 1789 and the German revolutions of 1848 and advocated a parliamentary state and laissez-faire economic policies. They were antimilitarist in a period when Germany was increasingly arming for war. The Progressive Party and its descendants bitterly opposed the principles of socialism and the Social Democratic Party. Hoverbeck is also remembered for his contribution to the development of East Prussian agriculture in his position as *Landwirtschaftsdirektor* (agricultural director) for the Department of Mohrenger, a position he held from 1862 until his death.

Wilhelm von Humboldt (Nidden)

1767 (Potsdam)–1835 (Tegel bei Berlin). Prussian liberal, education reformer, diplomat. Humboldt was steeped in the tradition of the Berlin Enlightenment. When he returned to Berlin after serving as the Prussian envoy to the Vatican (1802–8), he was made head of the department in charge of education. It was a period of reform as Prussia struggled to recover from its defeat by the French under Napoleon. Humboldt reformed the curriculum of the secondary schools; he established the University of Berlin; he was part of the Prussian delegation to the Congress of Vienna; and he briefly held the post of Minister of the Interior to work with Baron von Stein on Prussia's new constitution. Resigning from the civil service in 1819, Humboldt devoted himself to the study of languages, literature, antiquity, and political theory, all of which informed his ideas of *Bildung* (education, or in the broadest sense of the word, personal cultivation). For Humboldt, *Bildung* was the result of the cultivation of intellectual, social, and spiritual development so that the individual achieves his fullest humanity. Of the Courland Spit, Humboldt wrote in 1807: "[It] is so remarkable that one must visit it just as one must visit Spain or Italy if one's soul should is not to lack a wondrous image."

Engelbert Humperdinck (Nidden)

1854 (Sieberg, Hanover)–1892 (Neustrelitz). Opera composer. In 1893 his first, and best known, opera, *Hänsel und Gretel,* premiered. He was an associate of Richard Wagner.

"Inability to mourn" (The Königsberg "Cemetery")

Phrase from the title of the book *Die Unfähigkeit zu trauern (The Inability to Mourn: Principles of Collective Behavior),* published in 1967. The book by Alexander and Margarete Mitscherlich was instrumental in breaking the silence about the recent German past. It addressed the collective German difficulty in dealing with the recent history of the Third Reich. The two psychoanalysts used the phrase to explain people's psychodynamic process when they fail to work through grief and remain obsessively invested in their loss. People, they said, become sick due to their inability to mourn and refusal to recognize the problems they collectively faced arising from Germany's particular history in World War II. The authors insisted on the battle of remembrance and recognized the painful but necessary process of remembering.

Johann Jacoby (Conflicts and Personal Fates)

1805 (Königsberg)–1877 (Königsberg). Physician and political activist. Jacoby was first inspired by the Paris July Revolution of 1830 to become politically active and became the leader of the antifeudal opposition in East Prussia. In his 1841 pamphlet *Vier Fragen beantwortet von einem Ostpreussen (Four Questions Answered by an East Prussian)*, Jacoby called for a movement by the middle class to demand participation in the politics and national interests of a unified Germany; the pamphlet made him famous throughout Germany. He was active in the revolutions of 1848, which persuaded the king to reform East Prussia. On account of his advocacy of a constitutional monarchy at the Frankfurt National Assembly in 1849, Jacoby was later tried on the charge of high treason in Königsberg, but was acquitted. He was active in the cause of Jewish Emancipation: in 1838 he drafted a new *Synagogenordnung* (order of service) that was intended to reform the service to make it more "respectable."

SS Colonel Karl Jäger (Afterword)

1888 (Schaffhausen, Switzerland)–1959. SS officer in charge of the liquidation of the Jews in Lithuania. Jäger joined the Nazi Party in 1923 and the SS in 1932. Later he became commander with the rank of SS *Standartenführer* (SS Colonel) of the *Sicherheitspolizei* (Security Police) and of the *Sicherheitsdienst* for the General Commissariat of Kovno, Lithuania. He was, therefore, the person in charge of the extermination of Lithuanian Jewry. His report dated December 1, 1941, begins laconically: "On my orders and command, the executions carried out by the Lithuanian partisans . . ." and then lists in lapidary fashion the date of the action (all occurred between July 4 and November 25, 1941), the place, the number of Jews, Jewesses, children, Communists, and, on occasion, gypsies and Poles executed; at the bottom of each page there is a running subtotal, the grand total being 137,346. In reporting his success, he concludes that the solution to the "Jewish problem in Lithuania has been achieved." He describes the difficulty of the work and the administrative finesse necessary to overcome the "unbelievable obstacles." In 1943 Jäger was reassigned as chief of police in Reichenberg in the Sudetenland. After the war he hid under a false identity and became a farmer. When the December 1, 1941, report was discovered in 1959, Jäger was arrested, and while in prison awaiting trial, he committed suicide. The discovery was too late for the report to be used at the Nuremberg Trial or at the trial of the commanders of the *Einsatzgruppen*, but the report has been used in subsequent trials. In one federal case a U.S. appeals court wrote in 1996 "[Jäger's] account leaves one in a horror-driven state of shock."

Jewish Emancipation (Conflicts and Personal Fates)

The Jewish struggle to win civil, political, and social equality with gentiles in modern Europe began with the French Revolution and the spread of its ideas of liberty, equality, and brotherhood. By 1815 however, reaction set in and in Germany each state was permitted to enact its own laws concerning Jews. The question of Jewish Emancipation became one of German politics for liberal Jews, who saw possible relief in a united Germany and allied themselves with German liberals. After the failed revolutions of 1848, Jewish rights suffered a setback. Many liberal Jews then sought social and economic emancipation, not through laws and constitutions but in integration into German culture in general. In many Jewish communities, including Königsberg, the tension between the assimilationists and the religiously orthodox played out in the struggle to modernize ritual observance. (*See* Johann Jacoby.) Joseph Levin Saalschütz (1801–63) was a moderate reform preacher in Königsberg, who supported Jakob Mecklenberg's efforts to integrate different Orthodox and Eastern European groups together into one Jewish community. By the 1920s Jews were accepted as university professors in Königsberg: Felix Perles (1874–1933), who advocated assimilationist policies, was appointed honorary professor of modern Hebrew and Aramaic literature; and Ludwig Lichtheim, Julius Schreiber, Max Jaffé, and Alfred Ellinger were on the faculty of medicine at the University of Königsberg.

Joseph Joachim (Prologue)

1831 (Kittsee, Austria)–1907 (Berlin). Violinist and composer. Joachim studied under Felix Mendelssohn and was the concertmaster and solo violinist to George V, King of Hanover, and the director of music school in the Royal Academy of Arts in Berlin. He was the first major virtuoso to perform the works of many composers. He was influenced by Robert Schumann.

Wilhelm Jordan (Winter Storms)

1819 (Insterburg, East Prussia)–1904 (Frankfurt am Main). Poet and member of the National Assembly of 1848. Jordan studied theology and philosophy at the University of Königsberg. He was a newspaper correspondent in Paris in 1848, then in Berlin. After 1848 his poetry sought to revive German myths to express the new German identity. In his epic poem "Nibelunge" (started in 1867), he sought to use contemporary national subject matter to achieve a rebirth of medieval myth. He translated George Sand and Shakespeare into German.

July 20th Plot (Winter Storms)

The conspiracy to overthrow Hitler, culminating in the failed assassination attempt to kill the Führer at a war conference on July 20, 1944, in his headquarters in Rastenburg (the "Wolf's Lair"), East Prussia. Hitler had the conspirators tracked down. Some were brought before the *Volksgericht* presided over by Freisler, who sentenced them to an ignominious, painful, and slow death: strangulation by piano wire, their bodies hanged on meat hooks. Their last agonies were filmed for Hitler to watch. Other conspirators were shot by firing squad, including von Stauffenberg, who had placed a briefcase with a bomb on the floor beside Hitler. It is estimated that between 180 and 200 were killed as a direct result of the July 20th Plot, including Pastor Dietrich Bonhoeffer and his brother-in-law Hans von Dohnányi (legal expert), General Field Marshal Erwin Rommel, Adam von Trott zu Solz (counselor of legation in the Foreign Office), Dr. Carl Friedrich Goerdeler (former lord mayor of Leipzig and price commissioner), Dr. Albrecht Haushofer (author of the haunting *Moabit Sonnets*), and Christian Albrecht Ulrich von Hassel (Ambassador in Rome 1933–37).

Jungvolk (Aunt Fanny)

Junior division of the *Hitlerjugend* (Hitler Youth) for boys from the ages of ten to fourteen.

Mikhail Ivanovich Kalinin (Conflicts and Personal Fates)

1875 (Verkhnayay Troitsa, Korchev Region, Tver Province)–1946 (Moscow). Soviet politician. Kalinin was born a peasant and joined the Russian Social Democratic Workers Party in 1898. He participated in the Russian Revolution of 1905 in St. Petersburg. Kalinin became a member of the Bolsheviks' Central Committee and was cofounder of their newspaper *Pravda* in 1912. After November 1917 he became the mayor of St. Petersburg. He served in a number of high political positions and as Chairman of the Central Executive Committee of Soviets of the USSR from 1922 to 1938. This committee ceased to function when the new Soviet parliament, "the Supreme Soviet," was instituted, and Kalinin was elected chairman, a post equal to that of head of the Soviet state. Kalinin remained a loyal supporter of Stalin throughout his life.

Immanuel Kant (School Days 2)

1724 (Königsberg)–1804 (Königsberg). Philosopher of the Enlightenment. His works include *Kritik der reinen Vernunft (Critique of Pure Reason)* (1781); "Was ist Aufklärung?" ("What is Enlightenment?") (1784); and *Kritik der praktischen Vernunft (Critique of Practical Reason)* (1788), which held that fundamental freedom of the individual is freedom to obey consciously the laws of the universe as revealed by reason. In 1795 Kant published "Zum ewigen Frieden. Ein philosophischer Entwurf" ("Perpetual Peace: A Philosophical Sketch") to demonstrate the principles of philosophy prove that it is possible for idealism to prevail over realism in international relations and the pursuit of peace is not illusory.

Otto Klemperer (Prologue)

1885 (Breslau)–1973 (Zürich). Conductor. In 1927 Klemperer became the director of the Kroll Oper in Berlin, whose special mission was to perform new and recent works. He emigrated in 1933 to the United States, where he became the conductor of the Los Angeles Philharmonic Orchestra. He later became conductor of the Budapest Opera Orchestra and, in 1955, the principal conductor of the Philharmonia Orchestra of London.

Erich Koch (School Days 2)

1896 (Prussia)–1986 (Barczewo Prison, Poland). Party leader and *Gauleiter* of East Prussia. A member of the NSDP since 1920, Koch was appointed *Reichskommissar* for the Ukraine in 1941. He was responsible for four million dead, including the entire Jewish population. He sent another 2.5 million as slave workers known as *Ostarbeiter* (workers from the East) to Germany. After the collapse of the Ukraine, he returned in 1944 as the *Gauleiter* of East Prussia. In 1945 he slipped incognito into the British Zone of Occupation. In 1959 he was discovered and handed over to Poland. In 1959 he was tried and sentenced to death, but the sentence was commuted to house arrest due to illness.

Käthe Kollwitz (Nidden)

1867 (Königsberg)–1945 (Berlin). Sculptor and graphic artist. Her work is known for its Expressionist style and proletarian content. In 1919 she became the first woman member of *Preussische Akademie der Künste* (Prussian Academy of Arts), but in 1933 she was forced to resign because the Nazis disapproved of her work and politics. She lost her son in Flanders in 1914, and she lost her grandson in Russia in 1942.

Lev Kopelev (The Russians)

1912 (Kiev)–1997 (Cologne). Writer. Jewish. A Communist Party agitator during the forced collectivization in the Ukraine, Kopelev later criticized the Soviet regime. He studied German at the Moscow Institute of Foreign Languages. During World War II, he became a propaganda officer and translator in the interrogation of captured Nazi generals. He was arrested in 1945 and charged with "bourgeois humanitarianism" and "pity for the enemy" because he attempted to stop looting and raping by Soviet soldiers in East Prussia, and eventually served a term of hard labor. In the 1960s he became a dissident, supporting writers such as Solzhenitsyn. His first memoir *To Be Preserved Forever* began circulating as *samizdat*, then was smuggled to the West. In 1980 Kopelev and his wife, stripped of Soviet citizenship, left for Germany, where they settled in Cologne.

Fritz Kreisler (The Russians)

1875 (Vienna)–1962 (New York City). Violin virtuoso and composer. A child prodigy, Fritz Kreisler began his formal music studies at the age of seven. He was wounded in action during World War I and wrote "Four Weeks in the Trenches. The War Story of a Violinist" in 1915. He was enormously popular in the United States and Europe. Both as a performer and composer, he was noted for his brief encore pieces. In 1935 Kreisler revealed that a number of the pieces he had published as composed by old masters were really his own. In 1939 Kreisler, who was Jewish, became a French citizen and in 1943, an American citizen.

Peter Kreuder (Gleanings)

1905 (Aachen)–1981 (Salzburg). "King of the Evergreen." His musical career began with classical training and concerts. In the 1930s his popular music career began with the composition of light operas and musical comedies. He composed the music for 188 films. His first real success was his film music for *Mazurka* (1933) starring Pola Negri. In 1940 he went to Sweden for the premier of one of his operas, returning to Germany only in 1942. Immediately after the war, he began to tour South America. In 1950 Evita Peron honored him with the title of "professor." In 1955 he returned to Europe and in 1959 he became an Austrian citizen. In the 1970s he toured America, appearing on television with Perry Como, David Frost, and others. One of his most popular melodies "Für eine Nacht voller Seligkeit" [For One Night Filled with Delight] was composed in 1940 for the film *Kora Terry*. His musical hits continue to be available on compact discs.

Kreutzer Sonata (My School Days Are Over)

Sonata for Piano and Violin, op. 47, no. 9 (1802/1803) by Beethoven dedicated to Rudolphe Kreutzer (1766–1831). The French composer and violinist was a professor of violin at the Paris Conservatory who taught method; Kreutzer composed numerous operas, concertos, and sonatas, but is best known for his forty études for the violin.

Erwin Kroll (Nidden)

1886 (Deutsch-Eylau, East Prussia)–1976 (Berlin). Composer and music critic. Kroll studied in Königsberg and Munich. From 1919 to 1924 Kroll was repetiteur at the State Opera in Munich. From 1925 to 1933 he was a music journalist in Königsberg. During World War II Kroll led a precarious existence in Königsberg and was arrested toward the end of the war. After the war until 1953 he was active in the Berlin studios of the Northwest Radio station. He composed songs and chamber music but is better known for his musical biography writing, which includes *Musikstadt Königsberg* (The Musical City of Königsberg), which appeared in 1966.

Eduard Künneke (Berlin)

1885 (Emmerich am Rhein)–1953 (Berlin). Composer and conductor. Künneke studied with Max Bruch. From 1907 to 1911 he was the choral director at the Berliner Neues Operettentheater (Berlin New Operetta Theatre), then the Kapellmeister of theatrical music and the composer for the Deutsches Theater Berlin. He conducted the first known recording of Wagner's *Tannhäuser:* one act from the opera sung by Fritz Vogelstrom, in 1909. During World War I he was briefly a horn player in an infantry regiment before returning to civilian life and musical theatre in Berlin. His second marriage in 1920 was to the singer Katharina Garden. The operetta *Der Vetter aus Dingsda* (The Cousin from Whatsit) (1921) was not his first production, but it was the one for which he became famous. Before and after the Nazi regime, Künneke was president of the Verband Deutscher Bühnenschriftsteller und Bühnenkomponisten (Playwrights and Composers Association); in the years 1933–44 he was a member of the board. After World War II he was active in the organization he helped to found for German composers. He wrote a number of operettas, as well a number of stage plays.

KZ (The Chemical Factory of Gamm & Son)

Konzentrationslager or concentration camp. The term was first used, it seems, in connection with a policy of *"reconcentración"* by Arsenio Martinez Campos, commander of the Spanish garrison in Cuba in 1895 in a secret communication to the Spanish government on how to handle the Cuban insurgency; Campos recognized that the policy might lead to misery and famine, but would deprive the insurgents of food and support, thus effecting the end of the war. Campos' successor General Weyler y Nicolau put the theory into practice between 1896 and 1898, and in the miserable conditions that ensued it is estimated that some 200,000 *reconcentrados* may have died. By 1900 the term had been translated into English and was used to describe the camps in South Africa where Boer civilians were interned from 1900 to 1902 in order to deprive the insurgents of food and shelter from their sympathizers. Only four years later, the Germans used the technique in their African colonies in order to starve and work to death the Herero in what is now Namibia; by 1905, the word *Konzentrationslager* had entered the German language. In a chilling foreshadowing of what was to happen under Hitler, the Herero in these camps were the subjects of the first German medical experiments conducted on human beings by two of Joseph Mengele's teachers, Theodor Mollison and, to prove his theories about the superiority of the white race, Eugen Fischer. The first imperial commissioner of the colony Deutsch Süd-West Afrika was Dr. Heinrich Göring, the father of Hermann Göring, who set up the first concentration camps in the Third Reich. In the Third Reich the term referred to an elaborate system of labor and death camps. They were established as soon as the Nazis took power in 1933. Inmates included Communists, Jews, Socialists, Democrats, trade unionists, pacifists, Jehovah's Witnesses, gypsies, homosexuals, religious and even Nazi dissidents.

General Otto Lasch (Prologue)

1893–1971. Infantry General and *Festungskommandant* of Königsberg. After World War I, Lasch belonged to a Freikorps in Lyck, a city in the southeastern part of East Prussia, where his brother was the mayor. Lasch was appointed Festungskommandant of Königsberg on February 5, 1945. His orders were to defend Königsberg against the Red Army. He surrendered the city only after it had been destroyed, on April 9, 1945. On April 10, 1945, a German war communiqué declared resistance in Königsberg had ceased but there was no surrender; only three days after Lasch's surrender, on April 12, 1945, was there a German war communiqué announcing the surrender as well as the death penalty for the treasonous commander Otto Lasch. Lasch and 27,000 German soldiers were captured by the Soviets. The Soviets did not take Pillau until April 25, 1945. In the present-day remains of Lasch's bunker, the story of Königsberg's capitulation is told: 42,000 German soldiers and 60,000 Soviets and uncounted civilians perished in the final three-day battle. Lasch survived the surrender and then Siberia, returning to Germany to write his memoirs *So fiel Königsberg*, first published in 1958.

Johann Caspar Lavater (The Star of David)

1741 (Zürich)–1801 (Zürich). Theologian and mystic. Lavater's most famous work *Von der Physiognomik* (About Physiognomy) (1772) established physiognomy as a science, defended its usefulness, and set forth rules on how to interpret the shape of facial features such as the forehead, the eyes, and nose. Lavater's new science elaborated the rules for telling whether someone is stupid, cautious, lazy, etc. from the physical characteristics of the face.

Gotthold Ephraim Lessing (The Star of David)

1729 (Kamenz, Oberlausitz)–1781 (Braunschweig). Playwright and essayist. Son of a pastor, Lessing studied medicine and theology in Leipzig. Lessing began his literary career by writing for several newspapers in Berlin. In 1767 he was appointed dramaturge for the *Deutsches Nationaltheater* (German National Theater) in Hamburg; in 1770 he was appointed librarian in Wolfenbüttel. He wrote poetry, philosophical essays, and plays. The play *Nathan der Weise* (Nathan the Wise) (1779), set in the Holy Land at the time of the Crusades, was revolutionary in its day because it espoused the idea of religious tolerance and the ethical and moral equality of Christian, Moslem, and Jewish religions. The character of Nathan was based on Lessing's good friend Moses Mendelssohn (1729–86), the grandfather of the composer Felix Mendelssohn.

Theodor Lessing (Afterword)

1872 (Hanover)–1933 (Marienbad). Pacifist and educator. Lessing studied medicine, philosophy, and psychology. During World War I he wrote a pamphlet appealing to the "intellectual elite" of Germany to protest the war and the fanatical nationalism fueling it. He founded the first *Volkshochschule* (adult education center) in 1919. In 1925 Lessing published an attack on Hindenburg as unfit to be the new *Reichspräsident* and thereby unleashed a vitriolic campaign against him on the part of the nationalistic fraternity students. His colleagues at the *Technische Hochschule* (Technical College) in Hanover demanded that the government fire him. Right-wing students heckled his classes, chased him down the street, and attacked him. On March 1, 1933, Lessing fled to the Bohemian spa of Marienbad, where he continued to write and continued to provoke heated reaction. On August 30, 1933, two thugs in the pay of the SA sneaked in through his study window and shot him.

Max Liebermann (Prologue)

1847 (Berlin)–1935 (Berlin). Painter and sculptor. Liebermann studied in Berlin, Weimar, and Paris. The school of Dutch realism and later the French modernists influenced his style. He became a professor of the *Königliche Akademie der Künste* (Royal Academy of Arts) in Berlin in 1897. In 1927 he painted his well-known portrait of the Reichspräsident Paul von Hindenburg. In 1932 he was named the honorary president of the *Preussische Akademie der Künste* (Prussian Academy of Arts), but as a Jew he resigned the next year. During his tenure, he was one of the founding members of the Berlin Secession.

Longnose the Dwarf (*Kristallnacht* and After)

Fairy tale by Wilhelm Hauff (1802 [Stuttgart]–1827 [Stuttgart]). A private tutor, Hauff wrote a series of literary fairy tales. "Der Zwerg Nase" was one of four tales in the *Märchen-Almanach für Söhne und Töchter gebildeter Stände (Fairy Tale Almanac for Sons and Daughters of the Genteel Classes)*.

Konrad Lorenz (Prologue)

1903 (Vienna)–1989 (Altenberg, Austria). Professor of animal behavior. Lorenz studied medicine in Vienna and at Columbia University; he earned his Ph.D. in zoology from the University of Munich in 1933. In 1937 he was appointed lecturer in comparative anatomy and animal psychology at the University of Vienna. From

1940 to 1942 he held the chair for general psychology at the Albertus University in Königsberg. From 1942 to 1944 he served as a physician in the German army, and was a prisoner of war in Soviet Union until 1948. From 1949 to 1951 he headed the Institute of Comparative Ethology (study of the organization of individual and group behavior patterns) in Altenberg, Austria. In 1950 he established a comparative ethology department in the Max Planck Institute, Westphalia. From 1961 to 1973 he served as the director of the Max Planck Institute for Behavior Physiology in Seewiesen. In 1973 he was awarded the Nobel prize for physiology and medicine (shared with Karl von Frisch and Nikolaus Tinbergen) for discoveries concerning animal behavior patterns. His fame rests on his discovery of imprinting, made with Oscar Heinroth, and on two of his books: *King Solomon's Ring* (1949) and *On Aggression* (1963).

Martin Luther (Star of David)

1483 (Eisleben)–1546 (Eisleben). Protestant reformer and translator of the bible into German. Luther became a monk in the Augustinian Order in 1505, but he struggled with his own inner doubts. He came to believe that life comes by the gift of God, that is to say, by grace, that faith, not good works, is what God wants. Luther became the spokesman and the leader of the Protestant Reformation. Although Luther introduced a religious revolution, he expected loyalty to secular rulers; for example, he was horrified that the peasants rose up against their rulers in his name in 1524. In 1523 Luther wrote *Dass Jesus ein geborener Jude sei (That Jesus Was Born a Jew)*, hoping to convert the Jews to Christianity. Disappointed, Luther not only approved of anti-Jewish laws as their just punishment for denying Jesus as the Christ and for Jewish usury, but in 1543 he also published *Die Juden und ihre Lügen (The Jews and Their Lies):* Jews are "truly stupid fools"; "blind"; "thieves and robbers who daily eat no morsel and wear no thread of clothing which they have not stolen and pilfered from us by means of their accursed robbery"; "lazy rogues"; and they should be "eject[ed] forever from this country"; the government should "first, set fire to their synagogues or schools"; "their houses [should be] razed and destroyed"; "their prayer books and Talmudic writings . . . taken from them"; "their rabbis . . . forbidden to teach henceforth on pain of loss of life and limb"; "safe-conduct on the highways . . . abolished . . . for the Jews"; and their "cash and treasure . . . taken from them."

Marshal Edmé Patrice Maurice de MacMahon (Prologue)

1808 (Sully, Saône-et-Loire)–1893 (Montcresson, Loiret). Head of the French Army in the Alsace during the Franco-Prussian War. MacMahon was defeated by Prussian King Friedrich IV in the Battle of Wörth on August 6, 1870. To Bismarck's dismay, MacMahon supported the restoration of the French monarchy, a policy that came to naught.

Thomas Mann (Nidden)

1875 (Lübeck)–1955 (Zürich). Novelist, essayist, and short story writer. In 1929 Mann was awarded the Nobel prize for literature. While Mann was traveling in Switzerland in 1933, the Nazis seized power and Mann fled to the United States,

first to Princeton, then to Los Angeles. Although he had been a reluctant supporter of democracy and the Weimar Republic, Mann spoke out against the Nazi
regime.

mapach, pashto, munach, segol (*Kristallnacht* and After)

Musical tropes, known as *Teamim*. These are sets of graphic signs or cantillation
marks used when chanting texts in the synagogue. There is a set of cantillations
for the Torah and another for the Prophets. The names of the tropes allude to the
hand movements originally used by the *Tomech*, or helper; *pashto*, for example,
means "stretching." There are different sets for the High Holidays, for the Sabbath,
and for other holidays.

Karl May (Bar Mitzvah)

1842 (Hohenstein-Ernstthal, Saxony)–1912 (Radebeul bei Dresden). Author. Son
of a weaver, May became an elementary school teacher. When he was found guilty
of stealing a watch, he spent six weeks in prison and permanently lost his teaching license. He spent a total of seven years in prison for various frauds and scams,
such as posing as a physician, a police detective, and a notary's assistant. In 1875
he became the editor of various journals in Dresden. In 1878 he quit to write his
tales, many set in the Old West, where May had never set foot. His westerns, such
as *Winnetou* and *Old Shatterhand,* are beloved children's literature to this day. In
1900 May traveled abroad for the first time, enjoying fame and fortune from the
royalties pouring in. On his return he found his previously unpublished (and
naughty by Wilhelmine standards) novels published. In the ensuing scandals, May
was exposed as a former jailbird. He devoted the remainder of his life struggling
to regain his good name.

Memel (Nidden)

City and port in the Memelland, a district of East Prussia on the Baltic. The city
lies at the mouth of the Memel River, also known as the Niemen River. In 1919
the district was put under the administration of the League of Nations. Four years
later, in 1923, Lithuanian troops seized the district and in 1924 it became an
autonomous region within Lithuania. The electoral victory for the National
Socialists led to the German ultimatum in 1938 to return the district to German
rule and Lithuania complied. After the war, the district was restored to Lithuania,
which was by then part of the USSR. The "Memel" in German literature is often
the symbol for the easternmost point of German lands.

Moses Mendelssohn (Conflicts and Personal Fates)

1729 (Dessau)–1786 (Berlin). Philosopher. Known as the "Jewish Emancipator,"
Moses Mendelssohn paved the way for Jewish participation in German life in the
eighteenth and nineteenth centuries, writing about the necessity of tolerance; he
was the first Jew to translate the *Pentateuch* (the Five Books of Moses) into High
German. He was also the first to interpret the Jewish religion using the philosophical terms of the Enlightenment. He is considered to be the founder of *Haskala*
(Jewish Emancipation). On a brief visit to Königsberg, Mendelssohn was publicly

embraced by Kant, a minor occurrence that, however, gave the cultured Jews of the city the feeling that they were held in esteem by the gentile community.

Adolph von Menzel (Prologue)

1815 (Breslau)–1905 (Berlin). Painter and graphic artist. Menzel's early commissions were for his work as illustrator. He was a member of the *Königliche Akademie der Künste* (Royal Academy of Arts) in Berlin. His work reveals acute psychological insight into his subjects.

Agnes Miegel (Nidden)

1879 (Königsberg)–1964 (Bad Salzuflen). Novelist and balladeer. Known as the "Mother of East Prussia," Miegel was a teacher, nurse, journalist, and novelist. During the Nazi period she signed an oath of allegiance to Hitler. In 1945 she fled to Denmark. In 1954 she became an honorary citizen of Denmark. "Die Frau von Nidden" ("The Woman of Nidden"), one of her minor poems, celebrates the village and environs.

Bernard Law Montgomery, First Viscount (The Chemical Factory of Gamm & Son)

1887 (London)–1976 (Alton, Hampshire). British general and field marshal. The son of an Anglican bishop, Montgomery lived in Tasmania before the family returned to England in 1910. He studied at the Royal Military Academy at Sandhurst. He had a distinguished military career in World War I and early in World War II he led a division in France and commanded the southeastern section of England, where a German invasion was anticipated. In August 1942 Churchill appointed him commander of the British Eighth Army in North Africa, which Rommel had pushed back to Egypt. Montgomery restored morale and secured superiority in men and matériel. He forced Rommel's retreat at the Battle of El Alamein in November 1942 and finally defeated the German forces in Tunisia in May 1943. Montgomery shared major responsibility for the successful invasion of Sicily in July 1943 and, under General Dwight D. Eisenhower, led the Allied invasion of France in June 1944. He received the surrender of the German northern armies on May 4, 1945. First knighted in 1942 (K.C.B.), Montgomery was made knight of the garter and was created a viscount in 1946. He was deputy commander of NATO from 1951 to 1958.

Napoleon III (Prologue)

1803 (Paris)–1873 (Chislehurst, England). King, Emperor of France, and nephew of Napoleon. From 1850 to 1852 he was the President of the Second Republic and from 1852 to 1870, the Emperor of France. He surrendered at the Battle of Sedan and was deposed on September 2, 1870. Released by the Germans, he went to live in England.

National Polish Home Army (Winter Storms)

A major force in the Polish underground state. The National Polish Home Army, with its commander-in-chief subordinate to the Polish Armed Forces, was commanded from London. The main task of the National Polish Home Army was organizing actions against German occupation forces. On August 1, 1944, with a force of forty-five thousand partisans, it attacked the Germans in Warsaw and was soon joined by Warsaw civilians: the Warsaw Uprising began. The city had ammunition sufficient for only a week. On Stalin's orders, the Russian army, which was less than twelve miles away across the Vistula, did not attempt to assist and refused to allow Americans and British to use the Russian airfields to drop ammunition and supplies. After sixty-three days of fighting, the Germans had succeeded in virtually annihilating the National Polish Home Army as well as destroying over 80 percent of the city.

Nidden (Nidden)

A fishing village on the Courland Spit or Kurische Nehrung. Thomas Mann's essay "Mein Sommerhaus" ("My Summer House") (1931) describes his idyllic summers at Nidden.

Non-Aggression Pact between Germany and the USSR (The War Begins)

The treaty signed on August 23, 1939, by the USSR (represented by Molotov) and the Third Reich (represented by Ribbentrop). The Non-Aggression Pact stunned the world and assured Hitler that he would not be fighting a war on two fronts. The treaty's non-secret articles stated that the parties "obligate[d] themselves to desist from any act of violence, any aggressive action, and any attack on each other, either individually or jointly with other Powers." In secret protocols, however, the two sides agreed on their spheres of influence. "[I]n the event of a territorial and political rearrangement in the areas belonging to the Baltic States (Finland, Estonia, Latvia, Lithuania)," the northern border of Lithuania marked the boundary in the Baltic. Likewise, in such an event in Poland, the boundary was formed by the rivers Narev, Vistula, and San. The question of Poland's independence and its borders would be determined only "in the course of further political developments."

NS (National Socialism) (School Days 1)

Nationalsozialismus (National Socialism), also called Nazism. The ideology of socialist economic ideas mixed with rabid nationalism and opposition to democracy flourished among many right-wing groups in Germany after World War I, including the then very tiny *Nationalsozialistische Deutsche Arbeiterpartei* (National Socialist German Workers' Party). Hitler led the party after 1920, bringing it to power in 1933. The party's doctrine drew on racist ideas in which the Jew was the antithesis of the "Aryan"; the doctrine also drew on a perverted understanding of the Nietzschean superhero; and it glorified Germanic myth. The party's political policies aimed for total control in a corporatist state where labor, recreation, religion, thought, and the economy were regimented under party control, and "undesirables" were imprisoned or killed.

Max Pechstein (Nidden)

1881 (Zwickau)–1955 (Berlin). Painter and graphic artist. In 1906 Pechstein became a member of *Die Brücke*, a group of Expressionist painters. In 1918 he was one of the founders of the politically radical artists' group November Revolution. In 1923 he became a member of the *Preussische Akademie der Künste* (Prussian Academy of Arts). In 1925 he was the theater designer for Max Reinhardt. The Nazis forbade him to paint and seized 326 of his paintings for the 1937 exhibition of *Entartete Kunst* (Degenerate Art). In 1945 he was appointed professor in the *Hochschule für Bildende Künste* (Academy of Fine Arts) in Berlin.

Pre-Socratics (The "Charity")

Greek philosophers, beginning at the end of the seventh century B.C. before Socrates (469 B.C.–399 B.C.), who combined mythology with rational thinking to define the fundamental forces of nature, to explain the creation of the world, and to explain the process of change. Active in Greece, Sicily, and Asia Minor, the pre-Socratics developed concepts of substance, infinity, power, numbers, motion, being, even the concept of the atom.

Frieda Fromm-Reichmann (Conflicts and Personal Fates)

1889 (Karlsruhe)–1957 (Rockville, Maryland). Psychotherapist and psychologist. Reichmann came from a solid German-Jewish middle-class and talented family (her maternal grandmother played piano with Clara Schuman-Wieck), who moved to Königsberg in 1893. In 1914 she completed her medical studies with a dissertation on pupillary changes in schizophrenics that is still cited today. She completed her psychoanalytical training in Berlin, and in 1924 she opened her *Therapeutikum* in Heidelberg, where she treated, then married Erich Fromm. In 1933 she fled Germany to go to Strasbourg, then to Palestine, finally coming to the United States in 1935. She was a major pioneer in using an intensive therapeutic relationship with patients with severe mental illnesses. In 1950 her textbook *Principles of Intensive Psychotherapy* appeared, and she is fictionally celebrated as Clara Fried, whose empathy cures schizophrenia, in Joanne Greenberg's *I Never Promised You a Rose Garden* (1964).

Ernst Reuter (Berlin)

1889 (Apenrade, Schleswig)–1953 (Berlin). First mayor of West Berlin after World War II. Reuter was educated as a philologist. He joined the Social Democratic Party (SPD) in 1912. He was drafted into the military during World War I and taken prisoner by the Russians in 1916. After the Revolution he joined the Communist Party and served as Commissar of the Volga German Autonomous Workers' Commune in 1918. On his return to Germany, he became the secretary for the Communist Party for Berlin, but was soon expelled because he criticized the German party for becoming bolshevized. He rejoined the SPD in 1922 and was elected to the city assembly of Berlin in 1926. In 1931 he was elected mayor of Magdeburg and in 1932 he was elected to the Reichstag. After Hitler came to power in 1933, Reuter was arrested several times. He fled to England in 1935. From 1939 to 1945 he lived in Turkey, where he was an advisor to the Turkish government and was a professor of government in Ankara. After the war, he reorganized the SPD. He was elected mayor of Berlin in 1947, but Soviet opposition barred his taking office. Not until 1948, after Berlin was divided into an East and West sector, did he become mayor of West Berlin. On September 9, 1948, when the Soviets instituted a blockade, Reuter appealed to the world to save West Berlin from Soviet seizure. He became the face and voice of the embattled West Berliners. He was still in office when he died in 1953.

Ritterkreuz (Mirror Images)

"Knight's Cross." The Nazi regime created a series of medals to be awarded for bravery in battle modeled on the traditional German Iron Cross. There were six ascending grades: (1) *Ritterkreuz* (Knight's Cross); (2) *Ritterkreuz mit Eichenlaub* (Knight's Cross with Oak Leaves); (3) *Ritterkreuz mit Eichenlaub und Schwerten* (Knight's Cross with Oak Leaves and Swords); (4) *Ritterkreuz mit Eichenlaub, Schwerten, und Brillanten* (Knight's Cross with Oak Leaves, Swords, and Diamonds); (5) *Ritterkreuz mit goldenen Eichenlaub, Schwerten, und Brillanten* (Knight's Cross with Golden Oak Leaves, Swords, and Diamonds); and (6) *Grosskreuz* (Grand Cross of the Iron Cross), whose only recipient was Hermann Göring, after the Battle of France.

Erwin Rommel (Cabinetmaking)

1891 (Heidenheim an der Brenz)–1944 (Herrlingen bei Ulm). German general. Rommel was known as the "Desert Fox" in World War II. Already a highly decorated officer in World War I, he commanded the armored "Ghost Division" in 1940 in France. In 1941 he took the *Deutsches Afrika Korps* (German Africa Corps) to Libya. He was named a Field Marshal in June 1942. He was finally defeated by the British Eighth Army under Montgomery at El Alamein in November 1942; he was recalled to Germany before the Korps' final defeat in May 1943. At the beginning of 1944 he was appointed Supreme Commander of the *Heeresgruppe B* in France. Although he was never active in the July 20th Plot, the conspirators wanted him as chief of state. After his name was revealed, Hitler forced him to commit suicide in exchange for protection of his family and a state funeral.

Julius Rupp (Winter Storms)

1809 (Königsberg)–1884 (Königsberg). Pastor. Julius Rupp was a lecturer at the University of Königsberg and a pastor. His research in patristic studies led him to distinguish between external and inner religious values. In 1846 Rupp founded the Free Protestant Congregation in Königsberg. His little congregation of 118 was the first to break away from the state Protestant Church. The bronze relief created by his granddaughter Käthe Kollwitz on the Kneiphof next to the Königsberg Cathedral bore his words: "He who fails to live by the truth he believes is the most dangerous enemy of truth itself." The monument, destroyed in the war, has been replaced by a new one in the original style.

Samland (Nidden)

District in former East Prussia that forms a peninsula into the Baltic Sea, north of Königsberg. The Samland was known since Roman times for its trade in amber.

Pablo de Sarasate (Gleanings)

1844 (Pamplona)–1908 (Biarritz). Violinist and composer. A child prodigy on the violin, he made his concert debut at the age of eight. He studied at the Paris Conservatory. As a concert performer, he was known for his virtuoso technique. As a composer, he was known for his fast tempos, fantastic technique, and use of Spanish folk melodies. Max Bruch composed his Concerto no. 2 for him. One of Sarasate's best known works is *Zigeunerweisen* (Gypsy Melodies) for violin.

Friedrich Schiller (School Days 2)

1759 (Marbach am Neckar)–1805 (Weimar). Dramatist, poet, and historian. In 1781 Schiller's turbulent first play *Die Räuber (The Robbers)* was a sensation, bringing the wrath of the Duke of Württemberg down upon his head. To escape punishment for deserting his military regiment to see his own play in defiance of ducal orders, Schiller fled first to Mannheim, then to Leipzig. By 1787 he was living in Weimar where he became an intimate friend of Goethe. In 1788 he was appointed professor of history at the University of Jena. His plays deal with the themes of freedom and tyranny, such as *Don Carlos* (1787), *Wallenstein* (1800), and *Wilhelm Tell* (1804). The idealism of Kant forms the philosophical underpinnings of Schiller's plays. Schiller's ballads and plays are still perennial favorites in the German high school curriculum and in theater repertory.

Karl Schmidt-Rottluff (Nidden)

1884 (near Chemnitz)–1976 (Berlin). Painter and graphic artist. Schmidt-Rottluff's Expressionist style is marked by bright, solid colors. In 1905 with Ernst Ludwig Kirchner and Fritz Bleyl, he founded *Die Brücke*, a group of avant-garde Expressionist artists. In 1913 *Die Brücke* was dissolved. He served during World War I in Russia. In 1931 he was accepted into the *Preussische Akademie der Künste* (Prussian Academy of Arts) in Berlin. In 1933 he was excluded by the Nazis, who seized twenty-five of his paintings for the 1937 exhibition of *Entartete Kunst* (Degenerate Art). The Nazis forbade him to paint in 1941. In 1947 he was appointed professor in *Hochschule für Bildende Künste* (Academy of Fine Arts) in Berlin.

Arnold Schoenberg (Aunt Fanny)

1874 (Vienna)–1951 (Los Angeles). Composer. Schoenberg was known for his atonal or twelve-note serial music, and his influence can be found in the compositions of his students Anton Webern and Alban Berg. From 1925 to 1933 he was a member of the *Preussische Akademie der Künste* (Prussian Academy of Fine Arts) in Berlin. In 1933 he emigrated to the United States, where from 1936 to 1944 he was a professor at the University of California Los Angeles. In 1941 he became an American citizen.

Hans and Sophie Scholl (Air Raids over Königsberg)

Hans: 1918 (Ingersheim)–1943 (Munich). Sophie: 1921 (Forchtenberg am Kocher)–1943 (Munich). Deeply committed Catholics, the brother (a student of medicine at the University of Munich) and sister (a student of biology and philosophy) became part of the resistance group known as "The White Rose." They were denounced to the Gestapo by a janitor, who happened to see them as they were distributing leaflets condemning the regime at the University of Munich. Arrested on February 18, 1943, they were tried by Freisler and were beheaded within a few hours of the verdict.

Heinrich Theodor von Schön (Winter Storms)

1773 (Schreitlauken, Kreise Tilsit)–1856 (Arnau, East Prussia). Prussian liberal reformer. As the Germans began to forge a national identity after the Napoleonic Wars of Liberation, they discovered Gothic architecture as the German national style. Marienburg Castle, once the fortress of the Teutonic Knights, was one of the admired medieval structures chosen to be preserved. Oberpräsident (Regional President) von Schön directed the initial stages of its restoration and wanted to turn the castle into a national monument commemorating the Wars of Liberation and the Prussian reforms. He considered the castle, along with the four hundred new schools in West Prussia, the highpoint of his administrative career.

Schöneberger Rathaus (Berlin)

The city hall of the Berlin district Schöneberg, built in the years between 1911 and 1914. The district did not administratively become part of Berlin until 1920. From after World War II until December 2, 1990, it served first as the office for the Allied liaison officers, and then as the meeting place for West Berlin's House of Representatives. Americans know the building as the backdrop for John F. Kennedy's 1963 speech, declaring "Ich bin ein Berliner" ("I am a Berliner"), which assured West Berlin and Germany of the American commitment to maintain West Berlin free of Soviet control. After 1990 the government functions of the city of Berlin were moved from the Schöneberger Rathaus and it is, once again, the center of government for the district.

Franz Schubert (My School Days Are Over)

1797 (Vienna)–1828 (Vienna). Composer of chamber music, symphonies, church music, concertos, church music, and Lieder [songs]. His music interpreted rather than accompanied the poems he set to music, such as *Die Winterreise* (Winter Journey), *Die schöne Müllerin* (The Beautiful Maid of the Mill), and Goethe's "Erlkönig" (Erl-King) and "Mignon."

Clara Schumann-Wieck (Prologue)

1819 (Leipzig)–1896 (Frankfurt am Main). Pianist and composer. Clara Schumann-Wieck gave her first piano recital at the age of nine. Despite her father's opposition, she married Robert Schumann and continued to take care of him and their seven children. Her close friendships included Brahms and Joseph Joachim. After Robert's death she continued to give concerts. She taught piano and edited her husband's works.

Siegfried (School Days 2)

Hero of the medieval epic *Die Nibelungenlied* (c. 1203). Based on the Norse sagas, the *Nibelungenlied* is the story of Siegfried's deeds that win him his wife and defeat his enemies. He is invulnerable because he bathed in dragon's blood except for one spot on his back where a linden leaf had fallen. His wife Kriemhild knows of this and betrays her knowledge to Hagen, who kills Siegfried with a spear as he bends over a stream to drink.

Simonian Declaration (Prologue)

A waiver signed by Jewish students who studied at the University of Berlin. One can only surmise what this "Simonian Declaration" may have been. It might have been an administrative order; it does not appear to have been mandated by law. In nineteenth-century Germany, Jews were excluded from certain professions, from certain courses of study, and from full participation in civic life, exclusions that depended on when and where as the tide of liberalism advanced or retreated. In the eighteenth century, Jews were subject to severe restrictions. Under the shock of the defeat by Napoleon, Prussia instituted a number of reforms, including liberating Jews from the ghetto. In the Edict of March 11, 1812, for example, Friedrich Wilhelm guaranteed Jews the same rights as Prussian citizens, provided, among other conditions, that they adopt family names written in German or Latin letters and that they use only German or "other living languages" in their business ledgers, contracts, and other legal documents. The Edict allowed Jews who qualified as *Einländer* (legal residents) to buy real property "just as Christians do." The Edict also did away with all bars to professions and local office, but reserved the right to determine whether Jews could hold state and public positions. Only ten years later in 1822, another edict withdrew, on account of abuses, rights and freedom equivalent to those of Christians as well as permission to enter academic careers and to hold local office. At the University of Berlin the careers of Jewish academics now floundered. They found their *Habilitationsschrift* (post-doctoral thesis required for academic appointment) rejected or their advance up the professorial ranks blocked. One such academic was Karl Gustav Theodor Simon (1810–57), a brilliant medical researcher and practicing physician. When Robert Remak, a Jewish private docent on the medical faculty, finally won recognition of his *Habilitationsschrift* in 1847 after nine years of struggle, he applied for the position of "Extraordinary" professor; he was at first turned down as this would be unfair, according to the faculty, to older docents such as Dr. Simon.

Eduard von Simson (Winter Storms)

1810 (Königsberg)–1899 (Berlin). Parliamentarian. Son of converted Jews, Simson taught law at the University of Königsberg and belonged to the revolutionary generation of 1848. He was a member, then president, of the Frankfurt National Assembly. The parliament favored a constitutional monarchy: it adopted a liberal constitution and voted for an emperor. Simson headed the deputation to Berlin to offer the crown to King Friedrich Wilhelm IV. The effort was a disaster—the conservative newspapers scorned the offer of "beggars"; a court lackey denied Simson a requested glass of water; and the king mocked the Jewish member of the delegation Dr. Riesser: "Isn't it true, Herr Doktor, that you are also convinced that I cannot accept the constitution uncircumcised." However, when Simson as president of the Prussian Reichstag led a deputation to Versailles in 1871, Wilhelm I accepted the emperor's crown amidst great pomp. King Friedrich III raised Simson into the ranks of the aristocracy with a patent of nobility. He was the first President of the Supreme Court of the Reich or *Reichsgerichtpräsident* and a professor of Roman law. Simson was the first president of the Goethe Society, which was founded on June 20, 1885.

Baruch / Benedict Spinoza (Bar Mitzvah)

1632 (Amsterdam)–1677 (The Hague). Dutch philosopher. Spinoza was educated in the Sephardic orthodox tradition and was by trade a lens grinder. He also studied Latin and the works of Descartes and Hobbes. His pantheistic view of God was considered blasphemous; the Jewish community excommunicated and banished him from Amsterdam in 1656. Among his political and philosophical works, the *Ethics* (published posthumously in 1677) uses deductive reasoning from preliminary propositions to discuss the nature of God and the possibility of human knowledge. For Spinoza there is one essential nature that comprises all of reality and its attributes account for every feature of the universe. Knowledge, virtue, and power are one. Through German philosophers of the Enlightenment and Goethe, his philosophy influenced German idealism.

Professor Wilhelm Starlinger (The Reunion)

1898–1956. Physician and writer. Dr. Starlinger was responsible for setting up hospitals in Königsberg after World War II to combat epidemics. His book *Grenzen der Sowjetmacht im Spiegel einer West-Ostbegegnung hinter Palisaden von 1945–1954 (Limits to Soviet Power in View of West/East Confrontation from behind the Palisades)* appeared in 1956. It included a "Report of the German Epidemic Hospitals Yorck and St. Elisabeth Concerning Living and Dying in Königsberg, from 1945 to 1947: A Contribution to the Knowledge of the Course of a Major Epidemic under Primitive Conditions."

Staufer Empire (A Conversation)

1138–1268. A line of German kings and emperors of the Holy Roman Empire ruled in Northern Europe and Italy under the Hohenstaufens, whose name is derived from the castle of Staufen in Swabia. Memories of the family's greatness later became a powerful myth in German culture, in part due to an extraordinary flowering of German courtly literature at the time. Wolfram von Eschenbach's *Parzifal* and the poetry of Walter von der Vogelweide date from this period.

Claus Schenk Count von Stauffenberg (Winter Storms)

1907 (Greifenstein Castle, Upper Franconia)–1944 (Berlin). Military officer and conspirator in the July 20th Plot to assassinate Hitler. After being wounded early in World War II, Stauffenberg was appointed chief of staff of the Army Ordnance Department. He was open in his contempt of Hitler and Nazism and joined the conspiracy through the Kreisau Circle. He saw himself as a patriot, guided by his strong Christian principles and his anger at Nazi excesses. By early 1944 he was the active leader of the conspiracy to kill Hitler. His goal was to overthrow Hitler and replace his regime with a new social state that would restore the honor of his country. Stauffenberg attended the Rastenberg conference to give a report on the Home Army. He carried a British bomb in his briefcase, which he placed next to Hitler's chair before excusing himself to make a phone call. One of the colonels, feeling the briefcase to be in the way, pushed it under the table so that it rested behind a table support. The bomb exploded, killing several people but only slightly injuring Hitler. Unaware that Hitler had survived the blast, Stauffenberg returned by plane to Berlin. By midnight, he and three other officers were shot by a firing squad in a courtyard at the War Ministry.

Adalbert Stifter (The Chemical Factory of Gamm & Son)

1805 (Oberplan, Böhmerwald)–1868 (Linz an der Donau). Novelist. Stifter studied law, mathematics, science, and history but never took his university degree. He had wanted to become a landscape painter, but became a private tutor and eventually a school inspector. His novellas and novels extol the ethos of the classical ideal of the educated person. Nature as well as people are under the *sanftes Gesetz* (gentle law) of the universe, which manifests itself in the smallest as well as in the grandest aspects of life.

Der Stürmer (Cabinetmaking)

The Stormer. This virulent anti-Semitic, propagandistic newspaper (1923–45) was founded and edited by Julius Streicher, who was as an elementary school teacher in Nuremberg after World War I. He instituted the "Heil Hitler" for his pupils and was dismissed for conduct unbecoming a teacher in 1929. In his sometimes pornographically anti-Semitic *Stürmer*, he called for the elimination of the Jews from German life and, as early as 1938, the annihilation of the Jewish race. "Die Juden sind unser Unglück" ("The Jews are our misfortune"). Streicher was the paper's editor and publisher until 1933, when he was elected to the Reichstag. He organized the Jewish Boycott of April 1, 1933. He went on to become an important functionary in the *Reichssicherheitshauptamt* (Reich Security Main Office). At Nuremberg he called his trial "a triumph for world Jewry." The correspondent from the American weekly *Newsweek* reported that only Julius Streicher went to the gallows without dignity, having to be pushed across the floor while he screamed "Heil Hitler." As he stood on the gallows, Streicher "stared at the witnesses facing the gallows and shouted, 'Purimfest 1946.'" The reference is to the Jewish holiday of Purim, which celebrates the salvation of the Jews when Haman was hanged and the Jews of Persia were spared annihilation, as told in the biblical Book of Esther.

Sudetenland (The War Begins)

Portions of Bohemia and Moravia in Czechoslovakia with over three million Sudeten Germans, adjoining Germany, Poland, and Hungary. The Treaty of Versailles explicitly denied the Sudeten Germans the right to national self-determination. Although the majority in the area were German-speaking, the area had been made part of Czechoslovakia in 1919. On September 30, 1938, the conference in Munich resulted in the Munich Agreement, which sanctioned the annexation of Sudetenland territory into Germany (it also sanctioned annexation of portions of the Sudetenland into Poland and Hungary). Chamberlain returned from the conference, claiming the agreement meant "peace in our time." The German *Wehrmacht* marched into the Sudetenland on October 15, 1938.

Battle of Tannenberg (Winter Storms)

August 26–30, 1914. German victory, which later grew to mythic proportions, over the Russians in World War I. After the German defeat at the Battle of Gumbinnen a week earlier and the retreat beyond the Vistula, Hindenburg and Ludendorff regrouped the Eighth Army and succeeded in surrounding the numerically superior Second Russian Army under A. V. Samsonov near Tannenberg (now Stebark, Poland). The German victory was due to their having broken the Russian military code, to German superiority in artillery, and to the weakness of the Russian army, which had rushed into battle in East Prussia at the urging of the French before it had fully mobilized. The Germans sustained a comparatively small number of casualties (13,000), while 30,000 Russians were killed or wounded and 92,000 were taken prisoner. The Germans' booty amounted to over three hundred artillery pieces. With two fresh army corps pulled from the Western Front, Hindenburg then turned on the Russian First Army under P. K. Rennenkampf, attacking the Russians on a line from east of Königsberg to the southern end of the Masurian Lakes (September 6–15, 1914), and successfully routed the Russians. At home, the Germans wildly greeted the news. General von Hindenburg became the "Hero of Tannenberg," and in 1927, after Germany had lost the war, the Tannenberg Monument was built. The Nazi regime exploited the monument to glorify the nobility of war. On August 7, 1934, on the occasion of the burial of Reich President von Hindenburg, Hitler renamed the monument *Reichsehrenmal Tannenberg* (Tannenberg Reich Monument of Honor); as the Russians were advancing westward in 1945, Hitler had the architecturally pompous structure blown up.

German Knights of the Teutonic Order (Winter Storms)

Spiritual and military order. Founded at the end of the twelfth century by German merchants in Jerusalem to provide spiritual and medical care to German crusaders, the order was shortly thereafter transformed into a military one. When a duke in northern Poland requested the Pope's assistance to defend against attacks from the heathen Baltic Prussen, the German Knights were ordered to conquer and convert the Prussen in return for sovereignty over the lands it conquered, which included East Prussia. The order still exists and operates its own charitable hospitals in Germany and Austria.

Thirty Years' War (The Russians)

1618–48. The defenestration in Prague, when Protestants threw two ministers of King Ferdinand from a palace window, precipitated a series of conflicts between Protestant and Catholic powers that eventually encompassed almost all of western Europe. The Treaty of Westphalia brought peace by declaring the principle *cujus regio ejus religio* (whose country it is determines its religion), although certain exceptions were set forth. The religious and dynastic conflicts were fought mainly on German soil, and Germany was especially devastated by the destruction and cruelty. As a result, while France was consolidating under its king with a capital city in Paris, Germany remained fragmented in numerous tiny principalities for well over the next two centuries. The picaresque novel *Der Abentheuerliche Simplicissimus (The Adventures of Simplicissimus)* (1669) by Grimmelshausen provides graphic description of war atrocities not equaled in Europe until World War II and the poems of Andreas Gryphius are contemporaneous monuments to a land left in ashes and soot.

Turkos, Spahi, Gum, Zephyr (Prologue)

French regiments at time of Franco-Prussian War. The Spahi, for example, was an Algerian regiment.

Volksgenosse (Aunt Fanny)

"Racial comrade," i.e., "fellow countryman."

Volkssturm (Winter Storms)

Home defense units. All males between the ages of sixteen and sixty were subject to the draft into the *Volkssturm*. Although not officially armed, the men used whatever weapons were available or had been captured. The *Volkssturm* was an important part of the defense of Königsberg against the Red Army. As early as July 1944, *Volkssturm* units were deployed in the Memel area. When the Soviet forces had cut off the city by January 26, 1945, the *Volkssturm* were called upon to man the defenses as well as to assist the refugee evacuation. Gauleiter Koch sent a telegram to Hitler, saying that the Fourth Army was cowardly in trying to fight its way to the west. "I am continuing to defend East Prussia with the *Volkssturm*," he bragged and then fled the city on January 28. Even though General Lasch surrendered the city to the Soviets on April 9, *Volkssturm* units held the palace, and SS units and policemen held the citadel until April 10. Deputy Gauleiter Grossherr was killed when fighting "to the last man" with his *Volkssturm* battalion.

Richard Wagner (Cabinetmaking)

1813 (Leipzig)–1883 (Venice). Opera composer. Wagner's revolutionary ideas about music were set forth in essays he wrote after fleeing Germany to avoid arrest for participating in the uprising in Dresden in 1849. "Art and Revolution" (1849) and "The Artwork of the Future" (1849) discussed the complete union of music and drama. "Opera and Drama" (1851) defined his aesthetic ideas. In his essay "Das Judenthum in der Musik" ("Jewry in Music") (1850), Wagner wrote that Jewish music was without expression, was cold, indifferent, and trivial; the Jew lacked passion and therefore was incapable of artistic creation. Even admitting a Jew into the world of music would harm music. In "Deutsche Kunst und Deutsche Politik" ("German Art and Politics") (1867/68), Wagner bemoaned the baleful influence of Jewry on the morality of the nation: Jewish influence could subvert national morality, which was to be found in the German psyche.

Wannsee Conference (Prologue)

Secret meeting held on January 20, 1942, of Nazi leaders in Wannsee, a suburb of Berlin, to discuss and plan the Final Solution. Reinhard Heydrich, head of the

Reichssicherheithauptamt (Reich Security Main Office), opened the meeting called to implement the plan Hermann Göring had been instructed to prepare on Hitler's order of July 7, 1941; Adolf Eichmann transcribed the proceedings. The Wannsee Protocol, of which thirty copies were made for the record, stated that the "evacuation of the Jews to the east can now be substituted for emigration, after obtaining permission from the Führer to that effect.... the remnant [of Jews who survive the labor details] that is finally able to survive all this—since this is undoubtedly the part with the strongest resistance—must be treated accordingly, since these people, representing a natural selection, are to be regarded as the germ cell of a new Jewish development, in case they should succeed and go free (as history has proved). In the course of the execution of the Final Solution, Europe will be combed from west to east."

Erich Waske (Nidden)

1889 (Berlin, Friedenau)–1960? 1978? (Berlin). Expressionist painter. Waske was a member of *Die Brücke,* a group of Expressionist artists. The Nazis branded him a "degenerate painter." He is known for his very bright palette of colors. Many of his paintings were destroyed in air raids during World War II.

Werewolf (The Russians)

German partisan organization. Nominally under the SS headed by Heinrich Himmler, this group of partisans was, in the last days of World War II, operated by the Hitler Youth. The young men, often mere boys, were trained, sometimes for only a few days, to fight behind enemy lines. They mined roads, sniped at Allied Forces, and poisoned food stocks. Although their activities sharply diminished after the surrender on May 7, 1945, incidents were reported as late as 1947.

Horst Wessel Song (*Kristallnacht* and After)

1907 (Bielefeld)–1930 (Berlin). Nazi martyr. In 1926 Wessel joined the SA. He wrote the lyrics to the "Horst Wessel Lied," which the Nazis elevated to the status of a national anthem. It begins "Die Fahne hoch, die Reihen dicht geschlossen" [Hold high the banner! The ranks shoulder to shoulder].

West Prussia (Winter Storms)

Former province of Prussia along the Baltic Sea between Pomerania on the west and East Prussia on the east. Its capital city was Danzig. The Treaty of Versailles gave most of West Prussia to Poland, creating the "Polish Corridor," and made Danzig a free city. Germany annexed the whole territory in 1939 at the beginning of World War II; in 1945 the Potsdam Conference placed it under Polish administration; the Federal Republic of Germany confirmed its recognition of the territory as Polish after the fall of the Wall in 1989.

Dorothea Wieck (Prologue)

1908 (Davos)–1986 (Berlin). Actress. Trained by Max Reinhardt, she became a movie star. Her best known film is perhaps *Mädchen in Uniform (Schoolgirls in*

Uniform) (1931), in the role of Frau von Bernburg, the sympathetic teacher. Goebbels banned the movie, but she remained popular in the Third Reich. *Cradle Song* was her first movie made in the United States (1933); other movies made in Hollywood were *Miss Fane's Baby Is Stolen* (1934), *Man on a Tightrope* (1934), *A Time to Love and a Time to Die* (1958). After the war she continued to teach and act and made a guest appearance in the popular German television series *Der Kommissar* in 1973.

Henryk Wieniawski (The Russians)

1835 (Lublin)–1880 (Moscow). Violinist. A child prodigy, Wieniawski was admitted to the Paris Conservatoire at the age of eight. He was an extremely popular performer and composer, often playing at royal courts. He spent twelve years as the court violinist in St. Petersburg. He fell ill while on tour in Moscow, where he died at the age of forty-five.

Wilhelm Tell (Water and Electricity)

Legendary figure in the account of the liberation of Switzerland from the rule of the Habsburgs in the thirteenth century. In the legends, Tell came into conflict with the Habsburg representative, the Reichsvogt Gessler. Having refused to honor Gessler's hat, Tell was ordered to shoot an apple balanced on his son's head with bow and arrow. Tell did so, then murdered Gessler and fled, thereby precipitating the rebellion against Habsburg rule. In 1804 Friedrich Schiller's *Wilhelm Tell* premiered; it attacked tyranny and aristocratic privilege. Gioacchino Rossini (1792–1868) wrote the five-act opera *Guillaume Tell* in 1829. One movement of the overture is familiar to every American over a certain age who remembers the radio or TV cowboy serial *The Lone Ranger*.

Wilhelm Gustloff and Steuben (Siege of Königsberg)

Passenger cruise ships. The *Wilhelm Gustloff* was the first ship built expressly for mass pleasure cruises. Named after a high-ranking Swiss Nazi assassinated in 1936, the ship was launched in the presence of Hitler himself. In 1939 it briefly served as a hospital ship, then as the floating headquarters for the Second Submarine Training Division. On January 30, 1945, it was pressed into service to evacuate about 6,000 refugees, many from East Prussia. As it made its way unescorted across the Baltic, it was torpedoed shortly after 9 P.M. by a Soviet submarine. About 5,000 people died. Less than two weeks later, on February 10, 1945, the same Soviet submarine torpedoed the *Steuben*, a hospital ship carrying about 5,000 war wounded and refugees, of whom 3,500 died. Günter Grass's novella *Im Krebsgang* (Going Backwards), published in February 2002, explores the current recrudescence of the extreme right in Germany through a meticulous retelling of the history of the *Wilhelm Gustloff*.

Kaiser Wilhelm I (School Days 2)

1797 (Berlin)–1888 (Berlin). King of Prussia (crowned 1861) and Emperor of Germany (1871–88). After Napoleon defeated Prussia at the Battle of Jena and Auerstedt in a matter of hours, the royal family fled to Königsberg and then to Memel, where they remained for three years; after 1808 the family resided in the Königsberg Castle. As Prince of Prussia, Wilhelm earned the name of *Kartätschenprinz* (grapeshot prince) during the Revolution of 1848 when he was held responsible for the bloody suppression of the street fighting in Berlin. Under Wilhelm I, Bismarck's policies led to the military defeat of Denmark and the annexation of Schleswig-Holstein; to the military defeat of Austria and the restoration of the King's popularity; and to the military defeat of France and the coronation of the King as Kaiser in January 1871. The Second Reich under Kaiser Wilhelm I is also known as the *Gründerzeit* (literally, the Founders' Era to indicate the rapid industrial expansion of the period).

Willy Wolflein (Conflicts and Personal Fates)

Unknown. The *Encyclopedia Judaica* mentions Willy Wolflein in its entry under "Königsberg" in both the German- and English-language editions, along with Frieda (Fromm) Reichmann, as examples of professors forced to emigrate once the Nazis came to power. There is, however, no listing for Willy Wolflein in the standard list of academics in Germany *(Kürschners Deutscher Gelehrten Kalendar)*. He is not listed in the *Biographisches Handbuch der deutschsprachigen Emigration nach 1933*, edited by the Institut für Zeitgeschichte and the Research Foundation for Jewish Emigration. Willy Wolflein is absent from *Die Ausbürgerung deutscher Staatsangehöriger 1933–45 nach dem in Reichsanzeiger veröffentlichen Listen* (Expatriation Lists as Published in the *Reichsanzeiger, 1933–45*). The *Reichsanzeiger* or legal gazettes listed those who were stripped of their German nationality, including Thomas Mann, under the April 7, 1933, law *Gesetz zur Wiederherstellung des Berufsbeamtentums* (Law for the Restoration of the Civil Service), stripping non-Aryans of their civil service status, including academic appointments. Since there is no longer a University of Königsberg, it is impossible to check old course catalogs or lists of academic staff or students. The records of the old university that did survive the war now reside in less than desirable archival conditions in Olszteyn, Poland and, in part, in Vilnius, Lithuania; no easily accessible records that document the existence of Willy Wolflein could be found. It is as if he never existed except as a parenthetical phrase in an entry in the *Encyclopedia Judaica*.

Worpswede (Nidden)

Small village just east of Bremen, located between the Weser and Elbe Rivers. Worpswede was an artists' colony at the beginning of the twentieth century.

Bishop Theophil Wurm (*Kristallnacht* and After)

1868 (Basel)–1953(Stuttgart). Theologian. In 1929 Wurm became President of the Protestant Regional Church in Württemberg, and in 1933, Bishop. On April 22, 1934, he gave a sermon in the Ulm Cathedral, which marked the beginning of resistance by the Confessing Church. In 1943 he publicly protested against the destruction of the Jews. In 1945 he was one of the signers of the Stuttgart Confession admitting the failure of German clergy during Third Reich.

5,000 Taler Aria (Gleanings)

Aria at the end of Act 2 of *Der Wildschütz* (The Poacher) (1842). The opera by Albert Lortzing (1801–51), best known for his opera *Zar und Zimmerman* (The Czar and the Carpenter), (1837), tells the story of the aristocratic baron who lusts after the pretty bride of the commoner. In the "5,000 Taler" aria, the schoolmaster Baculus expresses his amazement at the offer from Baron Kronthal to purchase his bride for the extravagant sum of 5,000 talers.

Works Cited

Dieckert, Kurt, Major, and General Horst Grossmann. *Der Kampf um Ostpreussen. Der umfassende Dokumentarbericht über das Kriegsgeschehen in Ostpreussen.* Suttgart: Motorbuch Verlag, 1984 (5th printing); Munich: Gräfe und Unzer Verlag..

Gause, Fritz. *Königsberg in Preussen. Die Geschichte einer europäischen Stadt.* Munich: Gräfe und Unzer Verlag, 1984.

Geliebtes Königsberg. Porträt einer Stadt. Edited by Martin A. Borrmann. Munich: Gräfe und Unzer Verlag, 1967.

Königsberg in Preussen. Werden und Wesen der östlichsten deutschen Grossstadt. Edited by the Municipality of the City of Königsberg. Königsberg, 1924.

Lasch, Otto, General. *So fiel Königsberg.* Stuttgart: Motorbuch Verlag, 1984; Munich: Gräfe und Unzer Verlag.

Lorenz, Konrad. "Durch Domestikation verursachte Störungen arteigenen Verhaltens." In *Zeitschrift für angewandte Psychologie und Charakterkunde.* 59 (Heft 1 & 2) (1940).

Das Sonderrecht für die Juden im NS-Staat. Eine Sammlung der gesetzlichen Massnahmen und Richtlinien—Inhalt und Bedeutung. Edited by Joseph Walk. Motive, Texte, Materialien, Bd. 14. Heidelberg/Karlsruhe: C.F. Miller, 1981.

Starlinger, Wilhelm. *Grenzen der Sowjetmacht.* Würzburg: Holzner, 1954.

Quotations from *Der Kampf um Ostpreussen* by Dieckert and Grossman and from *So fiel Königsberg* by Otto Lasch have been reprinted with the kind permission of Gräfe und Unzer Verlag, Munich.